Exploring Forgiveness

DATE DUE

Exploring Forgiveness

Edited by
Robert D. Enright
and
Joanna North

With a Foreword by
Archbishop Desmond Tutu

THE UNIVERSITY OF WISCONSIN PRESS

The University of Wisconsin Press
1930 Monroe Street
Madison, Wisconsin 53711
www.wisc.edu/wisconsinpress/

3 Henrietta Street
London WC2E 8LU, England

2   4   6   5   3

Printed in the United States of America

Library of Congress Cataloging-in-Publication Data

Exploring forgiveness / edited by Robert D. Enright and Joanna North;
with a foreword by Desmond Tutu.
206 pp.   cm.
Includes bibliographical references and index.
ISBN 0-299-15770-9 (alk. paper)
ISBN 0-299-15774-1 (pbk. : alk. paper)
1. Forgiveness.   I. Enright, Robert D.   II. North, Joanna, 1958–
BF637.F67E86   1998
179'.9–dc21   97-49297

This book is dedicated to the memory of Fr. L. Martin Jenco,
who embodied forgiveness.

CONTENTS

CONTRIBUTORS

PAUL W. COLEMAN is a psychologist in private practice in Wappingers Falls, New York. He is the author of four books including *The Forgiving Marriage* and most recently *Getting to the Heart of the Matter: How to Halt Ongoing Marital Conflict Once and for All*. He is also a columnist for *Marriage* magazine. He has been married for twelve years and is the father of three children.

REV. DAVID COUPER was chief of police in Madison, Wisconsin, from 1972 to 1993. He retired from the police department to pursue a call to the Christian ministry. He is an ordained priest of the Episcopal church and is currently the rector of St. John the Baptist Episcopal Church in Portage, Wisconsin.

WALTER J. DICKEY is a professor of law at the University of Wisconsin–Madison. He directed the Department of Corrections in Wisconsin from 1983 to 1987. He has written extensively in the field of criminal justice and has supervised work on the Victim-Offender Reconciliation Program.

JOSEPH W. ELDER has been a professor of the University of Wisconsin–Madison Departments of Sociology and South Asian Studies since 1961. He has lectured and made documentary films about contemporary Hinduism, Buddhism, and Islam. On several occasions he has served as a member of Quaker teams carrying messages to and trying to maintain dialogues between parties that were at war with each other.

ROBERT D. ENRIGHT is a professor in the Department of Educational Psychology at the University of Wisconsin–Madison. He has pioneered the social scientific study of forgiveness within psychology. Within his own discipline, he has published, along with various coauthors, the first empirically based study on forgiveness, the first scientifically tested intervention on forgiveness, and the first article detailing a measure of interpersonal forgiveness that targets specific offenses and offenders. He organized the first national conference on forgiveness ever held within a university setting.

RICHARD FITZGIBBONS, MD, is a psychiatrist who trained at the Hospital at the University of Pennsylvania and the Philadelphia Child Guidance Center. In 1986 he published a seminal paper in the journal *Psychotherapy* on the clinical uses of forgiveness in the treatment of excessive anger. Over the past twenty years he has been in demand for conferences and workshops on the treatment of anger and the uses of forgiveness across the life-span. He maintains a private practice outside Philadelphia.

BEVERLY FLANIGAN is a clinical professor of social work who teaches and writes in the areas of professional ethics and substance abuse. Her qualitative research on interpersonal forgiveness began in 1980 (funded by the Kellogg Foundation) and culminated with Macmillan's publication of her book *Forgiving the Unforgivable,* which has been translated into German (Rowalt Press). A frequent trainer of medical and helping professionals, she is the author of *Forgiving Yourself* (Macmillan, 1996).

SUZANNE FREEDMAN is an assistant professor in the Department of Educational Psychology at the University of Northern Iowa. As a graduate student at the University of Wisconsin–Madison she wrote a brilliant dissertation in which she helped female incest survivors to forgive their perpetrators. That work is now published, with Robert Enright, in the *Journal of Consulting and Clinical Psychology.*

MARIETTA JAEGER has been giving presentations and leading workshops and retreats on forgiveness for twenty-one years and currently works for *THE WITNESS,* an ecumenical social justice magazine. She lives in the inner city of Detroit as a member of the Detroit Peace Community, a Catholic Worker-based group which advocates for peace, justice, and nonviolence. She is a board member of Murder Victims' Families for Reconciliation, whose primary mission is to abolish the death penalty.

JOANNA NORTH is a freelance writer living in England. She earned a master of philosophy degree from the University of London in 1984 and has written several articles on philosophical topics including forgiveness and is currently writing a doctoral thesis on the philosophy of forgiveness. She was the editor of a book, *The GCSE: An Examination,* published by Claridge Press, 1985. GCSE is the General Certificate of Secondary Education; this book was a critique of English secondary education. She has three children.

JULIO RIQUE is a graduate student in the Department of Educational Psychology at the University of Wisconsin–Madison. He has pioneered the psychological study of forgiveness in Brazil and is currently examining a measure of interpersonal forgiveness in northeastern Brazil.

DONALD W. SHRIVER, JR., was president of Union Theological Seminary from 1975 to 1991, and he continues on the faculty there as professor of Christian ethics. He spent ten years as a pastor and faculty member at North Carolina State University working in interprofessional and interdisciplinary research on ethically significant public issues. Among his eleven books are *Spindles and Spires: A Restudy of Religion and Social Change in Gastonia; Beyond Success: Corporations and their Critics in the 'Nineties*; and most recently, *An Ethic for Enemies: Forgiveness in Politics.* His wife, Peggy, is a staff member of the National Council of Churches, and they have three grown children and four grandchildren.

KEITH E. YANDELL is a professor of philosophy and South Asian studies at the University of Wisconsin–Madison. He has written four books, edited three, and published about fifty articles and book chapters. He teaches and does research in the philosophy of religion, South Asian philosophy, and the history of modern philosophy (the period of Descartes through Kant).

Without Forgiveness There Is No Future

Archbishop Desmond Tutu

Dear friends who are "exploring forgiveness" through this volume published by the University of Wisconsin Press, I am greeting you from South Africa, this new South Africa, this free, democratic South Africa. Forgiveness is one of the key ideas in this world. Forgiveness is not just some nebulous, vague idea that one can easily dismiss. It has to do with uniting people through practical politics. Without forgiveness there is no future. Of course, we here in South Africa are a living example of how forgiveness may unite people. Our history makes this surprising in many ways. Our miracle almost certainly would not have happened without the willingness of people to forgive, exemplified spectacularly in the magnanimity of Nelson Mandela. His forgiveness still leaves the world gasping at the sheer wonder of it, especially in light of his long imprisonment.

Forgiveness is taking seriously the awfulness of what has happened when you are treated unfairly. It is opening the door for the other person to have a chance to begin again. Without forgiveness, resentment builds in us, a resentment which turns into hostility and anger. Hatred eats away at our well-being. In Africa we have a word, *Ubuntu*, which is difficult to render in Western languages. It speaks about the essence of being human: that my humanity is caught up in your humanity because we say a person is a person through other persons. I am a person because I belong. The same is true for you. The solitary human being is a contradiction in terms. That is why God could say to Adam, "It is not good for man to be alone." No one can be fully human unless he or she relates to others in a fair, peaceful, and harmonious way. In our African understanding, we set great store by communal peace and harmony. Anything that subverts this harmony is injurious, not just to the community, but to all of us, and therefore forgiveness is an absolute necessity for continued human existence.

Forgiveness is not pretending that things are other than they are. Forgiveness is not cheap. It is facing the ghastliness of what has happened and giving the other person the opportunity of coming out of that ghastly situation. When you say to me, "I am sorry," in my Christian understanding

I am then constrained by the Gospel imperative to forgive. Yet, this is not the end of the story. You see, if you have stolen my pen and you say you are sorry, and I forgive you and you still retain my pen, then I must call into question the authenticity of your contrition. I must—as part of the process of reconciliation, of forgiving, of healing, of the willingness to make good—appropriate restitution. The world is on the brink of disaster if we don't forgive, accept forgiveness, and reconcile.

Forgiveness does not mean amnesia. Amnesia is a most dangerous thing, especially on a community, national, or international level. We must forgive, but almost always we should not forget that there were atrocities, because if we do, we are then likely to repeat those atrocities. Those who forgive and those who accept forgiveness must not forget in their reconciling. If we don't deal with our past adequately, it will return to haunt us. When something is unforgiven it has physical consequences for us. Unforgiven tension, unforgiven sin, actually has a deleterious impact on the person.

So I pray that you will be richly blessed as you examine the ramifications of forgiveness for personal life, for community life, for national life. I hope you continue exploring forgiveness long after you are finished reading this book. For example, I hope that one day you will have the opportunity of going to Hiroshima and seeing the memorial that the Japanese have erected for the atrocity that was perpetrated on the feast of the transfiguration, August the 6th. They are saying that the world must remember what happened—we must all remember—so that we do not repeat it, so that it will not ever happen again to anyone. God bless you.

Exploring Forgiveness

Introducing Forgiveness

Robert D. Enright and Joanna North

It is an obvious fact that we live in a world where violence, hatred, and animosity surround us on all sides. From nations at war with one another, to crime on our streets, to violence and cruelty in our families, there are none who are untouched by the atmosphere of fear and anxiety that these situations generate. The explanations put forward for these states of affairs are many and varied, and all are open to debate and criticism. Politicians, sociologists, psychologists, philosophers, journalists, judges, police officers, and social workers all find themselves at times in the public domain attempting to explain the causes of crime and violence in our societies and what must be done to prevent them. Accompanying this debate is the parallel concern with law and order, which discusses what is to be done with wrongdoers and criminals, how best to punish them, deter others from similar misdeeds, and rehabilitate the offender after he or she has been punished.

What is heard much less often in any of these debates, however, is any voice suggesting just how forgiveness might be useful in helping those who have been affected by cruelty, crime, and violence, and how it might play a valuable role in reconciling warring parties and restoring harmony between people. Occasionally a person speaks publicly about the wrong that has been done to him or her and declares his or her willingness to forgive the wrongdoer. Nevertheless, such instances are few and far between, and the task of forgiveness receives little support from public agencies. We hear much about the "social" causes of crime—poverty, unemployment, and illiteracy, for example. We sometimes hear about the need for tolerance and cooperation, compassion and understanding. But almost never do we hear public leaders declaring their belief that forgiveness can bring people together, heal their wounds, and alleviate the bitterness and resentment caused by wrongdoing.

In the academic world, too, many scholarly and learned articles and books are written concerning the origins of war, the psychology of aggression, and the social and psychological effects of violence. Yet, if one were to attempt to find all the articles and books on the topic of interpersonal forgiveness that have appeared in or been translated into English, starting with St. Augustine's writings in the early fifth century and ending in 1970, how many works could be gathered? In contrast with expositions on the related topic of justice, which would yield thousands of titles, we found only about 110 titles on interpersonal forgiveness—that is, people forgiving other people—within that time span. Even if we missed, let us suppose, a thousand titles, that would still amount to only about one published work per year. More realistically, it seems that works on forgiveness have appeared at a rate of only about one every ten to fifteen years. In other words, the volume you hold in your hands is rare within academia, because explorations of forgiveness have been scarce for almost sixteen hundred years.

Given our awareness then of the tremendous need for such a book as this, it is appropriate that this Introduction should explain the purposes of the various contributors and our overall aims and objectives. First of all, this is a *practical* book. While it is not a self-help manual or "how to do it" guide, one of its purposes is to examine and explain how the lives of ordinary, everyday people have been touched and even transformed by the practice of forgiveness. We concentrate on *interpersonal forgiveness,* the kind of forgiveness that exists between people, whether it be one individual forgiving another, family members engaged in mutual forgiveness, or even one nation forgiving another. We do not mean to suggest that this activity is incompatible with any spiritual dimensions of forgiveness, nor do we deny the important role that religious faith may play in helping people forgive others. We hope to show that forgiveness is possible for all of us regardless of the particular religious beliefs we may have, even if we have no religious beliefs at all.

Second, the chapters in this volume all attempt to give a *theoretical* grounding for forgiveness and to demonstrate that the nature of forgiveness can be clarified and illuminated through the various academic disciplines that are now beginning to explore the long-neglected topic of person-to-person forgiveness. What this book displays is the interdisciplinary focus of the work now being carried out on forgiveness in various settings. All the contributors, whatever their particular academic focus, demonstrate a willingness to share with and learn from others with different academic backgrounds and diverse personal experiences. For instance, when one scholar generates a definition of forgiveness, another may then apply that definition to helping people hurt by wrongdoing. One who helps *individuals* to forgive may find entirely new questions worth exploring when seeing how others aid *groups* in forgiving. This commitment to an interdisciplinary perspective should prove to be an exciting challenge to all those who examine the topic of forgiveness.

Thus, throughout the book readers will encounter the practical and theoretical commitments of the contributors and be struck by the richness of the study of forgiveness when viewed from many perspectives. The topic is huge and hugely exciting, and we hope that readers will catch something of the energy and enthusiasm with which we approach the subject. We also believe that it will provoke spirited discussion and debate and stimulate further exploration and research into forgiveness.

Before we discuss the main body of this volume, let us say a few words on how it begins. We are delighted to present a foreword by Archbishop Desmond Tutu, based on an address he delivered to the first National Conference on Forgiveness ever held on any university campus, at the University of Wisconsin–Madison from March 30 to April 1, 1995. Roy Lloyd of the National Council of Churches worked tirelessly behind the scenes to acquire Rev. Tutu's remarks on audio tape. We present here Rev. Tutu's ideas before the main chapters commence. We extend our heartfelt thanks to both of them. Following the Introduction is a second preliminary piece (chapter 2), which is Marietta Jaeger's poignant story of her journey to forgive the murderer of her daughter. Her love and fortitude are fine testimony to the difference which forgiveness can make in all our lives.

The remaining chapters in this book fall broadly into three main parts, which might be termed philosophical, psychological, and sociopolitical. Philosophy is an essential component within this project, because it is the discipline that guides us to basic definitions of forgiveness and imposes upon us the duties of both analytic clarity and conceptual rigor. Chapters 3 and 4 are, respectively, by Joanna North and Keith Yandell, two philosophers who explore here the concept of forgiveness and attempt to do justice to its full complexity through an analysis of its connections with freedom, responsibility, retribution, repentance, and reconciliation. Having offered a definition of forgiveness and outlined the typical stages in the process of forgiving, North goes on to examine the parallel process of *acceptance* of forgiveness on the part of the wrongdoer. Interestingly, one who accepts responsibility for his or her wrong and who feels the pain of guilt can accept forgiveness from another only if he or she experiences a form of *self*-forgiveness. An understanding of forgiveness, thus, will be of value to both victims and perpetrators of wrongdoing. In his reply to North, Keith Yandell further examines the notions of freedom, responsibility, and the nature of persons as agents of forgiveness. He argues that forgiveness, when offered and accepted, demonstrates our capacity to overcome evil and restore the common bonds of humanity so essential if we are to flourish as persons.

From the philosophical groundwork, the next part moves on to psychological issues. Chapter 5 by Robert Enright and colleagues and chapter 6 by Richard Fitzgibbons discuss issues in *individual* psychology and psychiatry. Enright discusses the extensive research he and others have carried out in the development of a model for the psychological process of forgiveness. He argues that thoroughness in the area of definition is vital if the practical help one gives other people is to be of lasting value. Theory and practice are inextricably linked: An incorrect or incomplete definition of forgiveness will naturally result in incorrect or incomplete advice for the person trying to forgive another. Of course, the process works both ways. Fitzgibbons offers us a fascinating glimpse of the practical uses of forgiveness in his account of his work in clinical practice. He reminds us that our concept of forgiveness must grow out of the real experiences of those struggling to overcome their hurt and anger.

In chapters 7 and 8, the role of practice in enabling us fully to understand forgiveness is explored in greater detail. These chapters examine the place of forgiveness within the family. After all, is it not in the privacy and intimacy of some homes that the deepest hurts are unfortunately and tragically perpetrated? Paul Coleman is a therapist who works with families. He describes how the recognition of the value of forgiveness in family therapy transformed his practical work. Growing out of his experiences, Coleman offers invaluable advice for all those interested in applying forgiveness within the context of therapy. In her reply to Coleman, Beverly Flanigan offers further critical insights into the use of forgiveness within families. She looks at those situations in which forgiveness seems most difficult and cautions us against the overoptimistic belief that full forgiveness is always possible. Instead she suggests that the degree of forgiveness possible is proportional to the degree of harm inflicted. Both the empirical study of forgiveness and the concept itself must develop to take into account its "degrees, forms, and subtleties."

From the family to the wider community, the third part of the book then moves on to consider how forgiveness can be applied to larger community injustices. Walter Dickey gives his views on the possibility of forgiveness within the criminal justice system. His and Couper's chapters perhaps are the most original in the book, because forgiveness within the criminal justice system is rarely explored. Both Dickey and Couper speak primarily from their own experiences, not from an examination of published works in their field, because those publications are practically nonexistent.

Dickey argues that the difficulties which many experience in accepting the idea that forgiveness might have a useful role in this area stem partly from a confusion over the nature of crime, the nature of the criminal, and the purpose of punishment. In addition, there are political pressures which act to marginalize forgiveness in the arena of justice. Nevertheless, Dickey sees some grounds for optimism in the development of the "restorative justice" movement, which aims to find room for forgiveness, for example, in reconciliation programs between victims and offenders. Where these programs work, Dickey has observed the incidence of understanding, empathy, and healing—precisely those processes which are crucial to forgiveness itself. In his reply to Dickey, David Couper combines his experience as a law enforcement officer with a strong Christian perspective and presents his own views of forgiveness and its role within institutions and communities. Indeed, he argues that it is not only individuals but also institutions, communities, and nations themselves that can practice forgiveness. This is so because they also can be doers and sufferers of wrong. Couper shows that it is essential to extend forgiveness beyond the individual to our institutional and community lives if we are ever to build a healthier and more human society.

The penultimate chapter, by Donald Shriver, Jr., carries this view onward into the international political arena. Shriver argues that forgiveness between nations, forgiveness between cultural groups, and forgiveness between communities are all possible once the necessary steps have been taken. These steps, identified also by other authors throughout this book, involve the following: first, complete honesty in the recognition that harm has been inflicted by one party on another; second, a willingness to forgo prolonging the hostility through acts of revenge; third, the development of understanding and empathy between the parties; and finally, the offer of renewed community in the future.

The final chapter in this book, by Joseph Elder, offers a summary of the main issues covered in all other chapters. He critiques definitions put forth and offers the challenging perspective that not all world views make room for forgiveness. Drawing on his knowledge of Buddhism, Elder argues that forgiveness may be a Western and a Judeo-Christian-Muslim phenomenon If this is true, he queries, then how can communities with widely differing views on forgiveness get together for mutual healing and reconciliation?

We asked Fr. Martin Jenco to contribute a chapter, but sadly, he died in July 1996 before he had a chance to start a work. He intended to relate his story of capture and imprisonment in Beirut in 1985 and his subsequent forgiving of his captors. Interested readers may wish to read Fr. Jenco's book, *Bound to Forgive* (1995, Notre Dame, Ind.: Ave Maria Press). From that book, he teaches us this: "Having forgiven, I am liberated. I need no longer be determined by the past" (p. 135).

A word on terminology that you may encounter throughout the book is in order. At times the various authors use different words that imply the same underlying idea. For example, in Joanna North's chapter, she refers to a developmental progression through a series of *stages* toward the endpoint of forgiveness. In Robert Enright and colleagues' chapter, the authors refer to a similar development progression through *units*. Whether termed a stage or a unit, both describe a particular part of the forgiveness journey. As an example, North describes an early *stage* in which a forgiver becomes angry over another's injustice. Enright and colleagues describe a *unit* of anger, also occurring early in a forgiveness progression. Different authors use different words to describe similar patterns of development toward the ultimate goal of forgiveness; this does not imply that the authors have radically different underlying meanings. Instead, the different terminologies signify that we work in different disciplines and that explorations of forgiveness are relatively new. Perhaps forgiveness will never become so scientific that all scholars in all disciplines will use common labels to denote movement toward a forgiving posture. One final point should be made. Just because the authors here talk in terms of development, you should not view any of the models as fixed in that a forgiver moves rigidly from point A to point Z. There are many twists and turns in any person's forgiveness journey.

To all who contributed to this volume, thank you. To Rosalie Robertson, editor at the University of Wisconsin Press, we owe our thanks for her open-mindedness, flexibility, and astute intellect in knowing how to shape the diverse material into a coherent unit. To our reviewers, Steen Halling and Clark Power, go our thanks for their penetrating critiques.

To Wendy Theobald we are indebted to her expertise and high energy in editing the sprawling bibliography. To Linda Shriberg for her administrative expertise, Barb Lienau and Karen O'Connell, who typed various parts of this manuscript, and to Nancy Enright for proof-reading, we are indebted. We are especially indebted to Philip and Christine Lodewick of Ridgefield, Connecticut, whose generous gift made this book possible.

In conclusion, despite the centuries of silence on the matter, it now is obvious that academia is ready to make a place for exploring forgiveness. This volume is evidence that forgiveness can and will be allowed a voice within the academy and beyond. We now must take steps to ensure its continued voice, a voice that is balanced, open to both change and correction, and ultimately helpful to all people embittered by injustice.

2

The Power and Reality
of Forgiveness: Forgiving the
Murderer of One's Child

Marietta Jaeger

It was to be the vacation we could talk about for the rest of our lives, our once-in-a-lifetime grand family vacation, camping for a whole month through the state of Montana. "It has everything you're all interested in!" my mom had said when she and my dad returned from a trip there the year before, and we were sure it did from everything we'd ever read or heard. So, when our five children were out of school for the summer, we were packed and ready to go.

After a week of travel, we arrived at our first campsite in Montana, the Missouri River Headwaters Park, nestled between mountain ranges and a sky that went on forever. My parents were there waiting, having traveled from Arizona to share this special time. And it surely was, with excellent weather, spectacular scenery, and, considering their wide range of ages, delightful camaraderie among all the children. We spent three wonder-filled days camped there, visiting all the scenic and historic sites. The last night, I went into the tent to settle the children, all of us excited about being on the move again in the morning. They were side by side in their individual sleeping bags, with their heads to the back of the tent. I knelt at their feet and crawled up to kiss each of them goodnight.

My youngest child, Susie, seven years old, was the most difficult to reach, tucked into the corner with camping gear piled at the foot of her sleeping bag. When I stretched over and around the pile, I still could hardly reach her, my lips barely skimming across her cheek. "Oh no, Mama!" Susie exclaimed, and crawled out of her sleeping bag and over her sister to kneel right in front of me. She hugged me hugely and kissed me smack on the lips. "There, Mama, that's the way it should be!" she happily exclaimed, scampering back to her sleeping bag and snuggling down, soon to sleep. I treasure that memory immeasurably, because that was the last time I ever saw my little girl.

During the night we discovered Susie missing, a hole slashed in the tent next to where her head had lain. We stumbled around the park in the dark with our feeble flashlights, desperately searching everywhere, but not a sign was to be found. My husband and father drove into the nearest town to get the town marshall, who, before he left his office, called the FBI and the Sheriff's Department. Within a short time the whole campground was swarming with law enforcement officers and citizens joining in the massive search and investigation.

A week later, a man called the home of one of the deputies assigned to the case, identified Susie by an unpublished birth defect so that we'd know the call to be authentic, and said he wanted to exchange her for ransom. The arrangements given for the exchange, however, were incomplete, and I soon appealed to the kidnapper through the media to make contact any way he wanted, telling him we were ready with the ransom and were willing to do whatever was needed for Susie's return.

The days dragged on with no word from the man. It seemed everyone else in the state was working twenty-four hours a day to find Susie. Deputies were searching homes, military men brought tracking dogs, Boy Scouts were hacking through thick underbrush with machetes, and search planes droned incessantly overhead.

The day came when they dragged the river right next to where we were camped. The boat would move a little bit and then stop, move on and then stop again. And every time the boat would stop, my heart would stop, terrified that Susie had been found there in the river, where I didn't want her to be. I watched the toll this terrible time was taking on my family, and I began to seethe with rage at this man who had done this to us. As an adult, I rarely expressed anger verbally, but while I prepared for bed that night, very consciously and deliberately and with much premeditation, I said out loud to my husband, "Even if the kidnapper were to bring Susie back, alive and well, this very moment, I could still kill him for what he has done to my family." I believed I could have done so with my bare hands and a big smile on my face, if only I knew who he was.

Almost as soon as the words were uttered, however human a response their sentiment was, I knew that to give myself to that ugly mindset would violate the principles and value system I held. Also, I'd learned enough about psychological well-being to know that hatred was not healthy. I knew myself well enough to recognize that, if I allowed that rage to engage my mind, it would obsess me and drain away all the psychic energy I needed to care for my family, cope with my own heartache, and, I hoped, help Susie process her own ordeal when she was returned.

Still, I was utterly furious. I felt absolutely justified in my desire for revenge, believing I'd have some input about what should happen to the kidnapper whenever he was apprehended. I knew the death penalty could be an option, and I was unabashedly convinced that this person should get "the chair." Susie was an innocent, defenseless little girl; I had every right to avenge whatever had happened to her. And so, round and round I went, wrestling with the worst and the best of myself.

Finally, because I'd been well taught always to reach for the highest moral ground, I surrendered. I made a decision to forgive this person, whoever he was. Yet, so saying, I clearly understood that this was not an accomplished feat by any means. The best I could muster was to choose to begin to make a serious effort to measure up to the call of my conscience. My choice seemed to lift an enormous burden from my heart, and for the first time since Susie had been taken, I actually was able to sleep soundly and felt rested in the morning.

After several more weeks had passed, we knew we had to return to Michigan, but the FBI agents handling the case in Montana would keep us informed. We immediately bought a recorder with a phone attachment so that, if the kidnapper called with final ransom exchange arrangements, it would be on tape and we'd be able to follow through with clear instructions and bring Susie home. Three months later, in a brief conversation with our oldest son, this man did indeed call, simply to say he still intended to exchange her for ransom, and when he figured out a workable way to accomplish this without getting caught, he'd call us again, goodbye. The call was traced to Wyoming, but there was no way of determining who'd made it.

Thus began many long months of waiting, of having hopes raised with sightings of little girls and suggestions of possible suspects, and then having hopes dashed when the girls were identified as children other than Susie and the suspects proved their innocence. It was a nearly unbearable time of stress and relentless psychological stretching to meet the challenge of coping with the anguish of Susie's absence and fate while being available to and involved with the rest of my family, who all still had ongoing lives in the midst of this abyss of not knowing.

Interminably, almost a whole year passed. The Montana media wanted to know what it was like to go for that long without knowing where my little girl was, how she was, even *if* she was anymore. When the reporter wrote his story, he quoted me as saying that I felt concern for the kidnapper, that I wished I could talk to him myself, but that I doubted I'd ever have the chance after all this time. The kidnapper read those words and was challenged by my statement. The night the report appeared, in the middle of the night—one year to the very minute he had taken Susie out of our tent—this man telephoned me at our home in Michigan.

He woke me from a sound sleep, but I knew who he was immediately. It quickly became clear he was calling to taunt me: "You wanted to talk to me? Well, here I am! Now what are you going to do about it? Because no one is ever going to find out who I am, and I am the one who is calling the shots. So, what does it matter if you get to talk to me or not?"

To my own amazement, as smug and nasty as he was being, something utterly unforeseen began to happen in me. From that time a year before, in Montana, where I had surrendered my rage and desire for revenge, I had truly tried to cooperate with moving my heart from fury to forgiveness. I had reminded myself repeatedly:

- that, however I felt about the kidnapper, in God's eyes he was just as precious as my little girl. I claim to believe in a God who is crazy about each of us, no matter who we are and what we've done, and I had to be unremitting in calling myself to that.
- that, even if he wasn't behaving like one, this man was a son of God, and, as such, just by virtue of his membership in the human family, he had dignity and worth, which meant for me that I had to think and speak of him with respect and not use the derogatory terms that came so easily to mind as I went month after month without knowing where my little girl was.
- that, as a Christian, I am called to pray for my enemies, a category for which he certainly qualified. In the beginning, that was the last thing I felt like doing, but as I sought to desire his well-being authentically and sincerely, the easier it became to do so. I realized how important it was that he experience good fortune and affirmation—the love of God—in his life. If he still had Susie, I wanted him to be good to her, and if he didn't have her, I wanted him to have the courage it would take to come forth and tell what had happened.

I've heard people say that forgiveness is for wimps. Well, I say then that they must never have tried it. Forgiveness is *hard work*. It demands diligent self-discipline, constant corralling of our basest instincts, custody of the tongue, and a steadfast refusal not to get caught up in the mean-spiritedness of our times. It doesn't mean we forget, we condone, or we absolve responsibility. It does mean that we let go of the hate, that we try to separate the loss and the cost from the recompense or punishment we deem is due. This is what happened to me, all that I had been working for, as I heard, for the first time, this man's voice in my ear—and neither of us was expecting it.

He was taken aback, backed off from his taunts, gentled down, and stayed on the phone for over an hour, even though he repeatedly expressed fear that the call was being traced and he'd be caught speaking to me. When I asked him what I could do to help him, he lost control and wept. Finally, he said, "I wish this burden could be lifted from me." I certainly knew the possibilities of what "this burden" could be, but I couldn't get him to elaborate. However, that's when I really understood the transformation that had happened in me. As desperate as I was for Susie's return, I realized I also wanted to reach and help this man.

Finally, the call ended and I was left holding the phone in the middle of the night. An attempt to trace the call failed, but in spite of my having been wakened out of a sound sleep, I'd somehow remembered to start the tape before I answered the phone, and the whole conversation was recorded. When the Montana agents listened to it, they heard, in that surprising milieu of concern and compassion, that he had let down his guard and inadvertently revealed enough information about himself to be identified.

Prior to his arrest, I was given the opportunity by the FBI to meet him and say face to face, not just to a voice on the phone, that I forgave him and hoped that he would use this opportunity to confess and receive the help he needed. He was sure he was going to beat this rap because he had passed both lie detector and truth serum tests, but finally, because of a second phone call he had made to me, this very sick young man was arrested, still insisting on his innocence. Once he was incarcerated, police went into his home with search warrants and therein found irrefutable evidence that he had committed murder. I learned that, even though he had talked all this time about exchanging Susie for ransom, in truth, Susie's life had been taken from her about a week after she'd been taken from me. She would never come home to me again, not in this world.

By this time, however, I had finally come to believe that real justice is not punishment but restoration, not necessarily to how things used to be, but to how they really should be. In both the Hebrew and Christian Scriptures whence my beliefs and values come, the God who rises up from them is a God of mercy and compassion, a God who seeks not to punish, destroy, or put us to death, but a God who works unceasingly to help and heal us, rehabilitate and reconcile us, restore us to the richness and fullness of life for which we have been created. This, now, was the justice I wanted for this man who had taken my little girl.

Though he was liable for the death penalty, I felt it would violate and profane the goodness, sweetness, and beauty of Susie's life by killing the kidnapper in her name. She was deserving of a more noble and beautiful memorial than a cold-blooded, premeditated, state-sanctioned killing of a restrained defenseless man, however deserving of death he may be deemed to be. I felt I far better honored her, not by becoming that which I deplored, but by saying that *all* life is sacred and worthy of preservation. So I asked the prosecutor to offer the alternative sentence for this crime, mandatory life imprisonment with no chance of parole. My request was honored, and when the alternative was offered, only then did he confess to Susie's death and also to the taking of three other young lives.

Though I readily admit that initially I wanted to kill this man with my bare hands, by the time of the resolution of his crimes, I was convinced that my best and healthiest option was to forgive. In the twenty years since losing my daughter, I have been working with victims and their families, and my experience has been consistently confirmed. Victim families have every right initially to the normal, valid, human response of rage, but those persons who retain a vindictive mind-set ultimately give the offender another victim. Embittered, tormented, enslaved by the past, their quality of life is diminished. However justified, our unforgiveness undoes us. Anger, hatred, resentment, bitterness, revenge—they are death-dealing spirits, and they will "take our lives" on some level as surely as Susie's life was taken. I believe the only way we can be whole, healthy, happy persons is to learn to forgive. That is the inexorable lesson and experience of the gospel of Marietta. Though I would *never* have chosen it so, the first person to receive a gift of life from the death of my daughter . . . was me.

3

The "Ideal" of Forgiveness:
A Philosopher's Exploration

Joanna North

Background

In 1987 I published an article in which I sought to provide a clear and coherent definition of the concept of forgiveness (North 1987). As a philosopher trained in the British analytic tradition, I present the following in an attempt to use the philosophical method of conceptual analysis to understand forgiveness and related issues in greater detail. To this end we must look at some approaches to the subject and try to see how they might be extended and developed so as to arrive, in the end, at a coherent, useful, and deep understanding of forgiveness. Paradoxically perhaps, my initial interest was stimulated by philosophical concerns with the nature of punishment and the related notions of retribution, deterrence, and rehabilitation, and by how these notions were being put into practice within the English legal system. In the 1980s there seemed to be a general confusion about the demands of justice and the purpose of the penal system. Many people, not least those working within the system itself, were unclear about the aims and goals of legal sanctions and penalties. For example, when we impose a prison sentence upon an offender, what exactly are we trying to do? Are we simply punishing him, making him suffer by administering a socially sanctioned form of public retribution? Are we aiming to deter others from similar crimes? Is our goal simply the protection of the public generally? Or are we trying to rehabilitate the offender, to make him a better and more socially useful member of society? Are we trying to do all these things at once, and if so, is a simple prison sentence likely to achieve so complex a result?

Amidst all this confusion (which to a large extent still exists) I detected the victim of crime, the one who had been wronged—the innocent, injured party. He appeared to stand alone, his feelings largely ignored, his needs unmet. I became interested in the range of possible responses which are open to an injured party and began to reflect upon the ways he or she might attempt to overcome a personal experience of having been wronged. My philosophical concerns include an interest in the philosophy of religion, and I began to see that the act of forgiveness might be of real practical help to those people who have been wronged by others.

What is forgiveness? Some have suggested that forgiveness is a wiping out of the wrong, a making undone what has been done. But how can this be achieved without requiring the wronged party simply to give up on his or her angry and hostile feelings toward the wrongdoer, feelings which are often extremely difficult to overcome and which, in any case, appear to be natural and indeed justifiable reactions to the infliction of harm? Another idea of forgiveness is that it involves, or requires, the forgoing of punishment. But is this not to condone the crime and to forgo the claims of justice? Yet another view of forgiveness equates it with *excusing* the wrongdoer. Rather than see the wrongdoer as a free agent, responsible for his crime, we are encouraged to see him as subject to natural or social forces way beyond his control. As a result, if he cannot be held responsible for his actions, then he cannot have done anything wrong at all. His misdemeanor was not morally reprehensible but only socially unacceptable. In such a view forgiveness is merely a response of pity and compassion, not a morally significant response in its own right.

Each of these views of forgiveness is, I believe, faulty and misguided. Forgiveness does not, indeed cannot, wipe out the fact of wrong having been done. Nor is it a matter of simply giving up one's right to punish (although this decision may in fact be a *result* of one's forgiveness of another person). Nor do we excuse the wrongdoer in forgiving him. We still see him as the perpetrator of the wrong and as the one who is responsible for it. Indeed, as Keith Yandell argues in the next chapter, there must be a real sense of the wrongdoer as responsible and the wrong as real if forgiveness is to be meaningful at all. After all, if there is no wrong and no wrongdoer, then there is nothing and no one to forgive.

A Note on Method

In what follows, then, I shall try to develop a coherent and persuasive account of forgiveness, analyzing the concept and discussing its related-ness to other issues such as "reframing," the acceptance of forgiveness, repentance, and self-forgiveness. In philosophy, apart from the realm of philosophical logic, there is perhaps no question of "proving" or demon-strating beyond any possible doubt that one's conclusions are correct. I present one approach to the topic of forgiveness, and there are, of course, other approaches and methods besides my own. The value of a book such as this is to present multiple perspectives on the subject, which it is to be hoped will stimulate further debate, disagreement, and argument. Only then will our understanding of forgiveness become fully rounded and profound.

At this point it would seem appropriate to acknowledge two debts. The first is to Robert Enright and his colleagues, whose empirical psychological research has allowed me to keep an eye on the "hard facts" of what people really go through when trying to forgive others. However, while keeping an eye on the empirical facts is crucial, such facts have to be grounded within a broad theoretical framework, and I have to make it clear that my orientation is influenced by thinkers such as Immanuel Kant and other philosophers of the "rationalistic" school. The view of the "person" which I adopt is that of a cognitive (in the sense of rational) being, capable of thought and self-reflection, capable also of exercising some control over emotions and emotional responses to given situations. I do not, however, hold that there is a complete split between the cognitive and the emotional sides of our nature, nor do I deny that there may also be a "spiritual" component. (This is not to say that religious themes are without value to forgiveness. Obviously not. My own personal belief is that human beings have a spiritual side, in which yearnings, hopes, and fears are expressed and experienced. Forgiveness is closely allied to this spiritual component of our nature and thus transcends the narrowly religious or denominational beliefs of individual religions. I also believe this spiritual side to be connected, in a complex way, to our capacity for morally significant feelings and actions. Thus forgiveness is of profound spiritual and moral relevance to all of us, regardless of whether we hold more specifically religious beliefs.) Such a view of the person is one which has been enormously influential in Western philosophical thought, and remains valid, I believe, even though I acknowledge that other conceptions of the person are possible. Once again this book is a great opportunity for furthering our understanding of ourselves and what it means to be human.

The Concept of Forgiveness

What we must remember is that a correct conception of forgiveness does not require that we forgo punishment altogether or that we should, in forgiving, attempt to annul the existence of the wrong done. Forgiveness does not remove the fact or event of wrongdoing but instead *relies* upon the recognition of wrong having been committed in order for the process of forgiveness to be made possible. As I said in my previous article: "What is annulled in the act of forgiveness is not the crime itself but the distorting effect that this wrong has upon one's relations with the wrongdoer and perhaps with others" (North 1987, p. 500). From the injured party's point of view, forgiveness will have the effect of preventing the wrong from continuing to damage one's self-esteem and one's psyche, so bringing to an end the distortion and corruption of one's relations with others.

Consider, for example, a woman who is unable or unwilling to forgive her attacker, a man who assaulted and robbed her on her way home one night. Someone might ask, "Well, why *should* she forgive him, after what he did to her? He is wicked, violent, and abusive. He deserves nothing but punishment and vilification. He has no right to compassion, sympathy, or forgiveness. She is completely justified in her hatred, her anger, and her bitterness toward him."

Well, quite. This reaction is natural enough, given the circumstances, and especially if only a short time has elapsed since the attack took place. But suppose we fill in the story with more detail. The attack occurred three years ago, and the victim, as I said, has not forgiven her attacker. She thinks about him every day, relives the pain and humiliation she felt that night. Every time she walks home, she is nervous, edgy, perhaps even panic-stricken when she hears someone walking behind her. She relives the attack in her thoughts by day and in her dreams by night. She has given up her job and has developed a more generalized fear of going out alone, even in daylight. Furthermore, the attack has affected her relations with men. Whenever she is with a man, she fears that he might attack her; she cannot trust him and cannot build a relationship with him.

It is clear that her experience of the attack has been devastating in its effects. It has affected every aspect of her life and, indeed, her whole personality. It is obvious that a real wrong has been done to her and that she has every reason to feel angry with her attacker. But it is not just anger that she is feeling now. She feels anxious, nervous, depressed, suspicious, and mistrustful. Is she justified in her fear, in her anxiety, in her inability to trust anyone she meets? Is she justified in depicting herself as a victim in all aspects of her life? We must, surely, say that, no, she is *not* justified in going this far. She is, in fact, a person who has intrinsic value, and, as such, she should regard herself with esteem and respect. She should be able to walk the streets without undue fear, without feeling more vulnerable than anyone else. She has allowed the original attack to dominate her whole existence, indeed, we might say, to *define* her very existence. Far from causing her an isolated and limited amount of harm at one point in her life, the attack has corrupted and all but destroyed her life. Its effects live on and thrive, because she cannot let go of the pain, cannot forgive the man who attacked her.

Through forgiveness the pain and hurt caused by the original wrong are released, or at least they are not allowed to mar the whole of one's being for all time. Once we recognize that an act of wrongdoing can have long-lasting and far-reaching effects, then we can see at least one aspect of the value of forgiveness as a response to having been wronged. If the woman in our example can forgive her attacker, she will, at the very least, be doing something of great value for her own self. In refusing to allow the wrong to cause her any more pain, she will be asserting her own value as a person. In forgiving the wrongdoer, she will in effect be saying, "This wrong you did to me caused me pain, but it is over now and I will not allow it to hurt me anymore. I will put the wrong in its proper place, as one thing which happened in my past, which I have dealt with, which I forgive you for, something which is only one small part of my whole life story."

The close relationship between self-respect and forgiveness is empha-sized in a paper by Margaret Holmgren (1993). She discusses a process of "responding to the wrongdoing" involving the recovery of self-esteem, recognition of wrong, and acknowledgment of feelings—a process which she sees as preparatory to the act or process of forgiveness. I prefer to see forgiveness itself as a complex process, which, in reality, cannot be neatly divided into pre- and postforgiveness phases. The rebuilding of one's self-esteem and self-confidence may not be completed until quite late in the process of forgiveness. Certainly, *enough* self-esteem must have been restored in order for the injured party to be willing to empathize and feel compassion for the wrongdoer, but it may be that the injured party's self-respect is restored in and through the act of forgiveness itself. This might be expressed in the realization: "If I can do this, forgive him, then I can't have been totally destroyed by his actions. I am something over and above the harm which he has done to me; otherwise I couldn't be offering him forgiveness here and now."

Of course, there is far more to forgiveness than this, and I am not suggesting that the moral value of forgiveness resides solely in its capacity to make the injured party feel better, as if forgiveness were simply a species of self-help therapy. Indeed, if this were a person's *sole* motivation in forgiving another, then he would be in danger of losing sight of the notion of forgiveness altogether. Forgiveness is not something that we do for ourselves alone, but something that we give or offer to another. The forgiving response is outward-looking and other-directed; it is supposed to make a difference *to the wrongdoer* as well as to ourselves, and it makes a difference in how we interact with the wrongdoer and with others. Even if the wrongdoer is no longer around—if he has since died, for example— our forgiveness is still directed at him as an object of our thoughts and memories, and our behavior *would* be different were it possible to meet him again. If we cannot meet him again, then forgiveness will typically have some outward manifestation in our behavior toward others with whom we come in contact. Examples of overt behavior which might constitute evidence or expression of forgiveness of those no longer present might include speaking of them favorably or fondly rather than with bitterness or anger, extending help and support to their remaining relatives or friends, visiting their graves, or simply telling someone else of one's change of heart.

But having said *this,* and having emphasized the giftlike quality of forgiveness, we should not decry the fact that in forgiving another we exercise some healing power over ourselves. If a man who is estranged from his erring father wants to forgive him, then it is at least partly because he, the son, suffers from the estrangement and wants to be rid of the pain he feels. There is no harm in the fact that, in giving to another, we take pleasure in the gift.

What these thoughts suggest is that the concept of forgiveness, and its moral value as a response to wrongdoing, is *multiperspectival.* A full examination requires us constantly to move between the perspective of the injured party and that of the wrongdoer in order to demonstrate the full complexity of the process of forgiveness. I shall return to this point in greater detail in the final section of this chapter.

The Active Nature of Forgiveness

Having reached some understanding of what forgiveness is *not* and suggested some of the elements underlying its complexity, I would like to emphasize another aspect of forgiveness. This is its *active* nature. As I said in 1987: "Forgiveness is a matter of a *willed* change of heart, the successful result of an active endeavor to replace bad thoughts with good, bitterness and anger with compassion and affection" (North 1987, p. 506). Forgiveness involves the overcoming of negative feelings (anger, hatred, resentment, desire for revenge) and their replacement with positive emotions (compassion, benevolence, even love). But, for the process to count as one of forgiveness, and therefore as having moral value, it has to occur in the right way and for the right reasons. If it were possible to take a pill which converted angry thoughts into kindly ones, this would not count as an example of forgiveness, nor would it be of any intrinsic moral value (although it might have desirable results, such as interpersonal harmony and reduction in crime). Nor is there any moral value in ceasing to be angry because one has become tired or bored with being so, or because one has forgotten the original injury, or because one has come to see that one was blaming the wrong person. The *mere* cessation of hostile feelings in such cases has nothing to do with forgiveness.

The overcoming of negative feelings involved in forgiveness must be the result of an *active psychological endeavor* on the part of the injured party, even while recognizing that a real injury has been inflicted and that the wrongdoer is to blame for the infliction. The active endeavor has as its goal the healing of the damage done to the injured party and of the damage caused to the relations which exist between injured party and wrongdoer.

This process of active psychological endeavor has, I believe, been very fully described by Robert Enright and the Human Development Study Group (Enright et al. 1992). They have proposed a four-phase process involving (1) "uncovery," (2) "decision making," (3) "work," and (4) "outcome." In the discussion which follows I shall adopt a similar strategy, breaking down the process of forgiveness into a number of stages, as represented in table 3.1. I must emphasize, however, that the experience of forgiving another does not necessarily follow each and every phase in the precise order which I have highlighted, and that the divisions between the stages are not always experienced as clear-cut and obvious.

The following are brief descriptions of each of the stages:

Stage 1

Injured party (IP) experiences negative feelings of anger, rage, hatred, bitterness, and so on. Initially, these may be repressed or not fully recognized for some reason. But recognition and awareness of such feelings and of one's *right* to them are essential if the process is to proceed.

Stage 2

IP demands justice, punishment, retribution. Public recognition of one's wrong helps IP to overcome his negative feelings to some degree. If justice is not done, on the other hand, IP is likely to feel frustration and perhaps an increase in the intensity of his negative feelings.

Stage 3

IP is still subject to negative, hostile feelings directed toward the wrongdoer (WD). He suffers from their influence and recognizes that the wrong still affects him. He is willing to countenance forgiveness as a way of healing himself. The point at which IP feels ready to forgive will vary according to a number of factors, including the extent and seriousness of the wrong done, who the wrongdoer was, the time elapsed since the wrong, and the nature and intensity of the feelings being experienced at the present time. Only IP can decide when the time is right for forgiveness, although, as I shall suggest later, certain circumstances may serve to motivate IP toward forgiveness, and he may even come to recognize a duty to forgive WD.

Stage 4

If IP is to forgive he has to look beyond himself to the wrongdoer. IP may recognize a moral or religious duty to forgive WD as a fellow human being or as one of God's creatures, like himself. That is, there may be some *impersonal claim* of this kind which encourages in IP a desire to forgive. IP may feel, "I ought to forgive WD because, as a human being, WD demands some measure of respect and consideration from me." Or IP may feel, "I ought to forgive WD because he and I are both sinners, both humble before God. I should forgive him because I want God to treat me in a forgiving manner."

Stage 5

Instead, or in addition, IP may recognize a *personal claim* on his forgiveness. This might depend on the relationship which existed prior to the wrongdoing or which perhaps has been built up between IP and WD since the wrongdoing. It may be, for example, that IP and WD are related through blood or marriage, and the fact of this relationship and what the relationship meant before the wrongdoing may itself be a reason for forgiveness to be attempted. IP might say, "He is my brother, after all. I ought to forgive him partly because of that fact alone." Thus family ties and bonds of close friendship are often sufficient motivation in themselves for the desire to forgive.

Stage 6

This stage is the *desire* to forgive, which arises out of or is itself a part of stages 4 and 5. IP recognizes not only that he *ought* to forgive WD but also that he *wants* to forgive him. He may experience more positive emotions toward WD, feelings such as compassion, pity, understanding, or love. The origin of such emotions may lie in several factors: IP's ability to see himself as similar to WD as in stage 4; IP's feelings for WD which arise out of the original relationship between them; the recognition that WD himself has suffered for the wrong he committed; WD's expression of penitence and his desire to be forgiven.

Stage 7

IP decides to try to forgive WD (or perhaps consciously acknowledges that this is what he is already in the process of doing). The positive emotions which may be experienced in stage 6 can be enhanced and nurtured through engagement in the process of "reframing" (identified by Enright and others). A fuller understanding of WD, his circumstances and outlook, his background and his beliefs and feelings, may all be considered by IP in his attempt to put WD and his action into perspective. Reframing is, among other things, a process whereby the wrongdoer can be regarded as someone over and above the wrong he has committed, a means of "separating" the wrongdoer from the wrong he has done. This is the most crucial stage in the whole process of forgiveness, and as such we ought to consider it in greater detail. Before doing so, however, we need to fill in the remaining gaps in the process.

Stage 8

As a natural result of stage 7, IP will typically offer some public form of expression of his forgiveness of WD. Often, where a close relationship exists between IP and WD, a mere friendly glance or touch of the hand might be sufficient to indicate forgiveness. What form the public expression takes will depend very much on the nature of the relationship existing between IP and WD at the time of the wrong. If they were strangers previously and unlikely to see each other again, IP might simply tell someone else that he has forgiven WD and that he no longer holds a grudge against him. If WD has been jailed for his crime, then IP might be willing to write to him or visit him in order to express his forgiveness in person. There are reconciliation programs which offer just such an opportunity for IP and WD to come together. Or IP's forgiveness may take the form of a public statement directed at WD and transmitted through the news media. We have seen this recently in England when the father of a victim of IRA terrorism publicly expressed his forgiveness of the terrorists and his willingness to meet with them in order to try to understand their perspective.

It is worth saying that the public expression of forgiveness may itself be a way of completing the internal process mentioned in stage 7. Public and private realms frequently inform and influence one another. We can see this in the cathartic nature of the public rituals and forms of mourning for a loved one who has died. The sharing of grief at a funeral enables the bereaved to release their private grief in a socially accepted way. In a similar manner, extending the hand to someone who has hurt you may be one way, not just of expressing existing forgiveness, but also of *experiencing* that forgiveness in the moment of contact. In physically making contact with another's hand, we make psychological contact with him, the wrongdoer, and allow the process of reconciliation to begin.

Stage 9

Finally, IP's negative feelings have been overcome and replaced with positive emotions toward WD. This completes the forgiveness process from the perspective of the injured party. It may be that WD is no longer around and cannot be informed of IP's forgiveness. This itself does not bar the forgiveness process, because forgiveness is principally an internal change of heart and mind, even while being other-directed. If WD *is* around, however, then the process will naturally or typically result in some contact between IP and WD that is a public expression of forgiveness. As a result the relations between them have been, at least partly, healed, although further work may be needed before complete trust and harmony can be experienced (although as Beverly Flanigan points out in her chapter, "complete" harmony may never be fully achieved). It is worth emphasizing, too, that the future relations between IP and WD may not take the same form as those which existed before the wrongdoing. The wife of an alcoholic who comes to forgive him for the years of misery he caused may decide that she cannot live with him and that their marriage is over, even though she is now able to view him with compassion and affection.

Reframing

I said earlier that stage 7 of the forgiveness process—that of reframing—is crucial to the whole enterprise. I would like now to examine some of the aspects of reframing which will help us to understand the process of forgiveness in greater detail.

Enright and his colleagues have described reframing as a process whereby the wrongdoer is viewed *in context* in an attempt to build up a complete picture of the wrongdoer and his actions. Typically, this involves understanding the pressures that the wrongdoer was under at the time of the wrong and an appreciation of WD's personality as a result of his particular developmental history.

For example, a man may dislike his father and resent him because when he was a child his father neglected him and failed to give him the love and support he craved. The son now wishes to forgive his father and to form a closer relationship with him. He begins to explore his father's own upbringing in more detail. He discovers that his father was himself deprived of affection from his own parents, that he grew up in a stern, rigid family environment in which expressions of love and affection were openly discouraged. Years of strict and authoritarian discipline took their toll on his father's personality, and he developed a cold, impassive persona as a way of coping with his lack of self-esteem and loneliness. He found it difficult to express his feelings of love for his own son, and although he was not harsh or tyrannical he made himself emotionally absent in his son's upbringing.

When the son has understood his father's background and personality in this deeper, more detailed way, he can see that his father's neglect was part and parcel of his own stunted emotional development. The father had developed a set of responses within interpersonal relations as a result of his own damaged psychological make-up, responses which involved a refusal to acknowledge the son's needs and a fear of expressing emotions. He did not want to hurt his son in the way that he himself had been hurt—through a strict and regimented upbringing—but the only way of dealing with his son that he could envisage or cope with emotionally was to be cool, distant, and detached, apparently indifferent and uncaring.

As a result of this reframing process the son now has a better understanding of the context of his father's attitude toward him and is now in a better position to encourage more positive feelings of compassion and empathy, and ultimately to forgive his father. It is important to distinguish this process from one of condoning or excusing his father's behavior. His father still did him real harm, and the father was responsible for it. He could have tried to change his responses and risked exposing his feelings for his son. But he failed to do so, and this failure was *his* and no one else's.

Consider another example. A man discovered that his wife had been having an affair, and he naturally felt betrayed, hurt, angry, and resentful. He insisted that she leave their home and refused to have anything to do with her. Then, as time passed, he realized that he missed her, that he still loved her, that he was suffering from their estrangement and wanted to forgive her and to be reconciled.

When he first discovered her infidelity his perceptions of her were focused solely on the wrong which she had done. He thought of how she had deceived him, how she lied to him, how she betrayed him, hurt him, and wronged him. He could not see beyond his pain and hurt, and his whole attitude toward her was clouded and defined in terms of the terrible wrong she had done to him. But if he was to forgive her, he had to regard his wife and her actions in context. She had not, after all, been deceiving him *all* their married life; the affair had begun at a particular point in time and in certain circumstances. When he was ready to try to forgive her, the husband could see that the affair had started at a time when he had been very busy at work, when he had been spending long periods away from home. He knew, too, that his wife had always needed a great amount of emotional reassurance of his love for her, and that she had always had a rather insecure sense of her own self-worth. He recognized now that his involvement in work must have been perceived by her as a form of emotional rejection and that she had felt increasingly lonely and unloved. The husband could now understand why she had sought love and reassurance from another man. He could see that her actions *made sense,* given the circumstances and given her personality. Of course, she should have spoken to him of her feelings of isolation, and she should have tried harder to cope with her feelings rather than embark upon an affair. But the process of reframing enabled the husband to see her actions in context and to overcome his feelings of anger and encourage more positive emotions. Forgiveness was now a possibility.

These two examples suggest that reframing is not just a way of putting the wrongdoer and his action *in context* but is also a way of *separating* the wrongdoer from the wrong which has been committed. When we are deeply hurt by another person we tend to think of him as a "bad person," as if his crime "shoots through," or defines, his whole personality. The son regards his father's whole being as devoid of love; the husband sees his wife as an adulteress; and the woman in my earlier example perceives her attacker as wholly vicious and wicked. But, in most cases, people are not wholly bad, and their actions result from a multiplicity of background factors. Reframing does not do away with the wrong itself, nor does it deny the wrongdoer's responsibility for it, but it allows us to regard the wrongdoer in a more complete, more detailed, more rounded way—in a way, that is, which does justice to the complexity of the wrongdoer's personality. The wrongdoer is not just an attacker, not just an adulteress, not just a bad father; rather, there is a whole story which may be told. The wrongdoing is one of many actions emanating from the wrongdoer, and it was done for a reason, under certain circumstances, and as part of a whole process of action and reaction reaching back into the past. The process of reframing then enables us to see the whole picture, or at least a richer picture, in which the wrongdoer is someone over and above the particular hurtful action. He is not simply or solely a wrongdoer but is a *person* who has done a particular wrong. We can now perhaps appreciate the thinking which lies behind the Christian dictum that we should hate the sin but not the sinner, that we should condemn the wrong but forgive the wrongdoer.

I have to pause at this point, however, to register a few reservations and to acknowledge the fact that there *may* be certain situations in which forgiveness is *not* possible. The nature of the impossibility seems to stem from the difficulty one has, in certain circumstances, in carrying out the reframing process just described, cases in which it is extremely difficult to separate the wrongdoer from the wrong which he or she has committed. There are two broad categories in which the difficulty seems to be most apparent.

The first category is that of certain horrific crimes where the wrong is of such magnitude as apparently to defy understanding. One might cite as examples cases of the torture and murder of children where the particular obscenity and horrible nature of the crime seems to militate against any attempt at reframing. Or there are other cases, such as genocide and mass extermination of whole races of people, where it is *the scale and extent of the wrong* which prevent victims and their families from attempting to understand and to forgive.

The apparent impossibility of forgiveness in such situations stems from the nature of the crime itself, which is so horrible or so extensive that it weighs far more in the balance than all the other aspects of the wrongdoer's past and personality put together. It is not that we are unable to carry out the reframing process; we can still see the wrong in its context and as an action which makes sense in terms of the wrongdoer's personality. Rather, it is that the reframing process, far from allowing us to separate the wrongdoer from his action, serves to reinforce the *identification* of the wrongdoer with his action. The more we understand, the more we come to regard the wrongdoer as culpable, as wholly and utterly bad. Any attempt to forgive in such situations may be doomed to failure because of the psychological difficulty of showing love and compassion for a person who could do such a terrible thing. Indeed, the impossibility of forgiveness in such cases may be a *moral,* not just a psychological, one. Martin Golding, for example, considers cases of wrongdoing such as the Holocaust in which "wrongs having this degree of culpability and enormity may put one permanently in debt to the victim such that the moral amends are unending and resentment is forever justified" (Golding 1984–85, p. 135).

The second, related, category of cases is that in which it is *the nature of the wrongdoer,* the person himself, which stands in the way of the possibility of forgiveness. Here I have in mind an individual who consciously, knowingly, and willingly chooses and adopts evil rather than good as the basic motivation for his life. Such a person might come from a good, loving background, have no social or educational disadvantages, have nothing in his background which might serve to explain his preference for bad rather than good behavior. He likes hurting others, he has no wish for friends, he delights in upsetting people and causing damage and destruction in the lives of others, he takes pleasure in others' pain. He is, we might say, a sadist, a psychotic personality, the personification of evil, the devil in human form. Mercifully, it is true that there are few examples of such people, but the type is conceivable and close approximations do exist. The unredeemability of such a person and his apparent relish for his crimes might incline us to regard him as so monstrous that we dismiss him from the moral universe which we inhabit. The result of this view, however, is that forgiveness becomes a *conceptual* impossibility, because the wrongdoer is not "one of us," not of the kind to which concepts of love, compassion, and forgiveness are applicable, not a person but a monster.

A similar view is taken by Margaret Holmgren, who depicts such a wrongdoer in Kantian terms as having "lost the capacity" for a good will. As such, and paradoxically, the thoroughly bad person cannot be regarded as a responsible agent: "Since the offender has lost the capacity to choose, she is not responsible for her violation. However, she remains a sentient being . . . the appropriate attitude to extend towards such an offender is simply an attitude of compassion" (Holmgren 1993, p. 350). In the example I have outlined, however, the wrongdoer has not simply lost the capacity for good but has *chosen* bad rather than good as a motivation for his actions and must, therefore, be regarded as responsible, that is, not simply a monster standing outside our moral universe. We should regard such a person, I believe, not as outside the moral universe but as defining the *limits* of that universe and as posing the ultimate challenge to our concept of forgiveness. Once again, the apparent impossibility of forgiveness seems to be moral as well as psychological, because the extent of the wrongdoer's own incorporation of wrong into his personality prevents the reframing process from revealing anything other than a bad person. We cannot forgive such a wrongdoer because he is so impenetrable in his moral corruption that we can find nothing to say in his favor.

Examples such as these and the difficulties which they pose to the concept of forgiveness merit closer attention and a more detailed analysis. However, I must return to the discussion of the forgiveness process and to the many, and more common, situations in which forgiveness, while difficult to achieve, is not itself open to charges of psychological, moral, or conceptual impossibility. I want to discuss that aspect of the forgiveness process which I mentioned earlier when I said that the concept of forgiveness, and its moral value, is "multiperspectival" in nature. This topic forms the subject matter of the next, final, section of this chapter.

The Multiperspectival Nature of Forgiveness

When we forgive another person we have to move from our own per-spective, of initial hurt and internal suffering, to that of the wrongdoer, the context of his wrong and his motivation for it as well as his present situation. Given the multiperspectival nature of the process of forgiveness as it is experienced, it seems natural to suppose that our understanding of the *concept* of forgiveness will be enhanced still further if we look beyond the perspective of the injured party to that of the wrongdoer and his view of both the victim and himself once the wrong has been committed. I believe that the process of forgiveness has interesting parallels in the process that the wrongdoer himself may undergo once he has committed the wrong. I would like, therefore, to examine the process of forgiveness from the point of view of the wrongdoer—the process of *being* forgiven, the process of the wrongdoer's *acceptance* of forgiveness from the injured party. As we shall see, acceptance of forgiveness requires the wrongdoer to perform his own variant of the forgiveness process, namely, that of *self-forgiveness*. Once we have brought the processes of forgiveness and acceptance of forgiveness into line, I believe that we will then have greater insight into the concept of forgiveness itself.

In table 3.1 I proposed an analysis of forgiveness in nine stages. I propose to treat the process of the acceptance of forgiveness on the part of the wrongdoer in a similar fashion. This process is represented in table 3.2. I shall now describe each of these stages in greater detail.

Stages 1–3 are the necessary stages of *repentance*. While I reject the view that forgiveness requires repentance on the part of the wrongdoer. I certainly believe that the wrongdoer's *acceptance* of forgiveness, if it is to be genuine and of moral value, must involve his being sorry for what he has done and determining to reform. We may forgive someone who is absent or dead and who expressed no sorrow for the harm they did to us. We can forgive someone in our hearts even though he may stand there in front of us throwing our forgiveness back at us. But reconciliation, which in some form is the desired goal on the part of the injured party who has forgiven the wrongdoer, is not possible unless the wrongdoer accepts that forgiveness, and acceptance, in turn, requires repentance for the wrong done. Acceptance of forgiveness is not a matter of cynically or calculatedly resuming relations with the injured party while still feeling glad for the hurt done him or while refusing to accept that a wrong was done. What is required is that the wrongdoer overcome his feelings of shame and remorse and allow himself to enter into harmonious relations with the injured party. But just as forgiveness of others has to occur in the right way and for the right reasons if it is to be of moral value, so too the process of accepting

Table 3.1. Forgiveness—the injured party's (IP) perspective

Stage 1	Stage 2	Stage 3
IP experiences negative feelings. Gradually recognizes and becomes aware of feelings experienced.	IP demands justice/ punishment/retribution. Perhaps feels some lessening of negative emotions.	IP willing to forgive, primarily to relieve his own feelings.
Stage 4	*Stage 5*	*Stage 6*
IP looks beyond himself to wrongdoer (WD). Recognizes some form of impersonal claim on his forgiveness.	IP recognizes a personal claim on his forgiveness.	IP experiences desire to forgive. Feels more positive emotions toward WD.
Stage 7	*Stage 8*	*Stage 9*
IP decides to try to forgive WD. Undergoes a process of "reframing" which helps IP to separate WD from his wrong.	IP offers or displays some public form of expression of his forgiveness.	IP's negative feelings largely or wholly overcome. Reconciliation now achieved or possible.

Table 3.2. Forgiveness—the wrongdoer's (WD) perspective

Stage 1	Stage 2	Stage 3
WD recognizes that he has done wrong. Also recognizes IP's right to punish.	WD experiences "other-oriented" regret or remorse for the wrong.	WD resolves to reform. Undergoes a process of reframing in regard to himself.
Stage 4	*Stage 5*	*Stage 6*
WD recognizes some measure of self-improvement. Process of self-forgiveness under way.	WD desires IP's forgiveness.	WD asks IP for forgiveness.
Stage 7	*Stage 8*	*Stage 9*
Some measure of self-forgiveness achieved. WD now awaits IP's response.	WD accepts IP's offer of forgiveness. Self-esteem restored, at least partially.	WD has overcome his negative feelings of self-hatred or disapproval. Reconciliation now achieved or possible.

forgiveness requires the wrongdoer to undergo certain stages—a *cognitive* stage of recognizing that he has done wrong, an *emotional* response of regret or remorse, and a stage involving the *determination to change* or to make amends. Together, these three stages constitute the process of repentance.

Stage 1 is the cognitive recognition on the part of the wrongdoer of the harm he has done. This may require quite a complex understanding of the meaning and full consequences of his action. A "joyrider," for example, may not fully appreciate what he has done if he sees it solely in terms of having stolen a car. If he learns that, as a result of his action, the car's owner was unable to visit her mother, who, in fact, had just collapsed at home, unable to call for help, and later died as a result of the delay, the wrongdoer should begin to realize the full seriousness of what he has done. While he may feel initial indifference or even euphoria for his action, the wrongdoer is likely to feel differently once he has seen the whole picture.

The recognition of having done something wrong is closely bound up with the recognition that one deserves punishment or some form of retribution. Even if the wrongdoer asks for mercy or pardon, he betrays his recognition that the injured party (or the judge on his behalf) has the *right* to punish him. What he wants is for that right to be set aside and for his pleas to be answered with compassion and benevolence.

Stage 1 leads us to stage 2, which is one of feeling emotions of remorse and regret for what one has done. It is important to emphasize that I am not suggesting that the stages are necessarily experienced by wrongdoers as a result of their actions; clearly and regrettably, many wrongdoers never accept that they have done anything wrong or, if they do, they do not care or, if they do care, they do not try to change. Of course, the apparent absence of a moral sense and a person's inability or unwillingness to try to change are serious matters and surely present severe practical difficulties for those who have to deal with the wrongdoer. But in describing the process of the acceptance of forgiveness, I am trying to uncover the *conceptual* links between the various stages and to examine the associations between the concepts of the recognition of wrong, the experience of remorse, and the willed change of heart that is prompted by these in cases where the wrongdoer *does* have a moral sense and *is* receptive to remorse. The fact that some people are incapable or unwilling to undergo the process of accepting forgiveness does not mean that the attempt to describe and analyze the process is futile. The process of forgiveness, similarly, may be beyond some people, but the understanding of how it would operate in those cases where it is possible for it to do so is still of value.

Let us continue, therefore, with the description of the process of accepting forgiveness. I said that the wrongdoer will, in stage 2, experience feelings of remorse or regret. This regret must, of course, go beyond mere self-pity and sorrow for having been caught in the act of wrongdoing. If regret is to be of moral value, it must be of the right kind and experienced for the right reasons. This has been recognized by Golding (1984–85), who identifies the response as "other-oriented regret," which may vary in its degree of intensity but which crucially involves an other-directed feeling of sorrow. Thus it is to be distinguished from self-pity in that it is sorrow for what one has done to the injured party.

For the process of repentance to be completed, a third stage must be experienced by the wrongdoer, namely, a volitional stage in which he resolves not only never to do such a thing again but also to become a better person (stage 3). Here we see an interesting parallel to the reframing process carried out by the injured party in relation to the wrongdoer. If the wrongdoer's determination to reform is to be more than an empty promise or a weak resolve, then he must engage in a process of self-examination and self-analysis comparable to the reframing process. He must examine his motivations for his action, understand the context of its occurrence, and analyze his own character and developmental history. He may come to see himself as having a serious flaw in his character or as having a tendency to react in a certain way as a result of something that happened in the past. He must deal with these influences, come to terms with them, and find ways of overcoming their effects upon his behavior if he is to change in the future.

The process of repentance—recognition of wrong, experience of remorse, and determination to change—is essential to the process of accepting forgiveness. It is, in fact, a *morally regenerative* process, enabling the wrongdoer both to see himself as someone who already has some moral worth despite the wrong which he has committed and, at the same time, to become more worthy of the respect and esteem which he wants the injured party to display toward him in forgiveness. Through repentance the wrongdoer has reached stage 4, a consciousness of some measure of self-improvement and a development of self-respect.

Once the wrongdoer has repented and feels worthy of it, he wants to be forgiven (stage 5). He has overcome his feelings of unworthiness and self-hatred sufficiently to allow himself to accept forgiveness if it is offered. There are cases where a wrongdoer feels so full of self-disgust and so lowered in his own estimation that he cannot accept that he is worthy of being forgiven. In such a case we would say that he cannot forgive himself and cannot regard himself as forgivable. He is stuck in the second stage of remorse and regret. That is why the parallel reframing process is so crucial here, just as it was in the injured party's process of forgiving another. Without the experience of such a process, the injured party is locked into his feelings of anger and bitterness, and the wrongdoer is similarly imprisoned in his own self-loathing. The process of reframing, on the part of the wrongdoer, allows him, at least in part, to forgive himself. In some cases this might have to do. If the injured party is unwilling ever to offer forgiveness to the wrongdoer, the latter may still be brought to a stage of self-acceptance, in which he finds it possible to live with himself in the future. If he has done all that he can to change and to make amends, I think we can concede to him the right to his own self-forgiveness. This is not to say, of course, that the injured party is obligated to offer forgiveness in return. But repentance and reform might well provide the injured party with a *motivation* to forgive the wrongdoer.

At stage 6 the wrongdoer may make a plea for forgiveness from the injured party. This request might be expressed in the following terms: "Please forgive me. I know I hurt you and I am sorry for it. I will never do so again. I want to change and indeed I have changed already. I am no longer exactly the same: I have disowned and reviled my past behavior. I hope and believe that I am worthy to accept your forgiveness." In desiring and asking for forgiveness after repentance, the wrongdoer demonstrates his separation from the wrong he has committed and his sincere intention to make amends through some form of reparation and a changed way of life.

By stage 7 the wrongdoer has achieved some measure of self-forgiveness and is awaiting forgiveness from the injured party in order for that process to be completed. Let us suppose now that the injured party offers forgiveness. The wrongdoer is now able to move on to stage 8, in which he accepts that forgiveness. He can do so because he feels worthy of the gift that is being offered. Having forgiven himself he feels able to be forgiven by another. Or perhaps the recognition of the injured party's willingness to forgive completes the wrongdoer's attempt to build his self-confidence and self-esteem. Here we see clearly the shift in perspectives between wrongdoer and injured party, which I mentioned earlier: the wrongdoer in effect says, "I can forgive myself now because *you* have forgiven me. In your eyes I am worthy, and I accept and adopt your perspective when I look at myself. If you can find it in yourself to give me this gift, then I must try to see myself as worthy of accepting it." From the injured party's perspective, what is being said might be expressed in the following terms: "I can forgive you now because I see that you are truly repentant, and if you are repentant, that must demonstrate your self-worth. I recognize that you are justified in your self-forgiveness and I accept and adopt your perspective when I look at you."

Finally, at stage 9 the wrongdoer and the injured party are reconciled, or at least some measure of interpersonal harmony has been reached. The act of forgiveness, offered and accepted, has enabled the two parties to reach a balance in their relations with each other. The wrongdoer, who through his action "cast himself down" in the eyes of the injured party, has been "raised up" once again in that party's estimation. He has become worthy of the respect and consideration of the injured party. The injured party, on the other hand, initially in a position of moral superiority over the wrongdoer, has, through forgiving him, metaphorically "lowered himself" to meet the wrongdoer, not at his original position of moral debasement, but at a position of moral equality, where both are equal in terms of the measure of respect, esteem, and consideration due them.

The process of the acceptance of forgiveness, like that of the offering of forgiveness, has been described here in ideal terms, of course. I use the word *ideal* in two senses. First, the processes are ideal archetypes, generalized patterns, which in their details map out typical stages that occur in most situations where forgiveness is offered and accepted. In reality, of course, each stage will be experienced in different ways by different people. Nor is there meant to be any suggestion of a specific time frame in which the processes occur or any exact matching between parallel stages at the same point in time. The process of forgiving another may be almost instantaneous or it may take years to achieve. In the same way, the process of accepting forgiveness, both from oneself and from another, is likely to take some time: indeed, self-forgiveness ought not to be accomplished too quickly if one is not to be suspected of insincerity.

The two processes are ideal in a second sense in that I propose them as goals toward which I believe we ought to strive. For Christians and non-Christians alike, the process of forgiveness enshrines common human values and virtues. Restoring affection and regard, overcoming estrangement and alienation, accepting and welcoming others: these are values which we should endeavor to realize in our dealings with one another. Through the effort to forgive and the effort to be worthy of forgiveness, we experience and put into practice the moral virtues of trust, compassion, and sympathy, which are the fundamental bonds of unity between all human individuals.

References

Enright, R. D., E. A. Gassin, and C. Wu. 1992. Forgiveness: A developmental view. *Journal of Moral Education* 21(2): 99–114.

Golding, M. P. 1984–85. Forgiveness and regret. *Philosophical Forum* 16(1–2): 121–137.

Holmgren, M. 1993. Forgiveness and the intrinsic value of persons. *American Philosophical Quarterly* 30(4): 340–352.

North, J. 1987. Wrongdoing and forgiveness. *Philosophy* 62: 499–508.

4

The Metaphysics and Morality
of Forgiveness

Keith E. Yandell

Whatever help philosophy can bring in principle to understanding for-giveness, any actual philosophical help obviously comes from particular philosophers on particular occasions. We are fortunate, then, to have the clarity and high plausibility of Joanna North's chapter (see chap. 3). I hope to extend the inquiry through a consideration of related topics of crucial relevance for the study of forgiveness. Forgiveness is a morally significant process that occurs between persons. This is not to deny that forgiveness can be spontaneous. Theoretically, a spontaneous act of forgiveness can be understood as the minimal limit on a process. Therapeutically, the possibility of spontaneous forgiveness gains its importance in the form of a warning that there is, relative to experienced time, probably no temporal limitation on how quickly forgiveness may occur.

For my purposes, I understand a person to be a being that endures through time and whose essence resides in being capable of a self-con-sciousness, which he or she typically experiences (Yandell 1995). A person has both a psychological and a moral dimension. Philosophy is relevant to a consideration of forgiveness, because forgiveness has necessary and sufficient conditions that are partly metaphysical and partly moral in nature. In what follows, I will say a bit about both sorts of conditions (see Yandell 1995, pp. 549–53, for definitions of conscious minds). One important topic that I will not do more than mention here is self-forgiveness; it deserves discussion on its own.

The Metaphysics of Forgiveness: What Sorts of Things Forgive?

It is obvious that there are conditions for forgiveness; in a world composed of only rocks, plants, and salamanders, there could be no forgiveness going on. Most obviously, it requires an offender who has done wrong and a victim who has been wronged. In the relevant sense of the terms *offender* and *victim,* both must be moral agents. The victim of a rock slide not caused by negligence or action on the part of some other person is not victimized by an offender. It is individual persons who are victims and offenders in the primary sense of these terms, and societies, nations, businesses, and other institutions are victims or offenders in an extended sense of the primary. This in no way diminishes the importance of communal forgiveness and reconciliation. However, this raises the question of what a moral agent is. There is controversy, of course, as to what the correct answer is, and it is worth saying a little in explanation and defense of a particular answer (Frankfurt 1988; Yandell 1988).

Determination

The world is a complex place, and we do not actually have anything like a description of everything that is true of the world at a given time. But the concept "a description of everything that is true of the world at a given time" is perfectly consistent, and it provides a nice way of saying what determinism is. A determinist holds that a description of everything that happens in the world at a given time, plus the laws of logic and the laws of nature, strictly entails any description of everything that is true of the world at any later time. (The laws of nature may themselves be thought of as true generalizations grounded in the natures and causal powers of natural objects.) The determinist slogan is: The past determines a unique future. There is a simple argument to the effect that it is logically impossible or self-contradictory that determinism be true and that persons have the sort of freedom that is required for them to be morally responsible for their choices and actions. The argument is this: One is not responsible for anything that one has no control over. One has no control over the truth about the past, the laws of nature, the laws of logic, or anything strictly entailed by any of these. According to determinism, everything true of the present is entailed by the truth about the past, the laws of logic, and the laws of nature. Hence, if determinism is true, no one has any control over anything, and thus, no one is morally responsible for anything. Since one cannot act rightly or wrongly if she is not responsible for her actions, if determinism is true, no one acts rightly or wrongly (Van Inwagen 1983).

Freedom

This argument that determinism precludes responsibility, brief and powerful, has another advantage relative to our present interests. It allows us to define the sort of freedom a moral agent must possess, even if determinism is true of the natural world. I shall reintroduce the notion of freedom, specifically *categorical freedom*: Jane has categorical freedom relative to a given action at a given time if and only if (1) she has it in her power to perform that action at that time, and (2) she has it in her power to refrain from performing that action at that time. She has it in her power to perform that action at that time only if her doing so does not require that she make false either some truth about the past, or some law of logic, or some law of nature; she has it in her power to refrain from performing that action at that time only if her doing so does not require that she make false some truth about the past, some law of nature, or some law of logic (Van Inwagen 1983). A moral agent has categorical freedom regarding morally significant actions (actions that are morally right, or else morally wrong, to perform) (Rowe 1991).

Persons and Natural Objects

These remarks also serve to make clearer the fact that, in a world of only natural objects, there could be no forgiveness. Consider a stone lying on the ground as a representative natural object. The stone might not have been located where it is; it is not part of its nature to lie there rather than somewhere else. But consider the rest of what is true about the world besides the stone's lying where it does; call all that the story around the stone. It could not be true, given the story around the stone, that the stone could lie elsewhere. Now consider an agent who exercises categorical freedom in speaking the truth. She could have lied; nothing in her nature as a person precludes lying, and had she lied she would not have changed species or gone "poof" out of existence. And consider the rest of what is true about the world besides our agent telling the truth; call that the story around the person. It could still be true, given the story around the person, that our agent lied. Typically, persons who tell the truth could have lied, even given their surrounding story; stones that lie in a given place could not lie elsewhere, given their surrounding story. That is a crucial distinction between persons and natural objects and a crucial distinction between worlds that contain persons and worlds that do not. Aristotle distinguished between things capable of volition and things not. Kant (1964) distinguished between things that can act only in accordance *with* a rule and things that act *from* a rule. Persons who tell the truth but could have lied possess volition, can act from a rule, are not natural objects. Forgiveness among natural objects, like squaring the circle, does not contain possible reality among its charms.

It is widely held that causal laws are probabilistic; the occurrence of a causing event only makes it probable to a high degree that the effect event will occur. This affects only how our present point is expressed. On the probabilistic account, it is only immensely probable that the rock lies where it does, given the rest of its story—given, that is, its environment, its environment's past, its past, the laws of logic, and the laws of nature. The rest of a person's story, however, is not related in that fashion to whether or not she lies.

Moral Agents

Possessors of categorical freedom, I have suggested, differ from natural objects.[1] Obviously, a possessor of categorical freedom is a person. She is a moral agent provided she exercises categorical freedom regarding morally significant actions. Forgiveness, in its primary sense, occurs among moral agents. This brings us to morality.

The Morality of Forgiveness: What Is It to Forgive?

Some Components of Forgiveness

Joanna North (1987) reminds us that forgiveness is possible among moral agents if there is a victim and an offender such that the offender has acted wrongly with respect to the victim. The victim must have negative feelings toward the offender because of the harm the offender did, and must at least be willing to lose those feelings, making an effort to do so. The failure to experience such feelings when one is harmed typically signals a lack of self-esteem. Full success in forgiving comes only when those feelings are gone, and this may (but need not) be a long process which the victim is not able to bring to a successful completion without help.

Forgiveness and Therapy

A psychological interest in forgiveness, I take it, tends to be victim-centered; its goal is therapeutic in the sense of being aimed at aiding the

---

1. Suppose that some nonconscious entity, X, is composed of parts Y and Z, that X's causal powers are not simply a function of Y's causal powers and Z's causal powers and the causal powers of X's environment, and that among X's causal powers are included ways in which X can affect Y, Z, and X's environment. The notion of such an entity, though highly abstract, seems perfectly coherent. For interactionist dualism, for which *human* persons are embodied minds, where a mind is one sort of substance and a body another sort of substance, a *human* person is related to its parts as X is related to Y and Z.

healing, the recovery from the effects of having been harmed, that forgiving brings to a harmed person. This orientation is obviously important, and it would be cruel and foolish to question it. Of course, it need not be the only interest. Offender rehabilitation may also be a concern. And, in this case, the process of asking for and *accepting* forgiveness is also of immense importance.

Some psychological orientations may not care to distinguish between the case in which an actual victim has been wronged and needs help in escaping from fixation on the *real* harm done to her and the case in which a supposed victim falsely believes himself to have been wronged and is fixated on the merely apparent harm done to him. The approach might be simply to treat the feelings with a view to their eradication, regardless of whether or not those feelings are justified or are responses to a real injury. A more "cognitively" oriented therapy (of the sort favored by Robert Enright and colleagues, chap. 5, and Joanna North, chap. 3) will treat the cases differently. The cognitively oriented psychologist will be concerned with the need for forgiveness of real, as opposed to imaginary, wrongs, and this will require a thorough examination of the beliefs and assumptions the victim holds about his or her attacker. Any theory of forgiveness that emphasizes "reframing" on the part of the victim, as the Enright-North view does, is obviously cognitively oriented. Here, then (though not only here), psychology and philosophy meet.

Letting Go

Often an important feature of a victim's forgiving an offender is that the victim's life is no longer dominated by thoughts, memories, and negative feelings regarding the harm done by the offender. The escape from lingering harm is central to the interest that psychologists and therapists have in forgiveness. Is this feature an essential part of forgiveness? The issue seems to me delicate and important, and quite possibly I will not get it right. Nonetheless, the truth of the matter, it seems to me, is that (with one provision) *escaping lingering harm* is neither a necessary nor a sufficient condition of forgiveness.[2] My reasons are these. Suppose that the victim

2. Suppose it is true that *The only way to get A is to do B*. It does not follow that *Doing B is part of getting A*. If the only way for Mary to see her grandmother is for her to take the bus, it does not follow that taking the bus is part of, as opposed to a means to, seeing her grandmother. Even if it is true that *The only way to let go is to forgive* it does not follow that *Letting go is part of forgiveness*. Consider this remark by Joanna North: "If it were possible to take a pill which converted angry thoughts into kindly ones, this would not count as an example of forgiveness, nor would it be of any intrinsic moral value (although it might have

is abused by an offender over a long period, and that the effect is that the victim has simply lost all self-esteem. The offender finally sees what he has done, is genuinely remorseful, and the victim, seeing his remorse, comes no longer to have negative feelings toward the offender. None of this need do much to restore the victim's self-esteem; the harm lingers though the negative feelings are gone. The victim's need for help is no longer the need to forgive. Whether she needs to forgive herself depends on whether she has knowingly harmed herself; if she has not, the closest she can come to self-forgiveness is learning that she does not need it and that the negative feelings she has toward herself do not fit anything she has done. The victim's forgiveness perhaps contains as an essential element her recovery from the harm done to her "insofar as this harm is constituted by or consequent upon the victim's negative feelings toward the offender," but it does not contain as an essential element "recovering from all the lingering harm the offender has done"; otherwise the victim cannot forgive the offender until she has escaped all the lingering harm the offender did her, and she cannot escape all that harm without forgiving the offender. Then she will be in a Catch-22 situation, needing to forgive when she cannot, in principle, do so. No correct notion of forgiveness can have that consequence.

Exactly how important keeping this sort of distinction in mind may be to therapy, I must learn from the therapists. But if the distinction is correct, it is important to the theory of therapy, and if the theory matters much to the therapy, then getting the theory right matters to the therapy.

The concept of God's forgiveness similarly, I take it, does not include as an essential element God's having cured the sinner of all the lingering effects of her sin; otherwise she will be forgiven, not upon repentance, but very much later. On such a view, going to heaven would (through grace) yield forgiveness rather than forgiveness (through grace) yielding going to heaven, and that would be a peculiar theology.

---

desirable results . . .)" (p. 20 in this volume). The perspective these remarks represent is correct; moral agents are beings who typically freely act rightly or wrongly over time, thus developing tendencies or dispositions to behave that partly constitute their moral character. Freely exercised effort in morally significant contexts is required if there are to be finite moral agents. But this is not enough to justify North's claim. Suppose that O harmed V by locking her in a room with a golden retriever, knowing that she is pathologically afraid of even the gentlest canines. V wants to stop feeling hate toward O, for O has repented, but because of her phobia she cannot. There is a North-pill that will destroy those feelings, though it will not cure the phobia. Learning this, V takes the North-pill, intending that it destroy her feelings of hate, which it does. Why, under these *circumstances,* should the fact of taking the pill get in the way of V's forgiving O?

Retribution and Rehabilitation

Punishment may target justice (the offender should get what he deserves) or correction (the offender should experience what he must in order not to be a habitual offender); so we have the notions of retributive punishment and rehabilitative punishment. In some quarters, retribution has come upon hard times, often being thought inhumane as well as uncultured. Yet rehabilitation without retribution is not even a favor to the offender and does no justice to the notion of the offender's responsibility for his wrong. Punishment as retribution has three key and invaluable elements. First, it insists that one be punished only if one is guilty; it recognizes the offender as truly a moral agent, possessing freedom and responsibility and thus meriting blame and censure. Rehabilitation alone seeks to *treat* the offender, as an object, as a patient, and as passive. It does not, by itself, without the idea of retributive justice, grant the offender the dignified status of a fully moral agent.

Second, granting that the notion lacks the clarity of the Pythagorean theorem, punishment as retribution requires that the punishment "fit the crime." It is easy to pretend not to understand this notion but, of course, that is merely a pose. Any intelligent person can rank crimes in terms of relative seriousness and punishments in terms of relative severity, and go on to roughly match punishment with crime in nonarbitrary ways without using an algorythm. Things are no less clear in this sort of case than in lots of other cases we deal with daily. Two points are crucial here. One point is that punishment as retribution, with its notion of the punishment fitting the crime, places intuitive limits on what can be done to an offender— limits neither as lucid as elementary logic nor only as clear as mud— which are essential to the humane treatment of offenders; rehabilitation places only the limit of what needs to be done in order to correct or cure the offender. The second point is that, if one then tries to build into punishment as rehabilitation limits of what can be done to cure an offender, one ends up considering the relative seriousness of crimes and the severity of cures, which is no closer to the intrinsic clarity of elementary logic than is matching punishment to crime, and indeed raises similar issues.

The third element of punishment as retribution is that it cares about justice being done. Desire for justice is not identical to desire for revenge. (The biblical concern for widows and orphans is based on appeal to divine justice.) Further, retribution and rehabilitation are not inherently competitive; the ideal punishment would be retribution that results in rehabilitation.

Forgiveness, Revenge, and Punishment

That the victim forgives the offender precludes the victim seeking or even favoring revenge for what the offender did to the victim. Since forgiveness is a process it can be more or less complete, and feelings of forgiveness may vie with desires for revenge. But if the victim is plotting or dreaming of revenge against the offender, the victim has not forgiven. Yet the victim may want, even insist, that the offender make restitution as a condition of forgiveness or that the offender be punished (perhaps for the offender's sake, or for society's) even though the victim forgives the offender.

A harder question is, Can the victim want or insist that the offender be punished other than for the offender's or for society's sake, even if the victim has forgiven the offender? Suppose that the offender will harm only the victim if the offender harms anyone, and that only by being punished for harming the victim can the offender be prevented from harming the victim again. Then surely the victim may forgive the offender and yet insist on punishment. This is a special case, and should be noted as such. Two problems remain. One is this: If the offender is justly punished for harming the victim, what is there for the victim to forgive? If justice is satisfied, is forgiveness needed? The other problem comes to light when we notice that, given the perspective of at least most monotheisms, the proposition "God forgives Adam and Adam is in hell" is self-contradictory. For God to forgive and exact full retribution is for God not to have forgiven after all. Neither of these points is encouraging to an attempt at an affirmative answer to the question, Can the victim want or insist that the offender be punished other than for the offender's or for society's sake, even if the victim has forgiven the offender?

The question is further complicated by the fact of secondary victims. If Ruth loves Tom, whom she knows Bill has harmed, she may find it in herself to forgive Bill the harm that he has done her by harming Tom and not find it in herself to forgive Bill for harming Tom; for that she may demand justice or even revenge. What seems true, then, is this: What the victim, primary or secondary, cannot do is both forgive the offender and demand that justice be done to the offender for her own sake, except in the special case.

Reframing

North and Enright, from different perspectives, stress the importance of what they call "reframing." Suppose it is true that (O1) the offender lashed out at the victim in anger though the victim had done nothing. When the victim begins to try to get over being the target of the offender's temper, the victim considers (we shall suppose) such truths as (O2) The offender is recovering from a peptic ulcer, and (O3) The offender found out today that a coveted promotion went to an incompetent colleague. It is easier for the victim to stop being hurt and angry in return, and to find forgiving a viable prospect, once the victim adds (O2) and (O3) to (O1). To reframe is to increase the scope of the basic narrative, adding more statements to the narrative under the constraint that the additions be *relevant* and *true*. Reframing, as exemplified in North's chapter, is a matter of increasing the relevant data base regarding the offender; we might describe it as increasing the offender's narrative.

There are other, perhaps equally important, sorts of reframing. Suppose that the victim starts with (V1) The victim was the innocent target of the offender's angry invective. Then the victim adds both (V2) The victim made no effort to express regret at the offender's losing the deserved promotion, and (V3) The victim did not inquire concerning the offender's health and had temporarily misplaced the offender's medication. It is easier for the victim to stop being hurt and angry in return, and to find forgiving the offender a more realistic prospect, once the victim adds (V2) and (V3) to (V1). Increasing the victim's narrative can be as significant as increasing the offender's narrative.

Again, there may be relevant relationships between the victim and the offender that do not hold between just any two persons. Victim and offender may be parent and child, or siblings, or friends. Suppose that the victim and offender are married, and the victim reflects that while (VO1) The offender has been highly inconsiderate, not just to anyone, but to a loving spouse; it is also true that (VO2) The offender faithfully nursed the victim back to health when the victim suffered a long illness, and (VO3) The victim and offender are linked by marriage vows and a long-term mutual commitment that nothing has really changed. It is easier for the victim to stop being hurt and angry in return, and to find forgiving the offender a more realistic prospect, once the victim adds (VO2) and (VO3) to (VO1). Increasing the relational narrative can be as significant as increasing the victim's narrative.

It is also possible, of course, that increasing the offender's, the victim's, or the relational narratives may make forgiveness harder, not easier. Perhaps, as North's chapter suggests, there are cases in which it would be wrong to forgive. Certainly there are cases in which it is unwise and/or impossible to reconcile. Christian theology traditionally has held that persons who permanently refuse to repent and be reformed are in this condition.

Yet again, there may be features, so to speak, of the world at large that are relevant. For example, if the victim is a Christian, while she may be incensed that (VC1) God has allowed her to be hurt yet again, she also believes that (VC2) God has created persons as free agents who are responsible for their morally significant actions and whose moral character is deeply affected by those actions, and (VC3) God in Christ has suffered, died, and risen again for the victim and has forgiven the victim's own sins. It is easier for the victim to stop being hurt and angry in return, and to find forgiving the offender a more realistic prospect, once the victim adds (VC2) and (VC3) to (VC1). Increasing the cosmic narrative can be as significant as increasing the relational narrative.

I make no pretense at having exhausted the kinds of reframing, let alone the varieties within each kind. Nonetheless, I suggest that relative both to "letting go" and to forgiving, two things should be said: (1) initial brief victim, relational, and cosmic narratives of the offense may be as important as an offender narrative of the offense, and (2) increasing the victim, relational, and cosmic narratives to fuller narratives may be as important as increasing the offender narrative to a fuller narrative. The importance of such narrative increases has various sources. They increase self-understanding and one's understanding of others. They place actions and reactions into a broader context, offering opportunity of a better understanding of their significance. They provide something of emotional distance from feelings that, however important and appropriate, can also be suffocating and destructive. They typically also offer justification or rationale for letting go and for forgiveness. They may also, far less typically, offer at least a caution about whether or not to let go or to forgive and, if done, how best to do so. These happy features depend, of course, on the constraint on narrative additions: that they be *relevant* and *true*.

Forgiveness and Reconciliation

While the ideal result of forgiveness is reconciliation, it seems plain that the reconciliation of victim and offender cannot, itself, be an essential element in the victim forgiving the offender. Were it so, the offender could prevent the victim from forgiving by simply refusing to reconcile. It is forgiveness that is an element in reconciliation, not reconciliation that is included in forgiveness. Nor can the offender's rehabilitation properly be the prisoner of the victim's willingness to forgive, though it is rightly prisoner to the offender's remorse and repentance, and possibly to the offender's making restitution and willingness to reconcile. The refusal of an offender to repent should not prevent the victim from forgiving, and the victim's refusal to forgive should not preclude the offender's restoration to rectitude.

Conclusion

The significance of forgiveness rests, perhaps, on two facts and a consequence. The facts are that people harm people (theologians place this fact under the rubric of sin) and that people are inherently social and cannot flourish in isolation. The consequence is that people either forgive one another or else wither as persons; they reconcile or perish. Reconciliation among sinners has forgiveness as an element—a necessary though not sufficient condition. So people learn to forgive, or they wither as persons, quite independently of the harm caused by the seeking of revenge.

References

Frankfurt, H. G. 1988. *The importance of what we care about.* Cambridge: Cambridge University Press.

Kant, Immanuel. 1964. *Groundwork of the metaphysics of morals.* Trans. H. J. Paton. New York: Harper and Row.

North, J. 1987. Wrongdoing and forgiveness. *Philosophy* 62: 499–508.

Rowe, W. 1991. *Thomas Reid on freedom and morality.* Ithaca: Cornell University Press.

Van Inwagen, P. 1983. *An essay on free will.* Oxford: Clarendon Press.

Yandell, K. 1988. Divine necessity and human goodness. In *Divine and human action,* ed. T. V. Morris, 313–344. Ithaca: Cornell University Press.

Yandell, K. 1995. A defense of dualism. *Faith and Philosophy* 12(4): 548–566.

5

The Psychology of Interpersonal Forgiveness

Robert D. Enright, Suzanne Freedman, and Julio Rique

For the past ten years, students and faculty in the Department of Educational Psychology at the University of Wisconsin–Madison have met weekly to discuss and debate the fine points of interpersonal forgiveness. We have focused on certain central questions that include: (1) What is interpersonal forgiveness? (2) Can we devise a model to help people forgive? (3) What are the psychological outcomes for those who forgive?

In this chapter, we first review our current answers to these three questions, gleaned over the ten-year period. Following this, we express some concerns about the direction the field of forgiveness studies seems to be taking regarding each question posed. We end with recommendations for future study in the area.

What Is Interpersonal Forgiveness?

This first question was masterfully addressed by Joanna North in chapter 3. It is our intent not to challenge her approach, but to try adding to it where possible. The question of definition is the bedrock query of the entire field of forgiveness studies, because, without a clear definition, forgiveness will be little understood and open to much confusion. When our group at the University of Wisconsin–Madison began exploring the construct of forgiveness in 1985, we read as many published works on the topic as we could. In a weekly seminar, now ongoing for over eleven years, we "sifted and winnowed," as we like to say at Wisconsin, until we felt we had a parsimonious and complete definition of interpersonal forgiving. Our quest took us through ancient texts (Jewish, Christian, Muslim, Buddhist, Hindu, and Confucian), modern philosophers' ideas, and the few case studies in psychology and psychiatry available at the time.

Enright and the Human Development Study Group (1991), following North (1987), define forgiving as a willingness to abandon one's right to resentment, negative judgment, and indifferent behavior toward one who unjustly injured us, while fostering the undeserved qualities of compassion, generosity, and even love toward him or her. Please note the following points about this definition: (1) The one offended suffered an unjust, perhaps even a deep, hurt from another. (2) The offended willingly chooses to forgive. Forgiving is volitional, not grimly obligatory. (3) The offender's new stance includes affect (overcoming resentment and substituting compassion), cognition (overcoming condemnation with respect and/or generosity), and behavior (overcoming indifference or the tendency toward subtle revenge with a sense of goodwill). (4) The offended may unconditionally forgive regardless of the other person's current attitudes or behaviors toward the offended, because forgiving is one person's volitional response to another. The sense of forgiveness as wiping away the negative consequences of the offender's injustice and as a merciful reaching out to the offender is consistent with ancient Hebrew, Christian, Islamic, and Confucian texts (see Enright and the Human Development Study Group 1991; Enright, Gassin, and Wu 1992). For other subtleties on the construct of forgiving, please refer to the following (mostly philosophical) sources: Downie (1965); Holmgren (1993); Horsbrugh (1974); Lewis (1980); Richards (1988); Smedes (1984); and Twambley (1976).

It is our position that forgiveness occurs only between people and not between a person and forces of nature. For example, one does not forgive a destructive blizzard in which friends may perish, because one does not foster the feeling of compassion, generosity, or love toward the blizzard. Forgiveness is a special case of mercy directed at an injuring person. Clinicians who help clients forgive remind us that the forgiveness journey may take time and be quite an intrapsychic struggle (Coleman 1989; Enright and the Human Development Study Group 1991; Fitzgibbons 1986; Hope 1987). Yet, despite this struggle, forgiving and receiving forgiveness may be positively transforming for self, the injurer, and our communities (see Gentilone and Regidor 1986 in particular on this point).

Forgiving Is More Than . . .

To further our understanding of forgiveness, consider four concepts that forgiveness is similar to but distinct from. First, forgiveness is more than simply *accepting* or *tolerating* the injustice. In contemporary culture people talk about "moving on" or "putting the past behind us." This alone is not forgiveness, because the attitudes involved need not make room in our lives or hearts for the offender. As North clarified in chapter 3, forgiving is "outward-looking and other-directed" (p. 19). When we forgive, we make room for the injurer. Second, forgiving is not the same as *forgetting*. A deep injustice suffered is rarely, if ever, wiped from consciousness. When someone forgives, he or she remembers, but in different ways from those before forgiveness occurs.

Third, forgiveness is more than *ceasing our anger toward the injurer.* Recall that a more complete forgiveness position includes not only the cessation of the negative, including anger, but also the inclusion of the giftlike positive qualities already mentioned. Thus, forgiveness is not a neutral stance toward our injurer. McGary (1989) disagreed with these points. In his view, a forgiver need do nothing more than cease resentment for the good of self and others with whom one interacts (but not necessarily toward the offender).

For McGary, giving a gift to the offender is going beyond the requirements of true forgiving. Yet, is it not possible that one can cease resentment and still be indifferently cold toward the offender? Cannot one, in essence, "write off" the offender and feel no resentment at the same time? It seems to us that the abandonment of resentment may be more easily accomplished by trying to ignore the offender than by offering moral love to him or her. We say this because offering moral love demands much of the forgiver, whereas "writing off" the offender asks less; thus the latter may be more easily embraced, especially by an angry person. If this is true and we accept McGary's reductionism, then forgiving may take place in a climate of veiled or even outright condemnation by the "forgiver," as long as resentment does not accompany the condemnation. Such an attitude seems more contradictory of forgiving than complementary.

For our fourth point, forgiving is more than making ourselves as forgivers feel good. McGary (1989), who diverged from us on the first two points, agreed. In his view, for example, ceasing resentment toward an employer may create a more peaceful atmosphere for family members. Forgiveness is a gift to others, not just to self. The paradox is that, when a forgiver abandons a focus on self and gives this gift to the injurer (or to people other than the forgiven, in McGary's view), the forgiver may experience psychological healing.

What Forgiving Is Not

To deepen the understanding of forgiveness further, consider three more points, in this case focusing on what forgiving is not. First, forgiving is not condoning or excusing wrongdoing. Because North already covered this point, we will let it stand. Second, forgiveness is not the same as legal pardon. Some are concerned that, when we forgive, we will open all the jail cell doors, letting the lawbreakers free to further their destructive aims. Yet, forgiveness is not really connected to the judicial system. A judge who deliberates on the fate of a criminal should never be the one directly hurt by the one breaking the law. Forgiveness is a personal response to one's own injury. The point here is that we can forgive and still bring legal justice to bear as required by the situation.

Third, forgiveness is distinguished from reconciliation. The basic philosophical distinction between forgiveness and reconciliation is this. Forgiveness is one person's response to injury. Reconciliation involves two people coming together again. The injurer must realize his or her offense, see the damage done, and take steps to rectify the problem. When both parties are guilty of injustice toward the other, both may need to forgive and realize one's own failures, with the intent to change. When already in a strong relationship with someone who offends, a forgiver usually reconciles. When in a chronic situation of abuse, a forgiver may not reconcile. Those who seem to advocate for forgiveness but nonetheless intolerantly "write off" the other, insisting on not reconciling in the face of obvious enduring, positive change on an offender's part, may be engaging in pseudoforgiveness.

False Forgiving

Pseudoforgiveness basically is a ploy to maintain or gain power over others. If we "forgive" a family member but then continually remind him of his injury to us, we are exercising a superiority that is incompatible with forgiving. If we "forgive" so that we will make the other perpetually indebted to us, we again misunderstand true forgiveness. When we forgive, we welcome the other into the human community; we see each other as equally worthy of respect.

Skeptical Views of Forgiving

Before any community embraces forgiving as valuable, perhaps the members of that community should consider two philosophical arguments suggesting forgiveness is immoral and dangerous. The first is from Nietzsche (1887), who claimed that only weaklings practice forgiveness. When one has no other choice because a more powerful person than ourselves has injured us, we reluctantly forgive. We can dismiss this idea when we realize that Nietzsche is describing a form of pseudo-, or false, forgiveness. Genuine forgiveness, in contrast, is centered in a courageous act of giving, as North (1987) argued. Holmgren (1993) further advanced North's work by eloquently arguing for forgiveness as an act of self-respect, as North discussed in chapter 3.

A second argument against forgiving is that it may work against justice and even perpetuate injustice. Suppose a person who is being battered by another person forgives. This may encourage the batterer to continue the abuse, whereas standing up and fighting may end the abuse. What is unrealized in this scenario is that justice seeking alone does not necessarily end altercations. The civil wars in eastern Europe, as just one example, have been fought for over four hundred years, with no end in sight. To forgive does not mean to acquiesce blindly to harsh demands. To forgive means to begin seeing the other in a new way, as a member of the human community rather than as evil incarnate. The new way of seeing and the offer of a gift of forgiveness leave open the possibility of the other's transformation, which opens the door not only for negotiation but also for heartfelt mutual goodwill. We do not claim that the pathway to forgiveness is easy, but has the pathway of destruction, for example, over the past four hundred years in eastern Europe been fruitful for any ethnic group?

A Concern about Definitional Drift

It took our group at Wisconsin several years of intensive study before we arrived at the definition of forgiveness and a response to critics. We tried first to understand what others have said about a definition of forgiveness before advancing our own. Of course, our definition is not "our own," because it appropriates ideas from ancient writings and modern philosophical sources. Our concern centers on what we are calling definitional drift. By definitional drift we mean that new definitions are being generated which seem to contradict existing views without showing how the new contradiction is an advance over the former views.

Consider three examples of current definitional drift. First is the current trend to see forgiveness, not as a gift to the offending person and to others, but as a gift primarily to self alone. Forgiveness as something you do for yourself is a clear message in the self-help literature (see, e.g., Simon and Simon 1990). If self-help is the exclusive or even the primary focus, we have lost the essential quality of forgiveness. Part of the definition is retained (the abandonment of resentment) while the essential other half is ignored (a response of goodness toward the offending person). Even McGary (1989), who opposed this view of goodness toward the offender, makes room in his definition for helping people other than the offender. If one can reduce resentment by going for a good jog, is the jogger forgiving in the running? Clearly, the absence of resentment must be supplemented if forgiving is to avoid confusion with a plethora of other ideas.

A second area of definitional drift is the current tendency in psychotherapy toward an emphasis on subjectivity. By subjectivity we mean that, when
we are offended, there is no objective wrong leading to our deep hurt and
resentment. It is our *subjective* perceptions that are primarily responsible for
the pain we feel. Forgiveness, therefore, is equated with faulty perception,
and our job is to change our perception, not to acknowledge and right
an objective wrong against us. For example, Albert Ellis, in his rational-
emotive approach to psychotherapy, works with people to change their
own expectations when they feel slighted (Ellis and Dryden 1987). He
believes our resentments are caused by our unreasonable demands that all
people *must* treat us with absolute fairness. When they do not, we become
deeply resentful. The point in Ellis' psychotherapy is to reduce expectations
that others be perfect and to change our perception that what happened
to us was not extremely awful but merely bad. Following these perceptual
changes, we are permitted to feel annoyed but not deeply resentful.

In our opinion, Ellis' exclusive focus on people's perceptions may be
an effective antidote to minor slights and in cases of pseudoforgiveness,
but not to experiences of extreme injustice, such as incest or capture
and torture. Is not anger sometimes a consequence of *rational* beliefs
of objective wrong? Ellis seems to think not. Such exclusive subjectivity
may be a second injury for a brutalized person, because she will now
blame herself for feeling bad: "If only I could alter my view of the incest,
I wouldn't feel so bad." Subjectivity denies objective wrong and may
pressure a person who is the object of radical injustice to blame himself.
Perhaps some caution is needed in readily accepting this new definitional
trend that places most or all wrongs against oneself in one's own head.

A third area of definitional drift is the benign neglect of tradition. When
this happens, some modern definitions seem to distort the meaning of forgiveness. Consider, as one example, Casarjian's (1992) ideas on forgiveness.
First, let us note that there is much that is accurate in her approach. She
equates forgiving with the offer of moral love and acceptance to those who
offend. At the same time, she overly generalizes the idea of acceptance to
include one's "forgiveness" of arthritic hands or a less-than-healthy body.
We understand and appreciate her attempt to help a person achieve a certain
inner peace in regard to a failing body. Yet, equating forgiveness with a
generalized acceptance brings the construct away from the interpersonal,
and thus away from the moral qualities of generosity and/or moral love.
A grounding in traditional definitions would help one avoid this.

Because definitional drift is occurring on at least three fronts, it could
intensify over the next decade. The difficult, moral work of forgiveness
could be forgotten or ignored if this trend continues. Let us examine some
of this moral work by turning to question two.

Can We Devise a Model to Help People Forgive?

The processes outlined in table 5.1 are our best estimate of the general pathway many people follow when they forgive (see Enright and the Human Development Study Group 1991). The model was at first rationally derived (e.g., one does not do the *work* of forgiving before *deciding* to forgive). We then brought our ideas to hundreds of people, asking them for feedback on the proposed sequence. Following minor revision based on the feedback, we devised educational applications of the model to test whether it is an effective pathway for bringing about forgiveness in people hurt by others' injustices.

Our educational programs were motivated, at least in part, by the observation that many people do not consciously consider forgiving when deeply hurt by another person. Our research suggests that people respond to injustice with various strategies to try reversing the injustice and with various healing strategies, but not with forgiveness (on this point, see the findings on the Willingness to Forgive Scale in the doctoral dissertations of Al-Mabuk 1990, and Freedman 1995). Our assumption based on Al-Mabuk's and Freedman's findings, that most people need to be taught about forgiveness to begin forgiving, is in contrast with Patton's (1985) articulate challenge that most people discover the idea of forgiving on their own.

We do not see our model as a rigid, steplike sequence, but instead as a flexible set of processes with feedback and feed-forward loops. Some may skip entire units in their process of forgiving. Units 1–8 represent the uncovering phase of change as the person becomes aware of the problem and the concomitant emotional pain associated with deep, unjust injury. Unit 1 represents a preforgiving state of denial. Many will not or cannot acknowledge that others have deeply offended them. Eventually, as these defenses break down even a bit, the person sees the injustice and reacts with characteristic negative emotions such as anger or even hatred toward the injurer (unit 2). Holmgren (1993) clarifies that a forgiver must accurately see and acknowledge the injustice, which, in her view, is a sign of self-respect. At times, an offended person experiences shame, guilt, or public humiliation (unit 3), which deepens his or her emotional pain. As the injured person tries to find a solution to the pain, he or she may attach excessive emotions to the situation, which can deplete his or her energy reserve (unit 4).

Cognitive correlates of these emotion-centered units include being aware that one is continually replaying the event in one's mind (unit 5), that one may be comparing one's own unfortunate state with the relatively comfortable condition of the offender (unit 6), and that one

Table 5.1. Psychological variables that may be involved when we forgive

Uncovering Phase

1.	Examination of psychological defenses (Kiel 1986)
2.	Confrontation of anger; the point is to release, not harbor, the anger (Trainer 1981)
3.	Admittance of shame, when this is appropriate (Patton 1985)
4.	Awareness of cathexis (Droll 1984)
5.	Awareness of cognitive rehearsal of the offense (Droll 1984)
6.	Insight that the injured party may be comparing self with the injurer (Kiel 1986)
7.	Realization that oneself may be permanently and adversely changed by the injury (Close 1970)
8.	Insight into a possibly altered "just world" view (Flanigan 1987)

Decision Phase

9.	A change of heart, conversion, new insights that old resolution strategies are not working (North 1987)
10.	Willingness to consider forgiveness as an option
11.	Commitment to forgive the offender (Neblett 1974)

Work Phase

12.	Reframing, through role taking, who the wrongdoer is by viewing him or her in context (Smith 1981)
13.	Empathy toward the offender (Cunningham 1985)
14.	Awareness of compassion, as it emerges, toward the offender (Droll 1984)
15.	Acceptance and absorption of the pain (Bergin 1988)

Deepening Phase

16.	Finding meaning for self and others in the suffering and in the forgiveness process (Frankl 1959)
17.	Realization that self has needed others' forgiveness in the past (Cunningham 1985)
18.	Insight that one is not alone (universality, support)
19.	Realization that self may have a new purpose in life because of the injury
20.	Awareness of decreased negative affect and, perhaps, increased positive affect, if this begins to emerge, toward the injurer; awareness of internal, emotional release (Smedes 1984)

Note: This table is an extension of Enright and the Human Development Study Group (1991). The references shown here at the end of each unit are prototypical examples or discussions of that unit.

may be negatively and permanently changed by the offense (unit 7). These realizations may lead to the conclusion that life is extremely unfair (unit 8).

At some point, the injured party enters the "decision" phase (units 9–11) by realizing that such preoccupations with the offense and offender are unhealthy (unit 9). The person entertains the idea of forgiveness (unit 10) and ultimately commits to forgiving the individual who caused such pain (unit 11). In committing to forgive, the injured gives up the idea of revenge, although complete forgiveness is not yet realized.

After this commitment, the injured party begins the "work" phase of the forgiveness process (units 12–15). The individual engages in "reframing" (unit 12) by striving to understand the offender's personal history, current pressures, and basic human worth. It is important to note that the outcome of reframing is understanding, not condoning. Often, such insight will be accompanied by emotional identification with the offender ("empathy," unit 13) and the willingness to share in the suffering the offender has experienced ("compassion," unit 14). Empathy and compassion may be seen as gifts to the offender, discussed in the definition of forgiveness. Acceptance or absorption of the pain (unit 15) is at the heart of forgiving and involves committing oneself *not* to pass on the pain of the injury to others, including the offender. The offended soaks up the pain, as a sponge does water, so that he or she does not fling that pain back to the offender or others. This unit, like the two preceding ones, emphasizes the affective nature of forgiving, as reframing emphasizes the cognitive nature. Also, unit 15, like the two preceding units, signifies the giftlike quality of forgiveness as the forgiver stops a cycle of revenge that otherwise may harm the offender and others. In essence, the forgiver is acting morally in the giving of these gifts.

While the injured party proceeds through the forgiveness process, he or she may notice personal benefits. We have termed these units (16–20) the outcome phase. The injured person may find deep meaning in the offense and forgiveness process (unit 16), perhaps appreciating a new sense of personal compassion that can now be easily extended to others. One may realize the self is imperfect and recall incidents in which it was necessary to receive others' forgiveness (unit 17). One may develop a keener understanding of an involvement in interpersonal support networks (unit 18), and a new sense of purpose or direction in life may emerge (unit 19). Ultimately, this entire process may lead to improved psychological health (unit 20), and it is here that the paradox of forgiveness is most evident: When we give to others the gift of mercy and compassion, we ourselves are healed.

When people forgive they seem to need time to accommodate slowly to the idea. We observe two patterns of change. In the first pattern, most people will consider forgiving another person when their emotional pain is so high that they must do something to change this uncomfortable situation. When they then decide to forgive, it is primarily a self-interested activity; the person forgives in order to feel better. Only after a period of time does the forgiver understand the giftlike quality of forgiveness. Only after a period of time does the forgiver focus more on the other person than on the self. Eventually people tend to generalize a specific forgiving episode and begin to forgive other people who have hurt them. Over time people who continue to practice forgiveness may actually alter their primary world view or their own sense of identity to integrate forgiveness into their philosophy of life and their view of themselves.

In the second pattern, we notice that once a forgiver focuses on the other, with the intent of forgiving, he or she operates by one of three moral principles. First, he or she finds the giving of *merciful restraint* to be sufficient. Merciful restraint here is the withholding of a negative response, such as punishment, when the offended has the power or the "right" to punish so. In merciful restraint, the forgiver gives up the notion of revenge or condemnation. Later, he or she may be willing to give *generosity* to the other. Generosity goes beyond refraining from the bad and adds the dimension of giving such good elements as occasional friendliness and attention to the offender. Still later, some forgivers give the gift of *moral love*, in which the forgiver willingly enters into the other's life in the hope of positively transforming the other and the community. As an example of community transformation, before a burglar is transformed, the people of a small community may live in fear of more break-ins; afterward, the community residents may feel more secure. The forgiver's degree of trust toward the other and the amount of time passed since the offense(s) play a part in these unfolding patterns.

An Example of an Intervention with the Model

In Freedman and Enright's (1996) study with incest survivors, twelve participants were given a written manual describing the various units of forgiving, similar to those in table 5.1 (at the time, the model included only seventeen units). Six of the randomly assigned participants met individually and weekly with one female instructor versed in the forgiveness literature and trained in helping people who had experienced sexual abuse. The other six were part of a wait-list control group and were free to seek therapy as they wished. All had extensive therapy prior to our program. Eventually, these six control participants became experimental participants; thus all twelve received forgiveness education.

In unit 1 of the manual the participants were introduced to the concept of psychological defenses and asked to explore such defenses as denial, suppression, repression, and displacement in their own case of injustice. The point was to see whether the injury and resulting anger were being pushed aside. In unit 2, the participants confronted their own anger. Some felt the emotion deeply for the first time. They saw that they had a right to the anger because of the betrayal. Next, they explored both shame and guilt (unit 3), shame over the public label of "incest victim/survivor," and guilt if any felt they played a part in the victimization by not informing others or felt pleasurable physical responses. The instructor pointed out that as a child (1) the survivor may have lacked the wisdom to know to whom she should turn, and (2) she in no way was at fault for the abuse. The instructor further elaborated that pleasurable physical sensations coupled with negative psychological reactions are not uncommon when being victimized. These insights were expected to reduce guilt.

In units 4 and 5 the survivors learned how both their preoccupation with the events of betrayal and their patterns of cognitively replaying those events in their minds kept the perpetrator ever before them; they were not free from his abuse. These insights served as a motivator to change course and try a new healing strategy. The other aspects of the "uncovering phase" also were examined, each at the participant's own pace. At the end of this phase, each survivor assessed her degree of emotional pain.

The next set of units constitute the "decision phase." At the beginning, before entering into the intervention, all participants said they would never forgive the perpetrator. The decision phase was intended to explore further the possibility of whether any would freely consider forgiving as a healing strategy. This necessitated examining various kinds of healing strategies, including forgiveness. Definitions of forgiveness were scrutinized, including what forgiveness is not. A commitment to try forgiveness was made by each participant only when she saw this as viable and reasonable. All decided to try it. For the first commitment, the instructor asked each participant to refrain from seeking even subtle revenge toward the perpetrator when this was possible. Revenge can include roundly condemning someone long after he or she is deceased.

The "work phase" began with reframing who the perpetrator is (or was, if he was deceased). The survivors examined the perpetrator's own childhood, searching for insights to the way he was raised. Some saw deep deprivation or abuse falling on the perpetrator as a child. They further explored the perpetrator's life during the period of betrayal. This was done not to condone his behavior but to see a confused person. As North said in chapter 3, reframing should help one separate the offense and the offender, seeing the offender in a larger context. Again, care was taken that the survivors continued to label his behavior as wrong.

Empathy and compassion began to emerge in most participants. For example, one sent her father a birthday card for the first time; one visited her father's grave for the first time; another visited her father in the hospital and helped with his care before he died. All willingly chose their own expressions of gift giving; some did not appear to show any outward sign of compassion. The instructor left this decision entirely to each participant.

In the unit on absorbing the pain, the participants tried to stop the cycles of revenge by taking on the pain rather than throwing it back to the perpetrator or others. One survivor related that, as she did this, she realized how strong she was emotionally. She then was able to see herself as a survivor rather than a victim.

For the "outcome phase," participants deepened their insights into forgiving by examining instances in which they had offended others and sought forgiveness. For some, this helped them appreciate the effort involved in both forgiving and being forgiven; it motivated further examinations of genuine forgiving. New meaning and purpose began to emerge for some. For example, several participants expressed an interest in careers to help other survivors. Many began to generalize their genuine forgiving (not the pseudoform described by Nietzsche) of the perpetrator to other situations. For example, one survivor related how forgiving the perpetrator helped her to forgive her husband for the small injustices in the marriage, thus strengthening an already-solid marriage. Another survivor stated that after forgiving her father, she was ready to try forgiving her mother for not protecting her. Other aspects of psychological healing in this sample are discussed below when we turn to the final question.

A Concern about Model Development

When we began this work in 1985 only a few published works existed describing how to forgive (e.g., see Linn and Linn 1978; Smedes 1984). In the decade since, literature on forgiveness has grown. We must realize that one's definition of forgiveness will strongly influence the advice one gives on how to forgive; if the definition is flawed, the model will be flawed.

As the study of forgiveness makes its way more and more into the research universities, we will probably see a proliferation of models describing how to forgive. If you will notice, we have deliberately avoided placing our model within the specific language of only one school of thought. Our model cannot be described as exclusively Freudian, psychodynamic, Eriksonian, cognitive developmental, or behavioristic. Our model has aspects of each of these theories. As different models emerge they probably will do so more and more within the specific language of a given theorist (Freud, Erikson, Piaget, Kohlberg, and so forth). There certainly is nothing wrong with having several good models, each expressed consistently within one psychological theory. The concern, instead, centers on the possible "turf battles" of academia likely to emerge with the ubiquitous wrestling for model supremacy. In our opinion, forgiveness can be successfully placed within the language of all the above theories because of the construct's broad appeal and utility. Yet, forgiveness belongs to no one model in particular. While models proliferate, we should try to avoid the relativism that is beginning to invade the definition of forgiveness. When a new model is developed, perhaps we should ask: (1) What does this add to existing models? (2) What flaws in the older model(s) are corrected by the new model? (3) Is the new model more parsimonious, more straightforward, or simpler than the older model? A concern we have is that in the name of progress we academicians tend to use more and more complex, specialized vocabulary to describe what used to be simple ideas open to many. In the name of forgiveness we should not inadvertently exclude those who do not have the specialized vocabulary. Forgiveness should be accessible to all.

Let us now turn to the final question to be addressed here.

What Are the Psychological Outcomes for Those Who Forgive?

Our model described in table 5.1 has been shown effective in several works to date. The Freedman and Enright (1996) study, already described, used a randomized, experimental, and control group design. Following the completion of the experimental group's educational program, the original control group commenced the education, thus becoming a second experimental group.

Three findings are worth noting. First, in comparing the experimental group with the control group after the first year of education, the experimental participants gained statistically more than the control group in forgiveness and hope. The experimental group decreased statistically significantly more than the control group in anxiety and psychological depression. The average participant upon entering the program showed moderate psychological depression. Upon finishing the program, the average participant was not depressed. This pattern held at the one-year follow-up.

Second, please recall that the control group after this first year became an experimental group for the entire second year. We thus could compare their outcomes within year two (as experimental participants) with their changes within year one (as control participants). This comparison yielded results similar to those described above: The changes within this group in year two compared with year one were statistically significant: greater gains in forgiveness, self-esteem, and hope, and greater decreases in anxiety and depression.

The third comparison examined the original (first year) experimental group scores at the one-year posttest with their scores at a one-year follow-up (one year after intervention ceased for this original experimental group).

These participants maintained their change patterns on all scales, thus showing that there was no washout effect.

Two other interventions also validate the model of forgiving in table 5.1. Al-Mabuk, Enright, and Cardis (1995) report positive mental health outcomes for parentally love-deprived college students following a short-term workshop on forgiveness education. Hebl and Enright (1993) demonstrated forgiving responses in the elderly following an eight-week program. In the latter study, both experimental and control groups decreased in anxiety. The overall pattern across these diverse samples suggests that the model of forgiving is effective in bringing people to a forgiving stance toward an offender.

A Concern about Choice of Outcome Variables

In the first generation of empirical studies on forgiveness, we chose to emphasize what a *forgiver* (not the forgiven) derives psychologically upon completing the forgiveness journey. We did this because the variables studied, such as anxiety, depression, and self-esteem, are specific, concrete variables with excellent scales already developed. If forgiving frees one from excessive resentments and internalizing psychological problems, we intended to measure this.

The exclusive focus on the forgiver's benefits might suggest to the casual reader of our studies that a forgiver is engaged in a pursuit of self-improvement, not necessarily in giving a gift to an offender. We did not intend to leave this impression, but given the definitional drift in the meaning of forgiveness (which we did not anticipate happening ten years ago), our outcome variables certainly are compatible with the overemphasis on self. Of course, we still must distinguish between the forgiveness *process* as a gift given to others and the *outcomes* of this process, which may include benefits to self.

To avoid any confusion in the future, we recommend expanding the kinds of variables studied as outcomes. We suggest a focus not only on a forgiver's psychological benefits but on the forgiven's benefits as well. Perhaps a person who wishes to receive and who genuinely does receive forgiveness will show reduced anxiety and an enhanced sense of well-being. We further recommend the examination of benefits for a forgiver's entire family and circle of friends. When a forgiver gives up displaced anger, we can envision his or her immediate community of family and friends benefiting from the transformation. In the future, we should cast our empirical net more widely in examining who benefits from forgiveness.

A Proposal for the Next Ten Years and Beyond

Our first ten years of study were rather lonely because few studied forgiveness on university campuses. The next ten years promise more participants in the research. As more come to investigate forgiveness, we should begin to examine carefully the problem of definitional drift, the complication of overly specialized language and turf battles (if these emerge), and the narrowness of our selected outcome variables.

If the new area of forgiveness studies is to thrive, we should be working together to advance knowledge and to help those hurt by injustice. Forgiveness is an important and special concept that lends itself to interdisciplinary cooperation. The study of forgiveness can be done in the social sciences, medicine, the political sciences, theology, and education. Forgiveness can be applied to the individual, families, neighborhoods, entire communities, and perhaps even to nations. Forgiveness casts a wide net.

A united approach to scholarship seems more desirable than the isolated and individualized. In this spirit, we have only recently developed the International Forgiveness Institute (IFI), dedicated to philanthropy, scholarship, and service to helping professionals. The IFI, as it is currently constituted, is a tax-exempt, public corporation in Wisconsin.[1] One purpose of the IFI is to provide grants to graduate students and professors who are studying forgiveness issues. We envision a yearly grant competition for interested scholars. Another purpose is to provide direct training in the latest ideas about forgiveness for helping professionals throughout the world who wish to implement forgiveness with clients. We envision having workshops in which we try to impart knowledge and share educational and therapeutic ideas with the helping professionals, who then would take the ideas back to their own communities.

The IFI has only recently begun fund raising. The board of directors is currently seeking funding strategies for a significant endowment to support the work. The work could include, for example, funding a professor in Belgrade who develops a program for bringing Serbs, Croats, Bosnians, Albanians, and others together to discuss issues of forgiveness and reconciliation. The work could further include funding a doctoral student at an African university in his or her efforts to introduce forgiveness to Rwandan communities. We could fund scholars—at Harvard, Emory University, the University of Wisconsin–Madison, or any other research community—who have innovative ideas for advancing forgiveness studies.

1. The address of the International Forgiveness Institute is P.O. Box 6153, Madison, Wisconsin 53716.

Within our institute, we could bring targeted groups together for the purpose of forgiveness education. As an example, if a situation like the Los Angeles riots blazes again, the IFI could be one voice amidst the healing that must take place. We could bring interested civic and religious leaders to the institute, discuss with them the meaning and specific implementation strategies of forgiveness, then send them back into their discordant regions. In this way, those already part of the culture would be the ones effecting change within that culture. Would this not enhance the opportunity for mutual healing, especially if forgiveness and mercy exist alongside the quest for justice?

Forgiveness is not an exclusive solution to human misery; yet, the latest philosophical analyses and social scientific research suggest that forgiveness deserves its place in effecting healing. For well over a thousand years academia has found a way to ignore interpersonal forgiveness as an area of consistent, penetrating inquiry. Because of this, the *study* of forgiveness is in its infancy. Perhaps our largest area of concern is that the voice of forgiveness continues to find a place in academic investigation. This volume and the formation of the IFI are hopeful steps in that direction.

References

Al-Mabuk, R. H. 1990. The commitment to forgive in parentally love-deprived college students. Doctoral dissertation, University of Wisconsin–Madison, 1990. *Dissertation Abstracts International—A* 51(10), 1991, p. 3361.

Bergin, A. E. 1988. Three contributions of a spiritual perspective to counseling, psychotherapy, and behavior change. *Counseling and Values* 33: 21–31.

Casarjian, R. 1992. *Forgiveness: A bold choice for a peaceful heart.* New York: Bantam Books.

Close, H. T. 1970. Forgiveness and responsibility. A case study. *Pastoral Psychology* 21: 19–25.

Coleman, P. W. 1989. *The forgiving marriage: Resolving anger and resentment and rediscovering each other.* Chicago: Contemporary Books.

Cunningham, B. B. 1985. The will to forgive: A pastoral theological view of forgiving. *Journal of Pastoral Care* 39(2): 141–149.

Downie, R. S. 1965. Forgiveness. *Philosophical Quarterly* 15: 128–134.

Droll, D. M. 1984. Forgiveness: Theory and research. Doctoral dissertation, University of Nevada–Reno. *Dissertation Abstracts International—B* 45(08), 1985, p. 2732.

Ellis, A., and W. Dryden. 1987. *The practice of rational-emotive therapy.* New York: Springer-Verlag.

Enright, R. D., and the Human Development Study Group. 1991. The moral development of forgiveness. In *Handbook of moral behavior and development,* ed. W. Kurtines and J. Gewirtz, Vol. 1, 123–152. Hillsdale, N.J.: Erlbaum.

Enright, R. D., E. A. Gassin, C. Wu. 1992. Forgiveness: A developmental view. *Journal of Moral Education* 21(2): 99–114.

Enright, R. D., E. A. Gassin, T. Longinovic, and D. Loudon. 1994. Forgiveness as a solution to social issues. Paper presented at the conference Morality and Social Crisis, Belgrade, Serbia, December.

Fitzgibbons, R. P. 1986. The cognitive and emotional uses of forgiveness in the treatment of anger. *Psychotherapy* 23(4): 629–633.

Flanigan, B. 1987. Shame and forgiving in alcoholism. *Alcoholism Treatment Quarterly* 4(2): 181–195.

Frankl, V. 1959. *The will to meaning: Foundations and applications of logotherapy.* New York: World Publishing House.

Freedman, S. R. 1995. Forgiveness as an educational intervention goal with incest survivors. Doctoral dissertation, University of Wisconsin–Madison, 1995. *Dissertation Abstracts International—B* 55(07), p. 3034.

Freedman, S. R., and R. D. Enright. 1996. Forgiveness as an intervention goal with incest survivors. *Journal of Consulting and Clinical Psychology* 64: 983–992.

Gentilone, F., and J. R. Regidor. 1986. The political dimension of reconciliation: A recent Italian experience. In Forgiveness, ed. by C. Floristan and C. Duquoc. *Concilium* (Special issue, Apr.): 22–31 (Edinburgh: T. & T. Clark).

Hebl, J. H., and R. D. Enright. 1993. Forgiveness as a psychotherapeutic goal with elderly females. *Psychotherapy* 30: 658–667.

Holmgren, M. R. 1993. Forgiveness and the intrinsic value of persons. *American Philosophical Quarterly* 30(4, October): 341–352.

Hope, D. 1987. The healing paradox of forgiveness. *Psychotherapy* 24(2): 240–244.

Horsbrugh, H. J. 1974. Forgiveness. *Canadian Journal of Philosophy* 4: 269–289.

Kiel, D. V. 1986. I'm learning how to forgive. *Decisions* (Feb.): 12–13.

Lewis, M. 1980. On forgiveness. *Philosophical Quarterly* 30: 236–245.

Linn, D., and M. Linn. 1978. *Healing life's hurts: Healing memories through the five stages of forgiveness.* New York: Paulist Press.

McGary, H. 1989. Forgiveness. *American Philosophical Quarterly* 26(4): 343–351.

Neblett, W. R. 1974. Forgiveness and ideals. *Mind* 83: 269–275.

Nietzsche, F. W. 1887. *The genealogy of morals.* Trans. P. Watson. London: S.P.C.K.

North, J. 1987. Wrongdoing and forgiveness. *Philosophy* 62: 499–508.

Patton, J. 1985. *Is human forgiveness possible?* Nashville: Abingdon.

Richards, N. 1988. Forgiveness. *Ethics* 99: 77–97.

Simon, S. B., and S. Simon. 1990. *Forgiveness: How to make peace with your past and get on with your life.* New York: Warner Books.

Smedes, L. B. 1984. *Forgive and forget: Healing the hurts we don't deserve.* New York: Harper and Row.

Smith, M. 1981. The psychology of forgiveness. *The Month* 14: 301–307.

Trainer, M. F. 1981. Forgiveness: Intrinsic, role-expected, expedient, in the context of divorce. Doctoral dissertation, Boston University, 1981. *Dissertation Abstracts International—B* 45(04), 1984, p. 1325.

Twambley, P. 1976. Mercy and forgiveness. *Analysis* 36: 84–90.

6

Anger and the Healing Power of Forgiveness: A Psychiatrist's View

Richard Fitzgibbons

Robert Enright and his associates in the Department of Educational Psychology at the University of Wisconsin–Madison have continued to make a significant contribution to the mental health field by their pioneering work in forgiveness studies. Forgiveness as a powerful psychotherapeutic tool has received little attention among mental health professionals because it has been viewed primarily within the domain of theology. In a previous article on the subject (Fitzgibbons 1986), I attempted to clarify the meaning of forgiveness and how it can be used effectively as a cognitive and emotive psychotherapeutic technique to diminish excessive anger in a number of clinical disorders.

For over twenty years in a very active practice of psychiatry I have studied the nature and degree of excessive anger in children, adolescents, and adults and have used forgiveness extensively and successfully to resolve hostile feelings and vengeful thinking. The psychotherapeutic uses of forgiveness have resulted in a significant diminishment in the emotional, mental, and physical suffering in our clients and have contributed to successful reconciliations in a variety of relationships. I am excited and enthusiastic about its use in numerous disorders, and I am also aware of its limitations. From this clinical background I will respond to three central questions: (1) What is interpersonal forgiveness? (2) Can we devise a model to help people to forgive? (3) What are the psychological outcomes for those who forgive? I will conclude with a few suggestions for research in the future.

The Nature of Anger

Before addressing the first question it is important to examine in some detail the powerful and complex emotion of anger, which forgiveness can be used to address. An understanding of the nature and manifestations of anger is essential if forgiveness is to be used appropriately. Anger is a strong feeling of displeasure and antagonism aroused by a sense of injury or wrong. Soon after a hurt or disappointment, this emotion occurs and is closely associated with a degree of sadness from the hurt. In Schimmel's (1979) historical analysis, the subjective feelings of the angry person include the pain of injury (sadness, fear, damage to self-esteem), as well as a certain pleasure at the expectation of revenge and of venting anger.

Anger develops as a natural response of the failure of others to meet one's needs for love, praise, acceptance, and justice, and it is experienced daily in the home, school, community, and place of employment. Anger begins in early childhood in relationships in the home and later is experienced in the community. Three basic mechanisms are used to deal with this emotion: conscious or unconscious denial; active- or passive-aggression expression; and forgiveness. Denial is the major method of dealing with anger in early childhood. As a result of denial, most people bring into their adult lives significant amounts of unconscious anger from their family of origin. The active expression of anger can be appropriate, excessive, or misdirected. The passive-aggressive expression of anger directs this emotion toward others in a covert manner while the person acts as though he or she is not angry.

The experience of anger leads to a desire for revenge, which does not diminish until the existence of the resentful feelings is recognized and subsequently resolved. Without this recognition and release, anger can be displaced for many years and erupt decades later in loving relationships with significant others. It will not be fully resolved until a conscious decision is made to let go of the desire for revenge and to forgive.

Many mental health professionals have viewed expression as the most appropriate way to deal with this emotion (e.g., see Freud 1963; Janov 1970; Rubin 1970; Novoca 1975; further discussion is in Fitzgibbons 1986). However, in my view, although the appropriate expression of anger is important and healthy, when relied on solely for relief, serious problems can develop because of the degree and strength of unresolved anger from previous disappointments encountered in childhood, adolescence, and adult life. The reenactment of past traumatic events with the expression of anger toward those who inflicted pain does not fully resolve the anger experienced in different life stages, nor does the expression of anger result in a true sense of justice or freedom from the desire for revenge. The excessive expression of anger can separate spouses by making them even more angry or aggressive with one another (Straus 1974), adversely affect children (Gardner 1971), increase guilt and shame (Lerner 1985), reinforce inappropriate ways of relating, ruin friendships, and aggravate psychosomatic illness (see Tavris 1984).

What Is Interpersonal Forgiveness?

North and Enright have given a definition of forgiveness which I endorse and support. I would like to add to it from my clinical experience. I will discuss the first aspect of their definition (the process of relinquishing one's feeling of resentment and thoughts of vengeance) and then the second aspect (the process of fostering compassion, generosity, and even love toward those who have inflicted pain).

Abandoning one's angry feelings and thoughts is not an easy task. Take, for example, the large number (almost 40 percent) of young Americans who do not have their biological fathers at home (Blankenhorn 1995). Most of these youngsters have great difficulty in understanding and forgiving their fathers for the pain of betrayal with which they struggle daily.

Forgiveness works directly on the emotion of anger (and related constructs such as resentment, hostility, or hatred) by diminishing its intensity or level within the mind and heart. Each time it is successfully applied to a disappointing or traumatic life experience with someone, it removes some of the anger from that hurt. Understandably, the more severe the emotional wound, the greater will be the time and effort needed to arrive at a control or resolution of the associated anger. An individual can be helped to move toward forgiveness by concentrating on a specific memory or a long series of painful memories. In the latter case, for example, the person might reflect, "I would like to try to forgive my spouse (or my mother or father) for all the ways in which she (or he) has disappointed me in my life." The process of forgiveness can proceed on one of three levels: cognitive, emotional, or spiritual.

In the process of cognitive forgiveness an individual, after analyzing the origins of his or her pain, makes a decision to forgive, that is, to let go of anger or the desire for revenge. This decision may occur for a variety of reasons. Initially the person may not feel at all like forgiving. Nevertheless, if there is to be progress, the individual requires some motivation. For example, someone may be motivated to relinquish hostile feelings in an attempt to protect a loving relationship from being harmed by misdirected anger from past disappointments in other relationships. Other motivations might involve the desire to overcome a depressive episode or to protect one's job. For most people the forgiveness process begins on this cognitive level and usually remains on that level for a period of time. I call this the *cognitive* level because the person *decides* to forgive, *thinks* it is good to do, but as yet does not feel compassion or love toward the offending one. As the anger level diminishes through regular cognitive forgiveness exercises, the intellect is afflicted less by the negative effects of anger and subsequently grows in understanding the offender and his or her weaknesses (this is one part of the process, described by North and by Enright and his colleagues as "reframing").

Emotional forgiveness is that phase of the forgiveness process in which one comes to understand deeply the offender and his life struggles, develops a degree of empathy for the "wounded boy or girl" within the adult, and, as a result, truly feels like forgiving. This level or stage of the process of forgiveness is usually preceded by a significant amount of time in the utilization of cognitive forgiveness exercises. Growth in understanding the weaknesses and life struggles of the offender is the major path which leads to emotional forgiveness. Some clients feel upset or even guilty when this process moves slowly. They may even think that cognitive forgiveness is not really forgiveness at all, because they don't truly feel like forgiving. Such individuals benefit from encouragement in the recognition that forgiveness is a process with several stages, that it is taking place, and that in time the feelings will follow. A therapist can err by pressuring clients to move too quickly to feel compassion for those who have hurt them and by failing to validate the effectiveness of cognitive forgiveness.

The third approach to the use of forgiveness is spiritual. This approach is used when someone suffers from such severe pain that he or she cannot let go of resentment against the offender either cognitively or emotionally. In utilizing a modification of the Alcoholics Anonymous' twelve steps, the person tries to reflect: "I am powerless over my anger and want to turn it over to God," or "Revenge or justice belongs to God," or "God forgive him, I can't," or "God free me from my anger." Many clients begin the forgiveness journey utilizing this method of relinquishing their anger, especially those who have felt severely betrayed by a parent, spouse, or employer. In the work of forgiveness individuals may find themselves utilizing each of these three approaches for resolving anger from a particular hurt.

The cognitive, emotional, and spiritual approaches to forgiveness in therapy can be employed to resolve anger from past hurts and from present stresses and to protect one in the future from overreacting in resentment. Clients also can use three types of forgiveness exercise for anger control: past forgiveness exercises; immediate forgiveness exercises; and preventive forgiveness exercises. Preventive forgiveness exercises diminish anger and decrease the likelihood that anger will be misdirected at inappropriate situations; at the school, at a loving relationship, or at the home. They can be used with children before going to school and with adults at the beginning of a new relationship, as well as on returning home after work.

The second parts of North's and Enright and colleagues' accounts of forgiveness include fostering the (perhaps undeserved) feelings of compassion, generosity, and even love for the person who inflicted the pain. This is the initial goal for most, but not all, clients. In some cases clients feel so betrayed and angry that they are incapable of understanding or feeling compassion toward their offender. For them, considerable anger needs to be resolved through cognitive forgiveness exercises before they are willing to move on to develop compassion, trust, or love for the offender.

Limitations of Forgiveness

Forgiveness does not resolve all emotional pain resulting from traumatic life events. In my clinical experience it has helped to diminish the degree of sadness from emotional wounds but has not seemed to heal the hope-lessness or despair associated with the severe pain of betrayal experienced by increasing numbers of people of all ages today. Also, forgiveness does not directly address a person's anger resulting from his or her character weakness, such as narcissism, grandiosity, impatience, and the absence of moral values. While it is a very powerful therapeutic tool, it alone cannot bring about a complete resolution of the excessive resentment, hostility, and hatred in our culture.

Unfortunately, forgiveness does not always result in even a neutral stance toward the offender, especially when that offender is unwilling to change his or her behavior. In a marital relationship where someone misdirects unresolved anger with one's parent at a spouse or is unwilling to change narcissistic behavior, it is essential that the victim does not remain vulnerable.

The discussion by Enright and his colleagues of false forgiveness as a way to control and manipulate others is an important contribution to the understanding of forgiveness. Related to false forgiveness is "superficial forgiveness," where individuals claim that they have resolved their anger from specific life hurts when in fact they have barely begun the forgiveness journey. They believe falsely that by simply deciding at a given time to forgive someone that all the anger will be instantly removed from their minds and hearts. Something similar occurs through psychodrama and Gestalt experiences in which people believe that all their anger is resolved simply by giving vent to it.

Devising a Model to Help People to Forgive

We move on now to the second question which I raised at the start of this chapter, namely, Can we devise a model to help people to forgive? Enright and the Human Development Study Group have developed a very important and much needed model for the process of forgiveness, with the four phases of "uncovering, decision, work, and outcome." This model will provide a solid basis for research and dialogue in regard to the specific aspects of the forgiveness process among mental health professionals. Another benefit of the model is that it could be used as a basis for developing educational materials on conflict resolution, which could in turn be used in our schools in the future.

On the basis of extensive clinical experience in the use of forgiveness at all age levels, I will make some additions to the different phases specified by Enright and colleagues.

Uncovering

In the uncovering phase we regularly discuss the nature of anger, the methods of dealing with this powerful affect, and the many forms which anger takes at various life stages. Correcting misconceptions about anger is important in this phase; they include the views that anger is an emotion which can be resolved only through expressing it and experienced only in the extreme and that the absence of blatant manifestations of anger precludes its presence.

The work of *uncovering* is facilitated by having all clients, regardless of diagnosis, complete at any early visit a questionnaire which allows the client to provide a subjective assessment of his current situation and his handling of feelings of anger. This measure assists client as well as therapist in understanding both the depth of the client's anger and his or her primary method for dealing with or expressing this emotion. We also might ask a family member to complete a similar anger checklist on the client if excessive anger is clearly a problem or if we suspect that the person is not being honest in the completion of the initial questionnaire. Parents routinely complete a childhood anger checklist when they bring a child into treatment.

In this phase we also explain to clients how they can resolve any anger which they may discover within themselves. Often people are more likely to stop denying their anger if they have an option for dealing with it that does not involve expressing it. Cognitive forgiveness exercises can be employed at this stage on the basis of the person's symptoms and history. The client may be asked to think about the option of forgiveness and the possibility of letting go of the anger toward an offending person. Initially the client may have no conscious awareness of hurt or anger. Cognitive exercises enable the client to recognize the existence of anger, perhaps previously denied, and so to commence the process of the healing journey. It should be noted that the relationship in which the greatest degree of denial takes place is that between parent and child (particularly between father and child).

We have learned that if the therapist can share how he or she came to realize the role of anger in his or her personal life and the benefits which accrued from facing and resolving it, the degree of trust in the therapist is often enhanced, so aiding the process of forgiveness therapy. At this early stage clients are expected to identify their deepest disappointments from different life stages and the anger associated with these hurts. It also is anticipated that they will examine ways in which they have misdirected their anger at others who did not deserve it and how this anger injured others.

Decision

In the decision phase the numerous advantages of forgiveness are presented as the preferred method for resolving anger. Frequently, successful case histories of others with conflicts are discussed to motivate the client.

Then we explain clearly what forgiveness is and what it is not. If the person's emotional pain and anger are intense, we normally discuss only the initial aspect of forgiveness, that of letting go of one's resentment and desire for revenge. As I said earlier, many people in the initial stage of their healing cannot consider extending compassion, generosity, and love toward those who have hurt them terribly. Such expectations would be asking too much of those who have been severely betrayed. Many will decide to begin the process only after they have been reassured that they do not necessarily have to become vulnerable toward the person whom they are trying to forgive and that forgiving does not preclude expressing anger or pursuing justice. It should be understood, as well, that the resolution of anger with an offender and the investment of trust toward that person are two related but different processes.

For those individuals who are not suffering from severe pain of betrayal, we will explain that, as they work at letting go of their anger, in all likelihood they will come to experience compassion and love toward those who have hurt them. We also explain that forgiveness is possible through a process of attempting to understand the emotional development and life stresses of those who have inflicted the pain. As that process occurs, there is growing awareness that the behavior of many offenders can be attributed to their own emotional scars, and perhaps that they loved as much as they were capable of loving and that the pain they caused was rarely deliberately inflicted. It is then possible to present the methods or stages of forgiveness—cognitive, emotional, and (possibly) spiritual—and the ways in which they differ from one another.

Work

In the work phase of forgiveness we describe reframing as understanding. For most people forgiveness begins as an intellectual process in which there is no true feeling of forgiveness. As their understanding of the offenders grows, especially the offenders' childhood and adolescent emotional wounds, the offended will experience more compassion and feel like forgiving. While cognitive forgiveness exercises are effective, the process may take considerable time. Our clients are expected to identify a number of areas in which they felt disappointment with each parent and to spend time forgiving the parent at different developmental stages. Although there is resistance to this initially, it is a basic aspect of the forgiveness process. Also, some people discover that they have been hurt so deeply that they cannot use the word *forgiveness,* and these people are more comfortable stating that they are willing to let go of their desire for revenge.

For those with very intense anger, the release of resentment can be facilitated by a process which begins with the physical expression of anger in a manner in which others will not be hurt. This is followed immediately by cognitive forgiveness exercises aimed at letting go of the desire for revenge. Relief from intense anger also may be experienced if the person imagines the expression of hostile feelings or impulses against the offender and then attempts to give up the desire for revenge.

In this stage we regularly review the major obstacles to forgiveness. These include: a lack of parental modeling for this process, significant others who continue to disappoint in a regular manner, and, on a personal basis, narcissism and a compulsive need to control. Also, since anger is often used to defend against feelings of inadequacy and fear, especially the fear of betrayal, many individuals are not able to move ahead with the forgiveness process until their self-esteem and basic ability to trust are enhanced.

When possible the willingness of the offenders to participate in the work phase can be very helpful in the resolution of the client's resentment. Attempts to explain behaviors, requests for forgiveness, and promises to change hurtful actions facilitate forgiveness. The engagement in therapy of fathers who live apart from their children can be extremely helpful in the healing process for many young people. Finally, the absorption of the pain is a very difficult process, because in reality what we may be expecting people to accept is profound sadness, hurt, and the betrayal pain of mistrust. Although forgiveness diminishes the level of anger, it does not completely heal the wounds of sadness and mistrust. For many who have sustained major loss, only a sense of being loved in a new and special way can enable them to accept the pain. However, a harsh reality may be that some have been betrayed so deeply that they may never be able to absorb the pain fully. This response to forgiveness is seen regularly in children or young adults who have been emotionally abandoned by their fathers.

Outcome

Enright and others in the Wisconsin group have made a major scientific contribution to the mental health field as a result of their pioneering research in forgiveness studies. Their research findings of decreases in anxiety and depression and improved self-esteem and hope in those who achieve forgiveness are extremely encouraging. They have proved what therapists knew from their clinical work but were unable to demonstrate empirically: Forgiveness has remarkable healing power in the lives of those who utilize it. Major advances will be made in the mental health field because of their work. The research on forgiveness by Robert Enright and his colleagues may be as important to the treatment of emotional and mental disorders as the discovery of sulfa drugs and penicillin have been to the treatment of infectious diseases.

We have seen many additional psychological benefits as a result of the practice of using forgiveness as a therapeutic tool during the last two decades. Significant among them are a decreased level of anger and hostility, increased feelings of love, improved ability to control anger, enhanced capacity to trust, and freedom from the subtle control of individuals and events of the past. Other advantages are a cessation of the repetition of negative parental emotional and behavioral patterns, improved sleep patterns, more confidence in relationships, improved academic and work performance, and a resolution of physical symptoms and illnesses caused by hostility (Barefoot et al. 1983; Shekelle et al. 1983). In addition, there are marked clinical improvements in a variety of psychiatric disorders in all age groups of persons who present a significant degree of anger and hostility. These disorders in children include: oppositional, defiant and disruptive behaviors; separation anxiety; and attention-deficit/hyperactivity disorder. In adolescents these disorders include: acting-out and sociopathic behaviors, substance abuse; and mood and anxiety disorders. Adult disorders include: bipolar, impulse-control, panic, factitious, dissociative, and adjustment disorders (particularly those related to job loss) and paraphilias. Finally, the use of forgiveness seems beneficial in treating those with personality disorders; these include the borderline, antisocial, histrionic, obsessive-compulsive, narcissistic, and paranoid types. Certainly more work must be done to understand more fully the interplay of disruptive symptoms, anger, and forgiveness, but our initial clinical observations are encouraging.

Choice of Outcome Variables

Enright and his colleagues need not criticize what they may perceive as an overemphasis on self in regard to their outcome variables. Their studies show us how to deal effectively with excessive resentment, anger, and hostility. The studies are extremely important in a world in which many individuals lack the skills to deal appropriately with resentment. Without a doubt the primary function of forgiveness is to help an individual gain control over anger and resolve it in an appropriate manner.

However, the benefits accruing from forgiveness reach far beyond the person doing the forgiving. There is reason to hope that in the near future the members of the Wisconsin group will cast their empirical net in many directions so that other people in the world of the forgiver can be studied, including the one being forgiven. Others in this volume indicate how the process of being forgiven might be experienced by the wrongdoer (see chapters 2, 3, and 4). With the resolution of anger in the life of the forgiver, the negative flow of resentment from this person toward others may decrease significantly. Subsequently, the forgiver's significant others may experience a diminishment in anxiety, muscular tension, and the physical symptoms of stress. Further benefits that might be researched include improved self-esteem, more energy and hope, and a great openness to a closer relationship with the forgiver.

The Next Ten Years and Beyond

A compelling need exists for the further training of mental health professionals, since the great majority have not received specialized training in the nature and treatment of excessive anger. We hope the work of the International Forgiveness Institute and others will help us support the development of such training.

To identify the implications for the use of forgiveness in therapy, it is necessary to detect the degree to which anger is present in various clinical diagnoses. Although the study of anger is in its infancy, there is evidence that anger is a significant factor in a wide range of clinical disorders. For example, in a study of 127 depressed outpatients at Massachusetts General Hospital (Fava et al. 1993), 44 percent manifested what the researchers referred to as anger attacks. The use of Prozac resulted in a diminution of anger attacks in 71 percent of the patients studied. In another study of 132 women with eating disorders, also conducted by Fava and colleagues (1995), 31 percent reported anger attacks, 4.8 per month on average. These researchers also found that those with eating disorders who have anger attacks had significantly more depressive symptoms than patients without these attacks. While this research is important, it did not evaluate the full extent of anger in these patients, since passive-aggressive resentment was not measured, a factor which can be significant, especially in those with eating disorders.

Another disorder in children and teenagers in which there is compelling need for anger research is attention-deficit/hyperactivity disorder. Today, the best estimates are that between 1.5 million and 2.5 million children in the United States take Ritalin for this condition. The number of children diagnosed with the condition is rather frightening, since studies show that approximately 25 percent of these youngsters will develop sociopathic personalities as adults. We need to offer these youngsters more than Ritalin and help them understand and resolve their anger without harming others. Perhaps genuine forgiveness may prevent the development of sociopathy in later years. Given the severe problem of excessive anger in our world today, such a premise presents a challenge for the urgent need to grow in understanding the nature of anger and its origins.

Perhaps researchers in the future will work to design psychotherapy research projects in which, for example, the process of forgiveness would be compared with Prozac in the treatment of resentment found in depressive and eating disorders, and with Ritalin in the treatment of the anger in attention-deficit/hyperactivity disorders. Second, researchers might develop evaluative and treatment protocols for excessive anger seen in various disorders included in the *Diagnostic and Statistical Manual of Mental Disorders IV.* Treatment protocols also could be established for certain physical illnesses, such as coronary artery disease, in which hostility plays a major role.

As conclusions are published and information is disseminated, there is every hope that therapists themselves will become more open to examine countertransference issues in the treatment of anger. The personal journey of the therapist in attempting to resolve anger at different life stages will be extremely helpful at various levels. Not least among them will be a greater ability to help others work through areas of resentment.

It is my belief that it is no longer possible to dismiss forgiveness as not having a role in the treatment of mental disorders. Forgiveness, it is hoped, will move into the mainstream of the mental health field, where it has been firmly placed thanks to Enright and his associates. Forgiveness has been defined and its healing power empirically supported. We now can expect that its voice and influence will become stronger and clearer both in academic investigation and in the clinical treatment of people of all ages in the years ahead.

References

Barefoot, J. C., W. G. Dahlstrom, and R. B. Williams. 1983. Hostility, CHD incidence, and total mortality: A 25-year follow-up study of 255 physicians. *Psychosomatic Medicine* 45: 49–63.

Blankenhorn, D. 1995. *Fatherless America*. New York: Basic Books.

Fava, M., J. Rosenbaum, and J. Fava. 1993. Anger attacks in unipolar depression, Part 1: Clinical correlates and response to Fluoxetine treatment. *American Journal of Psychiatry* 150(8): 1158–1168.

Fava, M., S. M. Rappe, J. West, and D. B. Herzog. 1995. Anger attacks in eating disorders. *Psychiatry Research* 56: 205–212.

Fitzgibbons, R. P. 1986. The cognitive and emotive uses of forgiveness in the treatment of anger. *Psychotherapy* 23: 629–633.

Freud, S. 1963. *Collected papers*. New York: Collier Books.

Gardner, G. E. 1971. Aggression and violence—the enemies of precision learning in children. *American Journal of Psychiatry* 128(4): 77–82.

Janov, A. 1970. *The primal scream*. New York: Dell.

Lerner, H. G. 1985. *The dance of anger*. New York: Harper and Row.

Novoca, R. 1975. *Anger control*. Lexington, Mass.: Lexington Books.

Rubin, T. I. 1970. *The angry book*. New York: Collier Books.

Schimmel, S. 1979. Anger and its control in Graeco-Roman and modern psychology. *Psychiatry* 42: 320–337.

Shekelle, A. B., M. Gale, A. M. Ostfeld, and P. Oglesby. 1983. Hostility, risk of coronary heart disease and mortality. *Psychosomatic Medicine* 45: 109–114.

Smedes, L. B. 1984. *Forgive and forget*. San Francisco: Harper and Row.

Straus, M. 1974. Leveling, civility, and violence in the family. *Journal of Marriage and the Family* 36: 13–29.

Tavris, C. 1984. *Anger: The misunderstood emotion*. New York: Simon and Schuster.

7

The Process of Forgiveness
in Marriage
and the Family

Paul W. Coleman

I always looked forward to the weekly session with Mary and Rick. On the brink of divorce when I had first seen them a year earlier, they were clearly happier now and more committed to one another. In one year's time we uncovered and disconnected emotional triangles, reworked family-of-origin issues, improved problem-solving and communication skills, and each partner stopped projecting his or her own attitudes onto the other and instead cultivated his or her self-focusing capabilities. Scars were not completely healed, however. Mutual trust was evident but episodic. Minor flare-ups sometimes occurred over mundane events, often spiced with resentments we all believed had been resolved. However, I had faith that our continued work together would be helpful. And it was, but not for reasons I would have predicted.

"Our last meeting changed how we view our marriage," Rick said enthusiastically in his opening remarks. "For all that's been accomplished this past year with you, your question to us about whether we'd ever forgive each other might be the most important thing you've ever said."

It took me a few seconds to recall what I had said during the previous session. Forgiveness? Yes, I remembered now, but I hadn't thought it was *that* important when I said it. In fact, the word *forgive* was not a part of my usual verbal repertoire, and I could easily have spoken about resolving one's anger or used some other synonymous cliché. It was disconcerting, especially since they believed it to be the most helpful thing I'd said in our forty-plus meetings together.

Over the next eight meetings I worked with a transformed couple. Forgiveness was their goal, and they worked hard on it. Resentments really did wither, hope emerged healthy and vigorous, and they were in love again. Six months after we terminated, they were still going strong. By that time I was knee deep in articles and personal notes on the forgiveness process. I introduced the topic of forgiveness to most of my clients and learned from their reactions. I raised the issue with colleagues at case conferences and sifted through their many and varied responses. Forgiveness was certainly not a new notion, and yet it rejuvenated my work. Now, almost ten years later, I'd like to report on the relevance and application of the forgiveness process in marital and family work.

Integrating Therapy and Forgiveness

The act of forgiveness presumes guilt. Guilt is something that many therapists shy away from in their work. (I'm not referring to the sense of *feeling* guilty that many clients report, but rather to the state of *being* guilty.) Therapists, in an effort to forge a therapeutic alliance, are less likely to tell their clients, "Maybe you feel guilty because what you did was hurtful or wrong." Therapists don't like to sound judgmental. Consequently, in the name of fostering unconditional regard for their clients, they may be not only overlooking some of the harmful things their clients might be doing but also giving tacit support to those actions. Recently, a male client of mine wanted to reestablish a relationship with his nineteen-year-old son from his first marriage. My client had divorced when his son was about four and had little to do with him thereafter. Now he realized his mistake and felt bad. But when his son snubbed him on his first major attempt at reconciliation, my client told me he felt angry and wondered, "Should I tell my son off?" I told my client, no, he should not tell his son off. I told him his son's anger was legitimate and that this is part of the dues he must pay. "You're not a bad person," I said sincerely. "And I applaud you for your desire to ask forgiveness and reconcile. But you are seeking forgiveness because you understand you were wrong to have ignored your son over the years. You blew it as a father. Your task now is to put his feelings ahead of yours, to care more about the pain you caused him than the pain he is causing you. And I'd like to help you with that."

Telling someone he or she is guilty goes against my training as a therapist, especially my training in the family systems approach. Systems therapists are likely to deemphasize individual dynamics and instead examine the relationship behavioral patterns that have evolved in a family. Systems therapists view causes and effects as interchangeable. Simply put, a needy or attention-seeking spouse may provoke his or her partner to back away, prompting the needy spouse to feel even needier. These feedback loops are important to a systems therapist and are eagerly searched out and examined. Systems therapists often try to reframe "bad" behavior into "good," as in the example where the actions of an irresponsible, acting-out young adult are reframed as his or her attempt to unite the usually distant parents. Many systems therapists see the condition of being guilty as a meaningless concept at best and a destructive concept at worst. Guilt breeds scapegoats (or so one line of reasoning goes), and the continuing presence of a scapegoat bogs down effective family therapy. I'm not for pinning blame on any family member, but I am for people ultimately accepting responsibility for their actions. I believe most other family therapists have the same view, and yet they tiptoe around issues of blame and guilt. I should point out that this has increasingly not been the case when the issue is one of physical or sexual abuse. Then, most therapists do point the finger of guilt at the abuser and do not allow rationalizations ever to justify abusive behavior.

Sometimes we systems therapists give clients mixed messages. I know I have. On the one hand we let them know that disruptive behaviors are a function of group interactions and that the question is not Who's to blame? or Who started it? but What can be done to disrupt the pattern? Yet, on the other hand, we convey that, if one person in the system changes for a sustained period of time, the system will change. In the first case we dilute the idea that one person can have so much impact on a family, and in the second case we strengthen it.

So where do guilt and forgiveness fit within a systems framework? Certainly, couples act in a subconsciously collusive manner, encouraging the very crimes they accuse each other of committing. Whichever way guilt is distributed within a family, each person must accept responsibility for his or her role in a problem. (Incidentally, I don't believe that family members bear equal responsibility for the perpetuation of some dysfunctional patterns of behavior. Some members are more powerful and thus more accountable—guiltier—than others.) When a working relationship between therapist and couple/family has developed, examining ways in which feedback cycles are operating to perpetuate painful interactions is a tried and true approach. Reframing techniques and exploring family-of-origin themes and patterns to see if they are emerging in the current context also can expand a couple's view of their problems. A broader perspective makes forgiving easier. But while some patterns of behavior may have occurred unwittingly, others occurred out of *conscious* anger or fear. And once a person becomes more aware of the origins and meanings of his or her actions, or once a person sees that he or she doesn't have to respond in her or her usual, dysfunctional way, the responsibility for the behaviors in question falls on that person's shoulders. It is then that the notions of guilt and forgiveness become more relevant from a therapeutic perspective.

For example, when I first saw Mary and Rick, clear, dysfunctional patterns of interaction emerged. Classically, she was overinvolved with the children, one of whom was mildly retarded. He was a workaholic with an impatient, overly logical exterior, animated by occasional bursts of anger at his wife's emotional helplessness. They had been this way for nine years. Predictably, the more emotional she was, the more analytical and irritated he became. She was pessimistic about the marriage and her retarded child's future happiness. He would minimize her concerns and suggest ways for her to cheer up. She resented that, viewing it as evidence of his lack of understanding. His attempts to downplay her concerns only reinforced her pessimism, and vice versa. We were able to halt the feedback cycles partly as a result of examining family-of-origin issues. As it turned out, when Rick was a boy, his job in his family-of-origin was to cheer up his parents and older siblings, who were still grieving the death of one of the children years earlier and who were also contending with Dad's alcoholism. Mary never knew that about Rick. She then viewed his tendency to block out sadness and trivialize her concerns with more compassion. His objectionable behavior was now reframed as an attempt to extend caring. She was then able to be more forgiving. But Rick could see that his style of responding still hurt Mary when what she needed was comfort and understanding. It was his willingness to own up to that, to express some remorse for behaviors that were now less instinctive, that helped them further. In other words, he didn't use his past or his good intentions to explain away or justify the continuation of his behaviors. He took responsibility for them and expressed remorse for those actions that were (even inadvertently) hurtful. He asked for forgiveness.

Thus from a systems view, stopping feedback cycles, evaluating family-of-origin patterns, and use of reframing allowed for and nurtured a forgiving attitude. Such an attitude, in turn, nourished further change. Although dysfunctional behavior patterns were altered, forgiveness appeared to be the glue that held the new behaviors in place long enough for other factors to be of influence.

Why Forgiveness?

In a family, the effort to overcome deep hurt and betrayal often includes a desire for reconciliation on at least one member's part. Forgiveness is not reconciliation. It is possible to forgive without reconciling, without coming together again in love and friendship. But it is not possible to reconcile truly without forgiving. Consequently, *forgiveness is a must in any family problem where there has been deep hurt, betrayal, or disloyalty. If there can be no reconciliation, forgiveness is the process that enables the forgiver to get on with his or her life unencumbered with the pain of betrayal.*

In forgiveness, you decide to offer love to someone who has betrayed that love. If the goal is to reconcile, then forgiveness provides a new context within which to nurture the relationship. Forgiveness is the changing of seasons. It allows you to let go of all that has been difficult to bear and begin again. When you forgive, you do not forget the season of cold completely, but neither do you shiver in its memory.

When forgiveness becomes a part of your life, little resentment is left. Anger may not vanish immediately, but it will wither in time. Forgiveness comes first as a decision to act lovingly even though you are justified to withhold your love. When you forgive, you are not saying that you approve of what was done, but you are saying that you will not reject the others outright for what they have done to you.

True forgiveness does not take place with strong sentimentality and sympathy at the expense of justice and dignity. There is certainly no justice or dignity if, in the name of forgiveness, one ignores the seriousness of some human actions.

Forgiveness involves a leap of faith, a willingness to risk being hurt again. But it does not demand that you knowingly lay yourself open to certain abuse. You can forgive but then limit or even end the relationship. Also, the one who is forgiven has no obligation to the forgiver as a condition of forgiveness. Forgiveness is not a quid pro quo deal. But if there is to be an ongoing relationship, then the one forgiven must try to learn from his mistakes and not reinjure the people that have offered their forgiveness.

Forgiveness and Game Theory

Game theory offers some insight into the process of forgiveness. Game theory examines when interactions between people result in payoffs that are obtained either through cooperation or through competition. In a zero-sum game, for instance, for there to be a winner there must be a loser. In a positive sum game, there is no loser, only winners. There, players may have to forgo a large individual payoff in order to maximize gains for all players in the long run. Healthy family relationships can be construed as positive-sum gains in that light. Even if a parent, spouse, or sibling must make personal sacrifices, the family's greater good is ultimately considered most important. Someone who feels that, if he offers forgiveness then the one who hurt him "won" or "got away with it," is operating from a zero sum game mentality. Someone who views forgiving as a process that can ultimately be beneficial for her or for the relationship, even if it is hard to accomplish in the short-run, is operating from a positive-sum game mentality.

Axelrod (1984) discusses a fascinating study about game theory and its relevance to relationships and forgiveness. His findings were also discussed in Heitler (1990) which is, in my view, rich with insights and practical applications for therapists. Axelrod wanted to examine when it is advantageous for a person to act in his own self-interest or to cooperate. Using game theory techniques, he arranged for players to act in a series of moves and countermoves, the goal being to determine which strategies of cooperation or selfishness would yield the highest score. He utilized the Prisoner's Dilemma model. In the Prisoner's Dilemma, two prisoners have been arrested and placed in separate rooms for questioning. Each faces a long jail term. Either can bear witness against the other. If Prisoner A bears witness against Prisoner B and Prisoner B remains quiet, then prisoner A will be released while Prisoner B will get the full jail term. If both prisoners inform against the other, both will suffer long prison sentences. But if both prisoners refuse to confess against the other, they will be convicted on minor charges and serve a brief jail term. The dilemma then involves the decision whether to cooperate or to act in one's self-interest.

Axelrod devised a scheme where two players must interact. At each player's turn, there is the choice to act "nice" and cooperatively for moderate gain or to act selfishly with the potential of receiving greater gains—or no gains at all. In his system, on any round that players cooperate, they each receive three points. On rounds where one player cooperates but one player "defects," which is Axelrod's term for acting solely in one's self-interest, then the "selfish" player receives five points while the cooperative player receives zero points. If both players defect, neither receives points. Axelrod invited game theorists from diverse fields to devise computer programs using this model. The winning program would be the one that earned the highest number of total points over several hundred rounds of play. Dozens of sophisticated programs entered the competition. The program that ultimately won the competition and was viewed as exceptionally powerful and robust, is named Tit for Tat—a disconcerting and rather offensive name to someone in the business of forgiveness. While its name connotes an "eye for an eye" mentality, I believe the specifics of the program have merit for family relationships and deserve some critical attention from the standpoint of forgiveness and its use within a family.

Basically, the first rule of Tit for Tat is to begin with a cooperative move (what Axelrod called "being nice"). That player continues being cooperative until the opponent acts selfishly, which causes a selfish response in return. It is possible in this model for players to become stuck in repeated patterns of selfish moves, neither one offering an olive branch to the other. Many warring countries and warring family members act that way, neither side willing to try to make repairs. However, in Tit for Tat, all it takes is one player to begin responding cooperatively and the rules compel the other to respond in kind. (Keep in mind that, however bothersome this notion of "an eye for an eye" is to you, this program offers the most successful long-term strategy for maximizing personal and relationship benefits. This is important from the standpoint of family relationships, because these relationships are typically long term.)

An essential rule to Tit for Tat is that "nice follows nice," even if there have been previous selfish moves. That is, imagine Player A responds cooperatively, but Player B then responds selfishly. Player A will respond in kind. But if Player B resumes a nice response, Player A is not allowed to "hold a grudge" and respond selfishly. Past offenses are quickly "forgiven" in this model, once cooperative playing has been resumed by the previously uncooperative player.

Susan Heitler (1990) concluded that the Tit for Tat program reveals several insights into human interactions. First, *niceness pays off*. If you begin interactions by being cooperative, instead of taking a selfish stance, the odds are better that the relationship can be beneficial to both sides over the long run. Second, *selfishness is costly*. Axelrod found that other computer programs that include in their rules the opportunity for sudden, unprovoked selfish moves result in the lowest scores among all the entrants. Third, according to Heitler *optimism*, or *the expectation that the other player will cooperate enhances the effectiveness of the Tit for Tat program, while excessive pessimism—the expectation that the other player will make a selfish move—diminishes the scoring potential*. To me, that finding parallels a dynamic of personal relationships. If people regard others as basically good and expect better things from each other, the odds increase that we will indeed act that way. In my experience, family members who chronically regard other members as bad or selfish or manipulative are more likely to foster an atmosphere for those undesirable behaviors to continue.

While this program allows for retaliation, *excessive retaliation decreases Tit for Tat's effectiveness* by lowering overall scores. In other words, excessive retaliation is costly, a finding observed in many unhealthy relationships we see today.

Even more fascinating from the standpoint of forgiveness is that the effectiveness of Tit for Tat is further enhanced if players use a modified rule of not responding selfishly to the opponent's selfish move without first giving that opponent a *second chance*. In other words, by *forgiving* the selfish opponent, which can be defined as the willingness to respond cooperatively at least one more time after the other player has defected, scores are highest of all. However, excessive forgiveness results in much lower overall scores, similar to strategies that use excessive selfishness.

A final insight gained by the Tit for Tat program is that clear and simple rules of interaction are more effective than vague or unpredictable rules. The rules of Tit for Tat are easy: Start by being cooperative and respond selfishly only if the other person does. Be willing to respond cooperatively the moment the first defector resumes cooperation. In many families, the rules of engagement are not at all clear or are ill-defined and confusing. Families that do a lot of mind reading or who change the rules of engagement inexplicably (as might be the case in a family where a parent is an alcoholic with unpredictable mood swings or reliability) will not have the highest payoff in terms of satisfaction.

I should point out that Axelrod's findings, however fascinating, probably don't account for all the subtle complexities of family functioning. In Axelrod's studies, when selfishness was met with selfishness, the selfish moves were given equal weight. In real life, family members may disagree on what constitutes a selfish move and may respond more harshly in retaliation to a perceived hurt. When that happens, debates of Who started it? or accusations of You're not treating me fairly! flourish and the simple rules of Tit for Tat fall to the side. Also, Tit for Tat might make better sense when discussing rules for maintaining a relationship or for reconciling, not when merely forgiving. In Tit for Tat, there is no rule that says if your opponent is too selfish you can quit the game and quit the relationship. Theoretically, someone who is routinely mistreated in a family may choose to forgive the perpetrator but leave the family environment. Tit for Tat, then, does not speak primarily of forgiveness but of how to have successful long-term relationships. However, forgiveness is viewed as an important component to successful family life.

In sum, game theory studies strongly suggest that for relationships to be the most rewarding and durable, participants must be willing to act cooperatively instead of selfishly but must be willing to assert themselves in some retaliatory way if a partner attempts to act unfairly. This is very consistent with Beverly Flanigan's (1992) notion of "balancing the scales" as a step in the forgiveness process. Flanigan recommends not so much a vengeful "getting even" response as a measured but punitive "teach him a lesson" response, which is consistent with the Tit for Tat rules.

Game theory also advises letting bygones be bygones and not holding a grudge. Finally, a willingness to give a partner a second chance before retaliating can yield even higher benefits for relationships.

Practical Applications

Before I discuss the typical phases of the forgiveness process, as outlined in Coleman (1989), I'd like to mention a few of the predictable issues or complications that occur within a therapeutic context when forgiveness is being discussed.

Don't Discuss Forgiveness Immediately

If the notion of forgiveness is mentioned by the therapist before a therapeutic alliance has been established, clients may feel angry and misunderstood. "Forgive him? After what he's done!" is a response I've too often heard. Another: "Well, what about me? I'm supposed to forgive her and get on with this marriage and just put aside my feelings? Don't my feelings count?"

If forgiveness is dealt with prematurely, before each spouse or family member has fully expressed his or her feelings and concerns and before the therapist has communicated an understanding of those feelings, the "victim" may rebel. A premature discussion of forgiveness insidiously places the entire burden for the resolution of the conflict on the person who sees himself or herself as the primary victim. (Even if each partner admits to being hurtful, there are some actions that are clearly regarded by couples as more serious than others, allowing one partner to feel more victimized.) The victim then feels doubly burdened. First, in that person's view, he or she has been unfairly betrayed. Second, he or she has had to struggle with finding forgiveness to mend the marriage.

As a result, I now wait until progress has been made in therapy before I raise the topic. (Progress is typically defined as a dramatic reduction in objectionable behaviors and an improvement in trust and communication.) And even then I say to the couple that forgiveness may feel like yet another unfair ordeal. I tell them that finding forgiveness is what they ultimately will do if they are to be happy and committed to each other but that now may not be the best time to start. The starting time is left up to them.

Particularly when there has been an affair, I have found that the spouse who feels betrayed may take several months before he or she is willing to move beyond expressing rage to the work of finding forgiveness. If a therapist suggests that expressing such rage will have adverse consequences, in my experience, the result is usually that the betrayed spouse feels disrespected and misunderstood.

The Process of Forgiveness Is Not Always Straightforward

There is no cookbook formula for forgiveness. Couples and families go through an overlapping and repetitive process of self-focus, self-disclosure, confrontation, and dialogue. Ultimately, forgiveness is a decision. I inform people that they must *choose* to be forgiving. If they wait until they *feel* forgiving before they choose to forgive, it may be a long and arduous wait. In my opinion, regarding forgiveness as a choice, as an *action* instead of a *reaction,* helps to empower the one betrayed.

A Self-Focus Is Critical for Forgiveness to Occur

The victim is aided not only by examining ways in which he or she may have unwittingly reinforced or enabled objectionable behaviors, but also by exploring how he or she is sensitive (perhaps oversensitive) to the hurt in question. Was he hurt that way before? When and how so? How did he handle it then? Greater awareness of his own issues and past relationships allows him not to let his spouse take the full rap for offenses that others committed before her.

Similarly, the "guilty" spouse must examine his or her motives. An automatic, defensive response to a confrontational spouse must give way to nonreactive responses. It is most helpful if remorse can be nurtured. It is difficult to forgive a spouse or family member who is not remorseful. Hand in hand with a self-focus is a willingness to accept responsibility for one's actions. No one "made you do it."

Anger Is Common

In the forgiveness process, angry flare-ups are common and do not indicate that forgiveness is insincere or lacking. The therapist can point out that flare-ups, while troubling, have occurred with less intensity and/or frequency as marital work has progressed and that the couple can now recover more quickly from them.

Excessive Punishment Is to Be Avoided

The guilty party, even if he or she admits remorse, may resent the spouse's inability to be forgiving over time. The guilty spouse tolerates the partner's anger and distance only so long before he or she claims, "I've paid my dues." The victim then feels infuriated over the partner's apparent insensitivity, and conflict continues. This is less likely to occur when each partner admits to many hurtful actions and attempts to make amends have been made. It is very likely to occur when the hurtful act was very serious, such as infidelity, and one partner views himself or herself as a fairly innocent, or at least benign, victim.

When that happens, I usually do two things. First, I validate the victim's anger, urge for retaliation, and difficulty in trusting. Then, I tell the guilty party that, while he or she appears eager for a reconciliation, a premature reconciliation would serve no purpose. I find that, if the guilty partner can disclose that he doesn't like the continued anger from his spouse but that he nonetheless understands and accepts it, there is a lessening of the victim's fury.

Mixed Feelings Are Typical

If a victim wants to stop retaliating against the partner but has mixed feelings, I've found it helpful to explain that, the more vengeful one spouse is, the less guilty the other spouse starts to feel. This awareness often reduces a spouse's desire for vengeance. I also explain that the better way to handle one's ambivalence is not to careen back and forth between extreme feelings ("Today I love him. tomorrow I know I'll hate him") but to allow for the presence of mixed feelings in the context. In one case, a remorseful husband who had had an affair wanted to take his wife on a weekend vacation. She had mixed feelings. On the one hand, she wanted to add something positive to their battle-weary marriage, but she wasn't ready to have fun and appear as though everything had improved. If she were to decline the invitation, her husband would be annoyed (and feel less guilty). If she were to accept, she feared giving him the wrong message. The solution was simple. She agreed to go but stated clearly her mixed feelings. She told her husband not to be surprised if she couldn't fully enjoy herself but that she was willing to make the most of it. With expectations clear, they allowed for the expression of a range of feelings on the trip without it ruining their weekend or sending their marriage into a tailspin.

Reestablishment of Love Is Built upon Caring

If partners have trouble finding love in their marriage, I ask them to put aside their concerns about love and focus on caring. Love is built on caring. You can care without loving, but you cannot truly love without caring. If caring seems too much, I suggest they make some efforts to show consideration for one another, to treat their spouse in a manner they'd like to be treated. You don't have to love the person you forgive.

Forgiving Other Generations May Be Necessary

Often, a spouse may have to forgive a parent or a grandparent before he or she can fully forgive his or her partner. As a rule of thumb, the longer a marital problem has existed despite repeated efforts to resolve it, the more likely it reflects unresolved hurts from one's childhood. It is therefore always important for a therapist to ask a husband or wife if similar hurts occurred at the hands of his or her parents or caretakers. Betrayal, abuse, deceit, unreliability, neglect, and criticism are common experiences for many children, who then grow up and reexperience those hurts from their spouse. And even in loving, nondysfunctional families, a child may experience pain associated with low income, the death of a loved one, or the chronic illness/disability of a family member, all of which may predispose that individual to certain hurts later on. For example, many children must "grow up too soon" and take on added responsibilities for the family when one family member is chronically ill. Such a child may grow up to be a responsible adult who nonetheless assumes too many burdens, is a "people pleaser" or a perfectionist, and may feel easily hurt or resentful when he or she perceives others as taking advantage of him or her or being inconsiderate.

It is a therapist's job to help a client realize when his or her anger at a spouse is really made more intense because of unresolved anger toward a parent. That doesn't mean that a client's anger at his or her spouse is illegitimate. It may be very legitimate but overdone. But in some cases it may be completely inappropriate. For example, one wife would often end arguments by stating she would discuss the issues later on, but then she would become furious when her husband complied and went off to do other things while waiting for her to resume the discussion. She wanted him to wait nearby. This caused years of problems for the couple, because the husband resented having to wait and often went about his own business. A simple inquiry into the wife's background and an answer to the question, What does your husband's behavior remind you of? revealed that, when she was a little girl and her parents argued, her father would leave the house and sometimes not return for days. She equated physical absence after an argument with abandonment. In this case, the wife understood that her husband was not wrong or hurtful for his dislike of having to wait for her to resume a difficult discussion and that he did not require forgiveness in this matter. She was able to make positive changes then with little fuss or fanfare, since she realized her anger was toward her father, not her husband.

To recapitulate, a therapist must make the following determinations:

1. Does a marital hurt appear to be similar to hurts experienced by one or both partners as children?
2. Is anger or resentment toward one's spouse legitimate and at an appropriate level? Is it legitimate but overdone? Or, is it, for the most part, inappropriate and unwarranted?

When it seems clear that hurts from one's childhood are interfering with a satisfying marriage, the need to forgive one's parents becomes a topic for discussion in psychotherapy. If the parents are alive and still hurtful to their adult child, it is very necessary that the adult child no longer put up with such hurts. That will require assertiveness and determination. A client who continues to tolerate abuse, criticism, or discourtesy from a parent will struggle in his or her marriage when his or her spouse acts in a hurtful or inconsiderate way. Or such a person may place unreasonable demands upon his or her spouse, wanting the spouse to compensate for childhood hurts and ongoing parental hurts.

It is often the case that asserting oneself to an abusive or insensitive parent will result in defensiveness and/or condemnation by the parent, at least temporarily. An assertive adult must plan for that consequence and rehearse various ways of responding. Attacking the parent in any way, however warranted it may seem, will be counterproductive. Simple phrases are best—phrases that clearly identify what the objectionable behaviors are and that firmly communicate what the consequences will be if the behaviors continue. For example: "Mother, every time you visit you find fault with my children. That hurts and I don't like it. I know they aren't perfect, but if you keep acting that way we will want to see much less of you."

Often, the awareness that anger toward one's parents is being displaced (at least partly) onto one's spouse is enough to jump-start the change process. Some clients may need to confront their parents (in a manner described in the next section) before lasting marital changes will result. If a client is steadfastly unwilling to forgive a parent, the therapist should attempt to understand fully and empathize with that decision. Still, the therapist may wish to point out that such an unforgiving stance may ensure that marital problems will persist and that the client will, in effect, be honoring his or her parents by refusing to unhook himself or herself from the legacy of anger that the parents imposed. Such a reframing may cause some clients to consider forgiveness as a therapeutic goal when they otherwise would not.

The Phases of Forgiveness

In my work with people who have tried to forgive others, I have discerned five phases of the forgiveness process.

Phase I: Identifying the Hurt

In phase 1 the injured party must identify the hurt, or "name the injury," as Flanigan (1992) terms it. This is by no means a straightforward or simple phase. Many injured people minimize or deny what was done to them. They make excuses to explain away the hurtful person's actions. Forgiveness is meaningless if there is nothing to forgive. Researcher and clinician Charles Figley (1989) states that the first question each family member must answer after having experienced some horrific loss or tragedy is, What happened? Because of defense mechanisms, answering that question can be difficult.

In my view, phase 1 of the forgiveness process is underway not only when the victim is able to articulate the specifics of what happened, such as "My father raped me' or "My wife had an affair," but also when the victim is able to examine the nature of his or her hurt. All hurt comes from loss, whether it is real or imagined loss; past, present, or anticipated loss. While it seems a tad simplistic to me to categorize loss in three ways, I believe these categories are accurate and helpful to a clinician or to someone wishing to find forgiveness. Essentially, when we are deeply hurt, our hurt is about one or a combination of three things:

1. loss of love or lovability; such as when a loved one dies or a relationship ends
2. loss of self-esteem
3. loss of control or influence

The person wishing to forgive must ask himself or herself, "What loss have I incurred?" Determining the area(s) of loss points the person in a direction of healing. It informs the person what needs to be repaired. For example, a person shattered by a spouse's infidelity may come to grips with the fact that his self-esteem or feeling of lovability has always been tenuous. Working on ways to improve his self-esteem then may help him in his task to find forgiveness. Probably in all cases of serious injury or betrayal, every victim feels a sense of loss of control over his or her life. The person who did the injuring made decisions that took control away from the victim. Forcing someone to do something against his or her will removes control from that person. Researcher Janoff-Bulman (1992) writes how someone who experiences a traumatic loss, injury, or betrayal discovers that many of the beliefs about life once held dear no longer have meaning. For instance, people who believe that if you work hard and try to be a kind person you will be rewarded are thoroughly disillusioned when something tragically unfair happens to them. In effect, these people are now stripped of a perception they once had of having some degree of control over their lives—control founded on their beliefs about how the world operates. The world doesn't work the way they once believed, perhaps even God is not working the way they once believed, and they feel a corresponding reduction in their perception of control. They now feel more helpless and unsure of themselves.

Often, when a victim feels a loss of control, he or she may withhold forgiveness as a way to regain the perception of control. By holding over the injurer's head the proclamation that he or she is unforgivable, the victim begins to believe he has more and more say over what has happened to him. Unfortunately, regaining control over one's life by withholding forgiveness is likely to undermine control in the long run, because the victim becomes further victimized by his own anger. To refuse to forgive is to choose to latch onto resentment, which can restrict one's freedom to love and trust and feel joy.

A simple but useful way for someone to begin to identify the nature of his or her loss involves a variation of an exercise recommended by Bloomfield (1985). Visualize the person who harmed you as sitting in front of you. Then say the phrase "I forgive you." Chances are, this will immediately be followed by a thought such as "But what you did was unfair" or "You don't deserve forgiveness." Repeat "I forgive you" and again pay close attention to the thoughts and feelings that immediately follow. Probably, these reactions are strong clues about what the nature of your hurt is and what issues you must resolve before you can feel fully forgiving.

When people have experienced a deep loss, they are forever changed. Even if they can forgive, even if they can rebuild the basic assumptions about life, love, and relationships that were shattered as a result of the injury, they are different. They must be in order to have successfully integrated what has happened to them into their scheme of things. Forgiveness offers a direction for healing that makes the "new" person less likely to become hardened and cynical, calloused by the hurts against him.

Phase 2: Confronting

In phase 2, you confront the one who injured you, either by letter (which may not necessarily be mailed, such as when the other person has died) or face to face. People often resist this phase, believing that they can readily forgive without actually confronting. It is possible to forgive without confronting, but for serious offenses it is a mistake to ignore this step. To confront is to confirm that you were deeply hurt and to make clear that the offense cannot be ignored. When a person holds back from confronting, she usually does so out of fear of making matters worse. In effect, she is minimizing what was done against her or is pretending it was not a big deal when it was. She may even be subtly conveying to herself the message that she is not *entitled* to express her anger or that it would be mean to do so. This process distorts the nature of the hurt and increases the odds that she will irrationally feel guilty about her anger, thereby contaminating the forgiveness process.

Researcher Pennebaker (1990) has demonstrated the powerful healing effects that come from writing or speaking about one's loss injury. In his studies, people who only thought about their injury suffered more symptoms than people who spent the same amount of time writing about or discussing their injury.

Phase 3: The Dialogue to Understanding

It is the senseless nature of some crimes against us or the fact that what happened could have been avoided that makes tragedy even more difficult to bear. Suffering is bad enough, but the meanest form of suffering is suffering with no meaning.

In phase 3 of forgiveness, it is important to come to some understanding of *why*. Making sense of our suffering is important in the healing process. And if we can learn why the other person harmed us, it can be easier to forgive.

I do not include the initial confrontation as part of this phase, because in the confronting phase the injured party is entitled to express anger without having to show understanding toward the other or listen to the other with any degree of compassion. And the injured party is entitled to confront over and over before showing a willingness to hear the other person out. But once phase 3 is entered, the concern on the part of the forgiver is to have a dialogue, a back-and-forth exchange of thoughts and feelings so as to understand better what happened and why.

A major trap the injured party sets for himself in this phase is to ask the question Why? and then conclude that no answer provided is good enough. When you think about it, asking an unfaithful spouse how he or she could have perpetuated a lengthy affair, even after the affair was discovered and the family—the spouse and children—were suffering because of it, puts that spouse in a no-win position. If he tries to come up with any answer at all, it will sound self-serving and appear to be an insufficient reason to damage the family. If he says nothing at all or "I don't know," he will appear evasive and insincere. The injured party who asks "Why?" when no answer could be good enough is focusing on the belief that what happened shouldn't have happened instead of focusing on the reality that it did indeed happen.

I usually explain to the injured person that he may never feel he's "gotten to the bottom" of what happened. That is so because every answer to a why question can elicit yet another question. Consequently, the injured party may feel uncertain and untrusting for awhile longer, because the complete answers he'd like to have may never be forthcoming.

Reframing is a useful tool in this phase of forgiveness. When we reframe, we essentially choose to overlook one feature of our appraisal of what happened and instead emphasize another feature. For example, it is hard to forgive people when we appraise them as malicious and selfish. It is a bit easier when we appraise those same people as weak. Do we regard hurtful parents as bad and unloving or as incompetent people who perhaps did what they could, given their own limitations?

In the dialogue to understanding, each side must try to allow emotional reactivity in the other. Too much strong emotion can bog down the dialogue, because anger, fear, or guilt can cause defensiveness or withdrawal and impede communication. But to expect that such emotionality won't occur from time to time is unrealistic. It is better if each party can develop some tolerance for the other's emotionality rather than getting defensive about it, because intolerance tends to fuel the very thing they are intolerant of. When communication starts to get out of hand, each person can stop and ask himself or herself, "What am I trying to do?" and "How am I trying to do it?" (Beavers 1985). If honest, people will see that what they are trying to say is being undermined by the way they are saying it.

I also alert people that during the dialogue, if they yell, feel angry, or want to withdraw, then they do not feel understood and are trying to express their frustration about that. However, by expressing their frustration in that manner, they increase the odds that the listener will not want to understand them once he or she becomes offended by the yelling or the withdrawal.

The dialogue to understanding sometimes reveals to the injured person that he or she too was hurtful and played a role in the relationship problem that led to his or her being deeply hurt by the other family member. Such a discovery does not excuse the behavior of the injurer, however. But it might make the injured party a bit more understanding and lead to a better idea of what changes each party needs to make to heal the relationship.

Forgiveness is made easier if there is agreement between the parties to make a plan of action—some plan that will improve the odds that the deep hurts will not occur again. It is not enough for a philandering spouse to say, "I will be faithful to you from now on." A plan of action takes into account all that was learned about why the harm was committed in the first place. Furthermore, research by John Gottman at the University of Washington reveals that negative actions outweigh positive actions by at least five to one. In other words, a couple or family who is making relationship improvements wipes away the effects of five positive interactions by the occurrence of just one negative interaction. To say it differently, a negative interaction is tolerable only if it can be paid for by at least five positive interactions. Therefore, in making a plan of action, family members must exert much energy doing as many positive things for one another as possible, since it is impossible to eliminate negative interactions completely.

Phase 4: Forgiving

Some people believe that forgiveness must flow naturally from you, that to be genuine, it must be an almost effortless, instinctive next step. But for most of us, forgiveness is found not by taking one final step but by making an awkward leap. If forgiveness is anything, it is a giant leap of faith.

When we forgive a family member, the likelihood is we will still see that person from time to time. Consequently, there is a willingness to trust embedded in the act of forgiveness where a relationship has not come to an end. I often tell people who are trying to regain trust that the process is similar to having lost a great deal of weight where the last ten pounds are the most difficult to lose. In regaining trust, people can become 80 percent and 90 percent trusting, but the final 10 percent is the hardest to achieve. It can be helpful to evaluate trust on a daily basis, such as "Today was he trustworthy? Did I feel trusting today?" instead of asking more global questions, such as "Can I trust him from now on?"

This phase of forgiveness is the shortest despite its importance. It is similar to the act of getting married. Saying "I do" takes no time at all, despite its importance. It is the courtship and life after the wedding ceremony that take the most time.

Phase 5: Letting Go

After you have forgiven the one who has hurt you, what remains is letting go of your pain of resentment. Despite genuine efforts to forgive, some remnants of the old hurts may remain. That doesn't mean you must retrace your steps of the forgiveness journey. For many, the memory of having been hurt will reappear now and again. Simply acknowledge that and remind yourself that the bad feelings may come but they will go soon. Letting go can be as simple as that.

When you can't let go of the pain, when the act of betrayal or brutality still burns in your memory, there is some unfinished business. That business is typically guilt or resentment. They are opposite sides of the same coin. When you feel guilty, you feel you owe somebody something. When you feel resentful, you feel that somebody owes you something.

If you feel guilty, are you irrationally feeling guilty about your anger, or are you truly guilty of something? Perhaps you realize a truth about your part of the relationship—a truth that is not very flattering. If so, you may need to own up to that and admit your mistakes.

If you are resentful still, you need to determine what you are owed by the person who hurt you. This is a serious and important consideration. It might be that you need further statements of apology. Many people who inflict harm but are then forgiven do not like the person they hurt to remind them of what happened. Consequently they come across as aloof or a bit insensitive, as trying to sweep the past under the rug.

It may be that what you are owed is not something the guilty party can repay. What if you lost your faith in God or in the benevolence of others? Your struggle then is to come to terms with those issues, to create a new theory about life and living, a theory that integrates what happened to you in a manner that is nonetheless optimistic and forward-moving. How does one achieve that? Well, one way to begin is to make your suffering have meaning. By that I mean that, even if the act against you was senseless, you can still make it meaningful. In my book *Life's Parachutes: How to Land on Your Feet during Trying Times,* I write that "meaningfulness begins as an idea, a *possibility* that *in spite of your suffering or even because of your suffering you will experience a quality to your life you might not otherwise have known.* It is the possibility that life has more to offer you and the possibility that the God you'd once befriended is beside you still" (Coleman 1993, pp. 116–117; emphasis modified from the original).

This gift of meaning is not like a piece of artwork that you contemplate and enjoy. Instead, it is a gift of lumber, hammer and nails, and a saw. You must build something. Making meaning out of what happened to you is seeing the possibilities that are now open to you as a direct result of your suffering.

- Isn't it possible that despite your injury, the love you are capable of giving can make a difference in the life of someone you haven't even met yet?
- Isn't it possible that with time and support you will have new ideas about how to live your life—ideas that are healing and life-affirming?
- Isn't it possible that God cares about how you are doing?
- Isn't it possible that your suffering is not permanent even if your loss is?
- Isn't it possible that because of your misfortune something very positive and good will happen in the future that never could have happened otherwise?
- Isn't it possible that the meaning of life is to make meaningful all that life has to offer and to live out your life accordingly?

The possibilities are endless.

Finally, as freeing and joyous as it may be to find forgiveness or be forgiven, it is a process that can also hurt a little.

There is the pain you feel when you hold back from retaliation. That pain is your anger at the injustice of it all.

There is the pain you may feel when the person you hurt chooses to forgive you rather than reject you. That pain is your shame and feelings of unworthiness.

There is the pain you feel when, in an effort to learn how the hurts came about, you learn something about yourself that is hard to accept. That pain is anxiety that comes from understanding that you are not above needing forgiveness.

There is pain you may feel when others try to persuade you that to forgive would be a sign of weakness. That pain is your self-doubt or need for approval.

There is pain when you open yourself up to trust once again. That pain could be the fear of looking foolish in others' eyes or in your own. That pain is also necessary if you are to give love.

Forgiveness is more than a moral imperative, more than a theological dictum. It is the only means, given our humanness and imperfections, to overcome hate and condemnation and proceed with the business of growing and loving.

References

Axelrod, R. 1984. *The evolution of cooperation*. New York: Basic Books.

Beavers, W. R. 1985. *Successful marriage*. New York: W. W. Norton.

Bloomfield, H. 1985. *Making peace with your parents*. New York: Ballantine Books.

Casarjian, R. 1992. *Forgiveness: A bold choice for a peaceful heart*. New York: Bantam.

Coleman, P. 1989. *The forgiving marriage*. Chicago: Contemporary Books.

Coleman, P. 1993. *Life's parachutes: How to land on your feet during trying times*. New York: Dell.

Figley, C. 1989. *Helping traumatized families*. San Francisco: Jossey-Bass.

Flanigan, B. 1992. *Forgiving the unforgivable: Overcoming the bitter legacy of intimate wounds*. New York: Macmillan.

Gottman, J. 1994. *Why marriages succeed or fail*. New York: Simon and Schuster.

Heitler, S. 1990. *From conflict to resolution*. New York: W. W. Norton.

Janoff-Bulman, R. 1992. *Shattered assumptions: Toward a new psychology of trauma*. New York: Free Press.

Pennebaker, J. 1990. *Opening up; The healing power of confiding in others*. New York: Morrow.

8

Forgivers and the Unforgivable

Beverly Flanigan

If there is any clear agreement among scholars who study forgiveness, it may be that this nascent examination is fraught with methodological, analytic, and conceptual difficulties. There are so many difficulties, in fact, that it may be that forgiving is not actually possible to study empirically. Still, those who attempt to do so must think the pursuit is worth some degree of professional risk. For, not only is forgiving difficult to study, but also those attempting to research it seem more comfortable than other researchers in making themselves vulnerable to the criticism that they bring to their work the subjective bias that forgiving has positive value. Students of forgiving seem to lack the unbiased objectivity expected of other social scientists—most believe that forgiving is desirable, not that it is neutral in value. For this bias, they can be criticized and, it appears, are willing to be, since they continue their projects.

The body of knowledge about forgiving has ordinarily been generated from three sources: conceptual treatises, qualitative research, and quantitative research. This being the case, I would like to lay out some limitations in each approach, some agreements generated from them, and then present a pair of propositions about forgiving that might be used to advance our understanding of it further. I will begin with limitations of qualitative research, many of which apply to limitations in quantitative studies.

The first limitation is the difficulty of finding or forming representative samples of "forgivers." Qualitative and quantitative researchers alike must cope with this problem. Qualitative researchers generally gather data from samples which are either clinical or purposeful. Clinical samples such as Paul Coleman's (1995) may be substantially different from those involving people who forgive without the assistance of professional helpers. That is, people in clinical samples may be found to have fewer coping skills than those persons who forgive each other without professional intervention. We could speculate that people in clinical samples have limited coping styles which are insufficient in the face of deep personal betrayal (for example, people who rely on problem-focused and not appraisal-focused coping, or emotion-focused and not problem-focused coping, may find their styles to be ineffective when they are required to forgive) (Moos and Billings 1982). Clinical subjects, too, may reflect the forgiving processes of clients from upper socioeconomic strata, who can afford therapy, thus missing entirely the process employed by those in the lower socioeconomic strata. Therapeutic clients may be more prone to the subjective experience of betrayal than nontherapeutic clients. In addition, clinical samples who describe past experiences of forgiving inform researchers through self-report and retrospective data. Self-reported data suffer a myriad of critical issues, not the least of which is frequent recision of reports of behaviors that cause people personal discomfort (Harrell 1985).

Clients in treatment (unlike people who are selected from case records) are being guided through forgiveness by a therapist. Therapists may observe the alteration of these clients' attitudes toward their injurers, but the question of validity becomes germane: Are changes in behavior or attitude toward offenders reflective of a natural process of forgiving, or are they reflective of a process that is subtly reinforced and shaped by the therapist, who defines these changes as "forgiveness"?

The findings about forgiveness generated from clinical samples should not be generalized to other samples; yet, glimmers of information about forgiving are so rare that we must look at them for their contributions to theory building. The same is true for inferences about forgiving drawn from purposeful samples (Flanigan 1992).

A purposeful sample, drawn through newspaper advertisements (or other types of request) soliciting people who believe they have completed the subjective experience of forgiving, is also severely limited in its generalizability to other samples. First, it can safely be presumed that people who answer newspaper advertisements are able to read, write letters of response, and are highly motivated. We might also infer that newspaper readers are of a certain educational level and interested in seeking information, not representative of the general public or a "universe of forgivers." Newspaper readers may also be more of one gender than the other. Data gathering from purposeful samples may also bias and limit generalizability of the results, even if the qualitative researcher attempts to collect data in a way that gives some measure of reliability to the information gathered. Regardless of whether the researcher uses structured, semistructured, or nonstructured interviews, each method limits the type and amount of data collected, and all are reliant upon retrospective data. In some cases, forgivers report quite recent experiences with forgiving; in other cases, they may report less recent information. Thus, these data produce more than the usual caveats germane to self-report. In addition, case-by-case analysis or content analysis may be used to generate theory, but either type is necessarily subjected to the theoretical perspective of the researcher. Whether the researcher comes from a theological, psychological, philosophical, or social science background delimits the theoretical interpretation of the interview content under analysis. What we currently understand about forgiving in this young phase of study reflects the biases of researchers; yet, these biases and differences in interpretation can and should engender robust and exciting exchanges among us.

Sample size also limits the utility of data on forgiving. In qualitative research, there is disagreement about the number of subjects needed to speculate about the meaningfulness of observations made; however, these researchers are hampered, in general, by small sample size. The above criticisms apply to my research on forgiveness just as the limitations of clinical samples apply to others. The size of forgiveness samples is usually quite small, and where not, they are often drawn from college student populations of limited cultural diversity.

The issue of validity is also relevant. If forgiveness is in some sense spiritual, then by definition spiritual matters cannot be measured empirically or quantified analytically. If forgiveness is a purely psychological process, it should reveal differences between sample populations as other psychological research does when applied to people of different ages, gender, ethnicity, attributional styles, and religiosity regarding coping with and adjusting to personal problems or trauma. Scales measuring forgiveness have, in some cases, been developed from items identified by undergraduate students, many of whom might not yet have been confronted with an offense that required forgiveness (Wade 1989, p. 5338).

Much of the theoretical information about forgiveness is drawn from the theology and philosophy of the Judeo-Christian tradition and culture (and the psychology of game and change theory) and informs the "American" concept of forgiving, which has been derived from Judeo-Christian culture, a culture that historically has been socially stratified, homogeneous, and largely lacking in gender equity, that is, patriarchal. Thus, the American lens focusing on forgiveness views it through these cultural atavisms. The question is, then, Do Judeo-Christian patriarchal or class-based accounts of forgiveness pertain to non-Christian, lower or working-class, female or children's subjective experience of forgiving other offenders? We cannot doubt, for example, that people in many cultures forgive each other without the assistance of either Jewish or Christian belief. In fact, the imposition of certain theoretical biases on the process may blind us to a deeper understanding of cross-cultural aspects of forgiveness.

Amy Tan (1991) speaks powerfully about cross-cultural conflicts with forgiving. Her protagonist, a middle-aged Chinese-American woman who had been ceaselessly and horrendously abused by her first husband, Wen Fu, chastises herself for her inability to forgive him because her Christian instruction says that she should.

> So you see, that's the way I am, easy to get mad, hard to forgive. . . . I can never forgive him. I can't excuse him because of that accident. I can't excuse what happened later. Why should I?
> . . . When Jesus was born, he was already the son of God. I was the daughter of someone who ran away, a big disgrace. And when Jesus suffered, everyone worshipped him. Nobody worshipped me. . . . I was like that wife of Kitchen God. Nobody worshipped her either. He got all the excuses. He got all the credit. She was forgotten (p. 322).

In spite of the problems we face, students of forgiveness do have some agreements about it: Forgiving, we believe, is a process; at its end, resentment is no longer harbored toward an offender. I agree with something Paul Coleman has expressed and want to expand upon it here: Injuries that are difficult to forgive disrupt or assault our belief systems. Put in another way, injuries that seem to be "unforgivable" shatter assumptions and for that reason are unique among injuries.

Paul Coleman (1995) focuses only on a clinical sample (couples) that experienced infidelity as unforgivable. My work in *Forgiving the Unforgivable* focuses on the unforgivable injuries described by a purposeful sample of just over seventy people ranging in age from seventeen to seventy, the majority of whom were harmed by a variety of family members, not only spouses. The injuries included infidelity but also spousal abandonment, theft, and the burning down of one's family home; parental incest, physical abuse, abandonment, and neglect; sibling battery; and children's abandonment and abuse of their parents; as well as other offenses. The problems of sample bias discussed earlier are present here. Still, there is cause for excitement in that, in both Coleman's (1995) sample and my own (1992), we both observed that beliefs are shattered as a result of infidelity and other injuries. To forgive, both Coleman and I agree, an injured person must rethink his or her beliefs, or, as Paul Coleman puts it, "create a new theory about life and living" (p. 93 in this volume).

For the remainder of this chapter, I will pursue the idea that certain offenses seem to the offended to be unforgivable precisely because they assault people's fundamental beliefs. Then I conclude with two propositions which will relate the depth of assault on people's assumptions and the various degrees of forgiveness those people are likely to achieve.

Coleman (1995) makes reference to Ronnie Janoff-Bulman's (1992) important work in trauma, in which she suggests that traumas such as rape shatter a person's bedrock "assumptive set, launching that person into a kind of 'cornered horror' for internal and external worlds are suddenly unfamiliar and threatening" (p. 63). The essence of trauma, Janoff-Bulman writes, "is the abrupt disintegration of one's inner world" (p. 63). My interviewees described their unforgivable injuries in the same way. Their worlds as they had perceived them came undone in the wake of infidelity, abandonment, abuse, lies, and/or other harms. Their unforgivable injuries can be viewed as a kind of "intrafamily trauma." Like traumas perpetrated by strangers or nature, intrafamily traumas assault people's fundamental beliefs, and as a result, their internal worlds come undone.

Janoff-Bulman (1992) describes the three fundamental assumptions of the bedrock assumptive set as these: "The world is benevolent/The world is meaningful/The self is worthy" (p. 6). In other words, when people experience traumas, their assumptions about themselves and their world are shattered. They question their self-worth, the meaning of life, and their presumptions of goodness. In my book, I described the kinds of beliefs and assumptions that "unforgivable" injuries shatter (Flanigan 1992, pp. 15–68). Some unforgivable injuries shatter certain of these assumptions; some shatter others. People's beliefs in personal control and rules of justice are shattered along with their self-worth and belief in the goodness of others, and depending upon the nature of the event that precipitates the unforgivable injury, the specific assumptions shattered in the injury vary from person to person in terms of which assumption is most affected, as do the range and degree of damage done to the assumptive set of the wounded person. One interviewee described very succinctly the damage that infidelity did to her belief system:

> What did I have to believe in anymore if I couldn't believe in a man I had come to know so well? So there was a loss in me of myself. Where had I been all these years? . . . I felt responsible because I wasn't aware of what was going on. . . . I lost faith in other people because their support was, "He was a lousy person, you're lucky." I lost faith in the professionals—the world of professional people who were supposed to be there when you needed them. My attorney was a schlock; my first psychologist didn't work. Now I'm a failure: now I can't even find support. So it was tough times. Everything was going. . . . And it wasn't because he walked out of my life; it was, maybe that was the cause, but the effects were the things I was dealing with. He was not the only thing in my life, but it did bring the rest of my world tumbling down.

In my sample, interviewees' perceptions of self-in-control and others-as-benevolent were shattered as often as assumptions about life's meaning were. Assaults on assumptions take us to the heart of forgiveness. For a person to forgive someone who harmed him requires that the injured person undertake the formidable task of relinquishing resentment toward that other person who, by his or her behavior, shattered the injured's bedrock assumptions about life. Forgiveness is not given to events, but to people who have altered a person's perceptions of his internal or external world and of how this world will be in the future. The primary bedrock assumption for those who perceive themselves to be unforgivably harmed may be that the world is a good place or that the self is valued and lovable. It may be the assumption that God will protect against harm or that one can control personal damage. It may be that a person believes there is some, albeit inscrutable, principle of justice that protects us from harm, but that it failed when harm was perpetrated on him or her. Assumptions and beliefs that fail in unforgivable injuries can vary from person to person. In one case a person's entire assumptive set can shatter, rendering an entire belief system failed; in another, a wounded person's assumptions about himself may be more damaged than assumptions about God or benevolence or justice.

The degree and scope of damage done to an injured person's belief system is related to the degree and scope of forgiveness a person is able to muster toward his offender. I will discuss the relationship between the damage to the assumptive set and the degree of forgiveness later in the chapter. First, however, I turn to observations on degrees of forgiveness from my work and from the work of Michelle Killough Nelson (1992). It became clear over the course of my interviews that people's perceptions of the subjective experience of forgiving differed from person to person. Thus, in *Forgiving the Unforgivable,* I describe people's accounts of forgiveness, not whether I considered their forgiveness to be complete or incomplete. It was the intent of my study to ascertain interviewees' subjective experiences of forgiveness, that is, to gather data recording their personal accounts of forgiveness and their subsequent definitions of forgiveness. I found that interviewees considered forgiveness complete when they had achieved one of these four end-states or some combination of them: (1) when they no longer harbored resentment or hatred toward the offenders; (2) when they felt neutral toward their offenders; (3) when they once again experienced some degree of trust in their offenders; (4) when they had reconciled with their offenders. The differences in their perceptions of when forgiveness was complete are reflected in their direct quotes; some of which are contained in my book (Flanigan 1992); "I wouldn't want my husband back on a silver platter, but I've forgiven him." "It's the ability to be free and live one's own life." "Forgiveness is having compassion, but I don't want to retrace my steps." "Forgiving means to write the person off. . . . It is not healing or reconciliation; it's just forgetting it and not giving it the opportunity to happen again." "Forgiving is being able to be at peace with yourself. I don't want to restore the relationship; I didn't even like it before all this happened."

In my work, I have not classified the various degrees of forgiving into a scheme or typology; however, Michelle Nelson has. She has introduced into the literature three types of forgiveness: detached forgiveness, limited forgiveness, and complete forgiveness. Detached forgiveness is "a reduction in negative affect toward the offender, but no restoration of the relationship" (Nelson 1992, p. 4381). Limited forgiveness is a "reduction in negative affect toward the offender and partial restoration of and decreased emotional investment in the relationship" (p. 4381). Full forgiveness includes "total cessation of negative affect towards the offender and full restoration and growth of the relationship" (p. 4381). Nelson analyzed postforgiveness levels of trust, satisfaction, commitment, loving, and liking, and found: "Results of the discriminant analysis . . . could be used to predict what type of forgiveness a subject had granted with a high degree of certainty" (p. 4381). Her findings suggest that the type of offense and degree of relationship prior to the offense are also predictors of the type of forgiveness a person is given. However, just as other research on forgiving suffers methodological problems, so does Nelson's. Her sample was composed of undergraduate students, many of whom might, by definition, have had limited life experience, and the majority of whom were single and who had had relationships of short duration with their offenders. Nevertheless, the types of forgiveness Nelson described are also reflected in the subjective accounts of forgiving described by individuals in my sample, who ranged widely in age and whose relationships, life experience, socioeconomic levels, level of education, and religiosity varied substantially.

My group, like Nelson's, described degrees of forgiveness, yet defined forgiving as subjectively complete and satisfactory. My interviewees were at peace, forward-looking, and continuing life without resentment or the expectation of compensation. Some had reaffirmed love for their offenders. They had reached complete forgiveness through the completion of tasks in various phases of the forgiving process (Flanigan 1992).

At the end of the process, though, the sample did not share a common operational definition of forgiving. What they did share was the experience of having cognitively restructured their bedrock assumptions so that their belief systems were intact and their assumptions about harm—to whom it can happen and at the hands of whom—were consonant with other bedrock assumptions. I was struck that almost every individual I interviewed said that nothing could be unforgivable again. Expectancy of the likelihood of being harmed had become a bedrock assumption, consonant with other assumptions about benevolence, personal worth, justice, and control. In other words, the constant of forgiving was not located in specific changes in affect or behavior. The constant of forgiveness was that forgivers underwent successful "paradigm shifts" that included injury as a part of the forgivers' bedrock assumptive sets. Family members who forgave each other did not assume they would never be hurt by the offender again. To the contrary, they assumed that injury might well happen again but that it would never again be unforgivable. Because they now expected the likelihood of being harmed, if harm were to happen, it would not shatter assumptions about the world's benevolence, life's meaning, or justice.

People who accomplish forgiveness of an offender may vary in the degree of positive affect toward their offender and the degree of emotional investment in their relationship with the offender. They also may vary in their continued commitment to the relationship. My work suggests, however, that they share the similarity of having created new assumptive sets in which the world again appears to be orderly and the self of inherent worth. In addition, control over harm and rules that govern harm are also revised to be included in the new assumptive set and to be consonant with its other assumptions. The subjective reports of forgivers reveal that forgiveness is extended in degrees. So, too, does at least one qualitative study.

I here propose a relationship between the degree of damage done to an offended person's assumptive set and that person's accomplishment of a certain degree of forgiveness:

Proposition One: The less damage done to an offended person's assumptive set, the more likely the offended person will accomplish full forgiveness.
Proposition Two: Given that there are three to five basic assumptions in a person's assumptive set, the more assumptions violated, the more likely a person cannot forgive or can attain only detached forgiveness.

It is conceivable that these propositions could lend themselves to empirical testing; however, let me suggest two vignettes that might make the propositions clearer.

Mary's husband, Sam, of twenty years, had a two-year affair with Mary's best friend, Susan. Mary drew much of her self-worth from her assumption that Sam would always be faithful. She believed that her marriage gave life meaning, since she had unwillingly remained childless. Mary also thought that her marriage was all that was good. While the world around her fell apart, Mary believed in good because of her relationship with Sam. Mary believed that God protected from harm those who kept their marriage vows and renewed their faith through prayer and church attendance. She also believed that she had some control over what Sam did, because she treated him well.

Teresa's husband, Max, had an affair with her best friend, Bertha. Teresa had always thought of herself as less pretty than Bertha. Her self-worth fluctuated depending upon her perceptions of personal attractiveness,. Teresa did not believe particularly that the world was just or good. She saw badness everywhere. Teresa struggled with the meaning of her life and had no particular religious faith. She did believe, however, that she controlled her own life and was responsible for what she made of it.

When Sam's affair with Susan was revealed, Mary's self-worth was shattered; and the meaning of life, so tied to her marriage, was also shattered as a result of the betrayal. The presumed goodness of people was shaken but not shattered. Both her faith in God as protector and her assumptions that she could control the pain in her life were shattered.

By contrast, when Max left Teresa for Bertha, her self-worth was assaulted but not shattered. Her belief in life's meaning was shaken but not shattered. Her presumption of benevolence was not assaulted, because she did not perceive the world to be necessarily good. Since Teresa had no particular faith or presumption that unjust things could not happen to her, she did not suffer assaults on those assumptions.

Sam shattered more of Mary's assumptive set than what Max shattered of Teresa's. Thus, when Sam asked Mary's forgiveness, she could not give it as freely as Teresa gave it to Max. In time, Teresa fully forgave. Mary, on the other hand, finally was able to give Sam only detached forgiveness. She no longer resented him or expected compensation, but she had no positive feelings toward him either. Both women, when asked, said they had forgiven their ex-husbands. Their subjective accounts reveal to an observer that one of them had reached one degree of forgiveness; the other, a different degree, even though they both, in their minds, at least, had "forgiven." I suggest that the relationship between the degree of injury to these offended people and the degree of forgiveness they were able to extend to their offenders represents the relationship between the extent of damage done to assumptive sets and degrees of forgiveness given.

Clinical Implications

I work with clients who have suffered "intrafamilial traumas." They come specifically to me to discuss forgiving and usually to attempt to forgive their offenders. If forgiving is a client's goal, then the issue of whether or not a clinician believes in degrees of forgiveness becomes critical to practice. Some therapists may believe that forgiving is accomplished only if a client harbors no resentment, carries no negative affect toward, or seeks no compensation from her offender; some think, in addition, that a client who truly forgives experiences positive affect or even compassion toward her offender. If a professional believes in only one degree of forgiving, he or she may subtly insist that a client's reported subjective accomplishment of forgiveness is not enough. The client's goals may become subordinate to the views of a therapist.

A clinician who holds that there are degrees of forgiveness, on the other hand, might guide the client to the point that forgiveness feels final, even if it seems incomplete. The clinician's mistake in this case might be if she fails to pursue the client's as yet unrevealed resentments. If my propositions are at all accurate, a clinician could forecast the type of forgiveness a client might likely achieve. Therefore, if a clinician is working with a client whose entire belief system has shattered as a result of his or her offender's behavior, she might work with that client to attempt to hold no grudges, seek no compensation, and put away resentment. If, on the other hand, a clinician finds few assumptions shattered in the wake of the unforgivable event, then the clinician might try to help the client reconcile the broken relationship and find compassion and renewed love for the offender.

Summary

We are only beginning to understand the process of forgiving. As we proceed, we need to broaden our examination to include questions of whether there are cultural variations in the process, whether men and women forgive differently, and whether socioeconomic status influences the nature of the process, its speed, and/or people's subjective definitions of forgiving. People who suffer intrafamily traumas undergo some of the most painful betrayals that can be experienced. If forgiveness does vary from culture to culture or gender to gender, and if people's subjective experience of forgiving is related to these and other sociocultural variables, then the continued examination of these variables could shed light on the methods that mental health and other helping practitioners might one day employ to expedite forgiving.

If forgiving is truly a tool of peacemaking, as many of us believe it is, then it seems imperative that we understand its various forms, degrees, and subtleties. When these are understood, we might be able to make forgiveness more accessible to more injured people. The knowledge that forgiveness can be achieved by harmed people seems to be the goal of researchers and practitioners alike, regardless of our disciplinary and cultural blinders. As we continue to remove the blinders of our own disciplines and methods of study, I believe there lies ahead of us tremendous potential for contributing to the possibility of peace—in families and in society. Regardless, then, of the limitations inherent in our methods of study, that possibility renders the pursuit well worth our efforts.

References

Coleman, P. 1995. The process of forgiveness within the family. Paper presented at the National Conference on Forgiveness, University of Wisconsin–Madison Extension, Madison, Wis., April.

Flanigan, B. 1992. *Forgiving the unforgivable: Overcoming the bitter legacy of intimate wounds.* New York: Macmillan.

Harrell, A. F. 1985. Validation of self-report: The research record. In *Self-report methods of estimation of drug use: Meeting current challenges,* ed. B. A. Rouse, N. J. Kozel, and L. G. Richards, NIDA Research Monograph No. 57, DHHS Publication No. ADM 85–1402. Washington, D.C.: U. S. Government Printing Office.

Janoff-Bulman, R. 1992. *Shattered assumptions.* New York: Free Press.

Moos, R. H., and A. G. Billings. 1982. Conceptualizing and measuring coping resources and processes. In *Handbook of stress,* ed. L. Goldberger and S. Breznitz, New York: Free Press.

Nelson, M. K. 1992. A new theory of forgiveness: Detached Forgiveness, Limited Forgiveness, Full Forgiveness. Doctoral dissertation, Purdue University, West Lafayette, Ind. *Dissertation Abstracts International—B,* 53(08), 1992, p. 4381.

Tan, A. 1991. *The kitchen god's wife.* New York: Ivy Books.

Wade, S. H. 1989. The development of a scale to measure forgiveness. Doctoral dissertation, Fuller Theological Seminary, School of Psychology. *Dissertation Abstracts International—B,* 50(11). 1990, p. 5338.

9

Forgiveness and Crime: The Possibilities of Restorative Justice

Walter J. Dickey

I am not a student of forgiveness or of the philosophy of moral development. I have spent my entire professional life working on criminal justice,
with an emphasis on corrections. My immediate interest in forgiveness and
the related, though distinct, qualities of empathy, compassion, mercy, and
restoration stems from my concern about their absence in criminal justice
policy and practice. Indeed, the original title of this chapter was "The
Absence of Forgiveness in Criminal Justice." I have chosen instead the
more optimistic emphasis upon its possibility, despite the fact that many of
the developments I will outline are hardly positive. I hope that the optimism
is not misplaced naiveté, but I believe that our society and our approach
to criminal justice are in a period of transition, which affords us important
opportunities. Hence the guarded optimism.

I believe that the criminal justice system reflects the larger society. To
understand the forces that shape most public institutions, including the
criminal justice system in this time of transition, and to explore where that
system may go, one must understand the economic, social, cultural, and
other forces which shape the society.

In a nutshell, the emphasis on punishment and vengeance, the limits
on individualized decision making, the abandonment of the rehabilitative
ideal, all recent developments in criminal justice, bespeak deep confusion
about the purposes of the system and the appropriate means to advance
them. Similar confusion is also evident in the disconnectedness of modern
life, manifested in many ways, including economic uncertainty, the lack of
national purpose, the absence of civil, searching dialogue on important issues, and the dominance of emotion in politics and policy making. Perhaps
our ongoing transition from authority-based institutions to participatory
ones is a response to these developments. Surely there are efforts by people
to be heard, in government, schools, and the workplace. Participation
creates the prospect for cohesiveness and community as well as personal
responsibility, which are all necessary if forgiveness and restorative justice

are to be introduced into the criminal justice system to any substantial degree.

By focusing on transitions and the possibilities they afford, I do not pretend to predict where our society and its criminal justice institutions will go. There is the possibility of more satisfying personal and community life, more connectedness in American life, which would allow forgiveness and related values to be introduced into, if not to flourish in, criminal justice. On the other hand, darker qualities may dominate; recent developments may merely portend further confusion about values not only in criminal justice but also more generally in American life.

In these comments, I want to outline more fully the recent changes in the criminal justice system and draw some parallels between them and deeper currents in our society. After this I will suggest what I think it will take for forgiveness, but particularly restoration, to play a more prominent role in criminal justice. Before this, however, I will provide some background about restorative justice and forgiveness and two examples of restorative justice in action.

Restoration and Forgiveness

Restorative justice defines justice as the restoration to wholeness of those whose lives and relationships have been broken or deeply strained by a criminal offense. This understanding of justice focuses on the harm the offense has caused to the victim, to the victim-offender relationship, and to the relationships of both the victim and the offender to the community. It asks: How can the harm be remedied? How can the victim's material loss be restored? How can the emotional trauma be healed? How can the relationship between the victim and offender, broken by the offense, be repaired?

Restorative justice is a model still in formation. It rests on the notions that (1) community, interpersonal wholeness, and social and individual healing must be fostered by any system that purports to administer justice; and (2) apology, forgiveness, and restitution are important components of any restoration or healing that occurs.

Enright (1995) provides a helpful definition of forgiveness as the "willingness to abandon one's right to resentment, negative judgment, and indifferent behavior toward one who unjustly injures us, while fostering the undeserved qualities of compassion, generosity and even love . . ." (p. 1).

Forgiveness, then, plays a role in restorative justice. As Joanna North (1987) has written, "What is annulled in the art of forgiveness is not the crime itself but the distorting effect that the wrong has upon one's relations with the wrongdoer and perhaps with others" (p. 499).

To the extent that forgiveness seeks repair of these relations, it is part of the process of restorative justice. Restorative justice, however, seeks to go beyond forgiveness. It includes an apology and acknowledgment of responsibility by the offender. It is not merely one person's response, the victim's; it is also relational and seeks reconciliation.

Restorative justice has much in common with forgiveness. It is not forgetting; it is not condoning or pardoning; it is not indifference or a diminishing of anger; it is not inconsistent with punishment; it does not wipe out the wrong or deny it. Indeed, it relies on recognition of the wrong so that repair can occur. It also relies on the taking of responsibility for the wrong in a personal and social way.

Perhaps restorative justice and its relation to forgiveness can best be understood in the two real-life examples that follow. Both involve cases in which the offender received a sentence to prison, the second a quite substantial one.

The first case is one in which the offender burglarized a church. The meeting between victim and offender occurred during a furlough from prison, given for purposes of the meeting. The reports are those of the mediator who brought the victims and offenders together.

Case One

A victim offender reconciliation meeting was held between Johnny Singleton and Rev. Harry Davis on January 9, 1993. The meeting was held in Rev. Davis' home in Milwaukee, Wisconsin, and lasted approximately one hour.

The reconciliation meeting began with a review of the purposes of the Victim Offender Rehabilitation Project (VORP) and a summary of the agenda for the meeting. Mr. Singleton then began with an explanation to Rev. Davis of how and why he had committed the burglary. Mr. Singleton explained his involvement with drugs prior to the incident. He stated that he hadn't realized the building was a church at the time he burglarized it. He also stated that the morning after the burglary he had felt great remorse for the offense. He explained to Rev. Davis that his own father was the assistant pastor of a church and that, after speaking with his father on the day after the burglary, he had decided to turn himself in. Mr. Singleton also expressed to Rev. Davis his apologies for the offense.

Rev. Davis responded to Mr. Singleton by saying that he could understand why Mr. Singleton had not realized he was burglarizing a church, because the building was formerly a firehouse and was just beginning to be converted to a church building. Rev. Davis then described the consequences of the offense to himself and the members of the congregation. Rev. Davis mentioned the recent shooting that had occurred in a Milwaukee church, leaving one church member dead, and stated that many church members were beginning to feel very fearful while in church. Rev. Davis also stated that, although property damage had occurred and items had been stolen, the damage amounted to only a hundred dollars and was covered by insurance, and the stolen items had been returned.

Mr. Singleton responded to this, stating that he wanted to do what he could to relieve the fears of the congregation and to demonstrate his remorse. He said he would be willing to speak to the whole congregation and apologize if that would help. He also stated that he would be willing to work for the church, mowing lawns and cleaning up, if that would be helpful.

Rev. Davis said that he thought Mr. Singleton was sincere in his remorse and that he would forgive him and that he would not hold the offense against him. He stated that he didn't believe it would be necessary for Mr. Singleton to work for the church, since he had now forgiven him for the offense. He further stated, however, that he would like to see Mr. Singleton attend church services for a period of time.

Mr. Singleton stated that he would be glad to attend church services. Mr. Singleton then again stated that he would like to make amends to the church in a tangible way and that he would like to work around the church if such work was available.

Rev. Davis stated that a work group composed of church members convened on most Saturdays to help with the remodeling program. He stated that Mr. Singleton would be welcome to help out if he desired. The parties agreed upon a hundred hours of community service work to be performed by Mr. Singleton at the church during the first year of his parole supervision. Ms. Spors-Murphy stated that she would be willing to monitor this agreement as a condition of Mr. Singleton's parole supervision.

As the reconciliation meeting drew to a close, Mr. Singleton again expressed his remorse to Rev. Davis, and Rev. Davis again stated that he believed Mr. Singleton was sincere and that as far as he was concerned the matter was settled. Rev. Davis stated that he had not known what length of sentence Mr. Singleton had received and that he hoped things would go well for him in the future. He stated that sometimes good results from being placed in a hard situation. Mr. Singleton acknowledged that he had found that to be true.

This was a very successful victim-offender meeting for several reasons. First, a helpful exchange of information occurred relating to both the facts of the offense and the consequences of the offense for the victim. Second, a fairly high degree of reconciliation occurred in this case as a result of Mr. Singleton's sincere expressions of remorse and Rev. Davis' willingness to extend forgiveness. Finally, the meeting resulted in a tangible contract for a hundred hours of community service work, which will be of direct benefit to the victim. The meeting was also successful because of the supportive role of Mr. Singleton's probation agent, who arranged for an evaluation of Mr. Singleton at DePaul Hospital and for his placement at Bridge Halfway House following the drug abuse treatment program.

Case Two

The victim in this case ("TC") is a twenty-seven-year-old white female. At the time of the offense (March 18, 1991) she was married and had one adopted daughter, then age seven. She and her family lived in their home in the country in northwest Wisconsin. The offender ("WR") is a twenty-eight-year-old single, white male who had prior arrests for burglary.

In short, WR raped TC at gunpoint and threatened her with a knife in her country home after gaining access to her home by a request to use the telephone. Facts important to his report and not stated in the complaint include TC's belief that she was going to die that day. While raping her, WR inserted the gun into TC's mouth and told her to count the bullets because he was going to use them on her. He also continually ran the length of the hunting knife over her throat and body.

TC began their meeting by asking WR some general questions about his life at the prison, what he did and how he spent his time. This was done as a way to break the ice and avoid diving directly into the heavy issues which lay ahead of us. TC then explained the consequences of the rape. Her losses include first and foremost her family. Her husband blamed her for opening the door for WR and for not struggling sufficiently. He considered her to be "damaged goods" and had no interest in her sexually from that point on. He very quickly turned into a workaholic to stay away from TC, which eventually led to their eating at different times, and so on. This led to their divorce, through which TC's husband won custody of their adopted child.

The loss of her daughter was bad enough, but even more painful was the fact that the little girl had been in seven different foster homes and had just begun to believe that TC and TC's husband would really be her mother and father forever. Thus, the separation of the family not only devastated TC but also shattered the world their adopted daughter had just begun to have faith in. Their daughter eventually sought therapy because of her extreme difficulty in dealing with the divorce and the rape itself (she blamed herself and believed if she had been home it wouldn't have happened). As a side note, for the rest of that school year, every day when TC's daughter left home for school she would yell back to her mom that she'd be home after school and *not* to open the door for any strangers.

During TC's recovery she was admitted to mental hospitals on three occasions. The last was in an effort to counteract what the doctors believed to be a suicide attempt by TC: she refused to eat any food for about six weeks. TC explained this was a response to being forced to perform oral sex on WR and afterward being unable to put food into her mouth. As a result of these repeated mental concerns, TC was heavily drugged and now complains of having lost a certain portion of her memory because of this drug use. She also complains of suffering significant withdrawal pains because her medication was suddenly cut off.

TC concluded this portion of her remarks by stating that, while it is WR who is incarcerated formally, she suffers an even greater loss of freedom than he does through all the humiliation and shame imposed upon her in this process. She feels as though she has been victimized not only by WR but also by the criminal justice system, the hospitals and doctors, and her family and friends.

TC then began asking WR some questions. First, why did he choose to rape her if he hadn't raped before and only came to burglarize the house? WR responded that he truly didn't know. He hadn't planned it when he approached the house but once inside had decided to do it. TC asked if he had actually made a phone call. WR stated, no, he had just debated whether to rape her or not. TC expressed her immediate anger at WR for *not* killing her because of how terrible her life has become since the rape. She stated that no amount of restitution would be able to compensate her for what she has gone through and for how she must now live her life as the "rape victim."

TC then explained how she has even lost the ability to enjoy nature. She used to love long walks in the country and camping and being alone. Now she fears being alone and can't enjoy nature or that type of solitude. This has contributed to the feelings she has of herself being the one who is really imprisoned.

WR responded to this series of questions, indicating that he knew that anything he said would sound "lame" but that he felt he could relate to her losses on a certain level because some are similar to what he has gone through, although in no way can he comprehend what she must have gone through. He shared how he loves nature and now cannot enjoy that, but admitted it is for a much different reason. Now he has worked hard at reordering his priorities simply to aim at healing himself so this will never happen again (it was clear during this time of the meeting that, although WR was attempting to provide an appropriate response, he felt totally inadequate to do so).

The conversation then turned to a discussion of the judicial process, with TC asking several questions about why WR had pleaded guilty to the last set of charges, what he had admitted to, and similar questions. Many of his answers were revealing and helpful to TC, who felt very shorted by the system. WR's answers appeared to put some things in a different perspective, making it easier for her to understand and live with the way she had been treated by the system.

One aspect of this conversation was WR's revelation that he had decided not to go to trial after a hearing at which TC read a poem about how the rape had hurt her. It was only then that WR (partly) realized what he had done and began to connect with women in his own family who had been raped. He decided to take the plea, because his attorney told him what they would need to try to do to TC on the stand during trial, and the attorney didn't feel TC could stand up to that type of beating. WR said he didn't want to do that to her and felt he could not have lived with himself if he had allowed his attorney to try to do that type of thing to TC.

The conversation then turned to WR, who began to reveal much about his past and why he had taken the life of crime he had. He stated he is glad he was arrested so that he can get help and so he won't hurt anyone else, and that he wishes there were a way to take it all back but knows there is no way he can. He related that about four to six months before the offense he had found his fiancée (of two years) in bed with his then best friend. This was a very traumatizing experience for him and one he thought he had put behind him by the date of the offense (at least he stated that it was not consciously on his mind at the time of the offense). He told of being beaten by his father, who used the "strap" on him repeatedly for his own transgressions as well as for the errors of his younger siblings, for whom WR was responsible.

His relationship with his father worsened as he grew older. His father was a Green Beret and had wanted WR to join the Marines also. However, WR lost the hearing in one of his ears at the age of nine and thus could not pass the military physical. This resulted in his father calling him "wimp" and other similar demeaning names. His father had also hated his fiancée, always telling WR how bad she was for him and how she would really hurt him someday.

WR then moved on to discuss his future plans, and we spent a lot of time talking about his expected release date, where he would live, notice to TC, and his future work. TC was engaged in this, clearly appearing to be interested in protecting herself and being assured that she would know of any parole decisions and WR's location if released. WR explained that he would like to work somewhere that would allow him to do something for society and make small efforts at repaying people for all he has done.

(As one aspect of VORPs, I am committed to approaching the issue of forgiveness where appropriate. When preparing the participants for these meetings, we rarely speak of the offender saying "I'm sorry" or of the victim's forgiveness. However, in most cases it is an issue that just seems to come up, with the parties eventually bringing it up themselves to some level of resolution. Thus, we find it to be a natural component of these meetings. More important, most often it is crucial to the healing and reconciliation process. If nothing else is accomplished by these meetings than an offender saying he is sorry for the offense and asking forgiveness from the victim, we have started to create a real opportunity for true healing and justice. The words themselves are important, as is the control and power that are shifted back to the victim. Whether the victim actually forgives or not [of course, if he or she genuinely can it is all the better] is not as important as having the right simply to make the decision.)

After a break, we reconvened and WR began by reaffirming the issues regarding his ultimate release and attempting to assure TC that she need not fear him in the future (TC countered that, while that sounded great, it is a bit hard for her to believe all that, coming from a guy who had stuck a gun in her mouth and told her to count the shells). WR then turned to the forgiveness issue, explaining that he has sought God's forgiveness and is not sure that he will ever get it. Also, he has worked at forgiving himself but still has been unable to do so. But he hopes that at some time in the future she may be able to bring herself to forgive him. WR went on to say that he is truly sorry for what he did, and that if there were any way to take it back or remove her pain he would do it.

TC responded that, no, she didn't feel she could forgive him at that time, but that she is working on it and hopes she can some time in the future. TC explained that she had been a fairly devoted Christian (which was why she had opened the door) but, since the rape, has struggled with how there can be a God that allows this to happen. As a result she has fallen away from Christianity but has turned to her Native American roots (she is a quarter

Native American) and to spirituality to heal herself. However, forgiveness is a part of that too, and she will continue to work on it.

TC shared that after the rape she had written a poem entitled "Silent Scream" (WR also shared that he has written a great deal of poetry). She wanted to bring it with her to the meeting but in the end could not because it was simply too painful to do so. It is based on the guilt and shame she has felt for never screaming out during the rape. At the time, she felt she did everything she could to defend herself but, afterward, was condemned by her family and husband for not doing more. It is the guilt and blame she associates with not screaming that have haunted her for so long. However, she now thanks WR for not killing her, because she has grown to understand how much she has to live for. She knows that she survived so she can counsel other rape victims. Otherwise, she might as well be dead.

We ended the meeting and rose to leave. As WR was exiting he turned to TC and thanked her for sharing all of this with him because, although he had heard some of these things from his doctors at the prison, it was never real to him before. But now, watching her tell her story, he can feel what he has done to her and the pain she has suffered and, through that, her pain and suffering has become real for him in a way that he believes he can use to help heal himself.

TC expressed repeatedly how helpful the meeting was to her and how grateful she is that it occurred. Two follow-up contacts with her reveal that she believes she is now much more understanding of what happened to her and why and much more able to carry on with her life.

Developments in Criminal Justice

The major developments in criminal justice during the past two decades are several. While restorative justice has come to greater prominence and use in the past five years, most recent developments are of quite a different character. The rehabilitative ideal and the indeterminate sentence have largely been abandoned, and the objectives of the system are now limited to punishment and vengeance. While attempts to advance the rehabilitative ideal were never substantial enough to test it, it did serve to introduce broader objectives into the system and ameliorate the historical emphasis given punishment and vengeance. Recently, sentencing systems have been changed to limit the discretion of sentencing authorities, especially judges and parole boards. We now rely heavily on depersonalized sentencing matrices and grids, which greatly limit the individualization of decisions. Limits on discretion, while imposed in the name of fairness and equality, really reflect distrust of individual decision making and appear more unjust, particularly to minority group members, than any sentencing systems we have ever had. One consequence of these changes is that they move responsibility for sentencing out of the hands of those closest to offenders, judges and parole boards, to the distant and more political state legislatures. As a result, politics, rather than individual behavior, plays a more dominant role in sentencing. The unintended consequences of these policies for the roles of actors in the system, for the nature and quality of important decisions, and for offenders, taxpayers, and victims have been profound.

A related development is the renewed emphasis on the use of the formal system at a time when we should be using the system less. The volume of cases in the criminal justice system has always created great pressure to "process" them rather than deal with them thoughtfully. Today, the volume in the system far outstrips its ability to deal with cases with any degree of care. There are many consequences of this, but one of great significance is that cases are dealt with in perfunctory ways, without any engagement between those making the decisions and those affected by them, especially victims and defendants.

Driving these changes is the politicization of crime, most vividly apparent in the Willie Horton issue during the 1988 presidential election. Sadly, the crime issue has been polarized, like so many other issues, into a set of false choices—whether we should be tough or soft, when the real question is far more complex. As recent experience in policing suggests, when we redefine our goals in terms of personal and community safety and improved quality of life, we redefine and refocus the role of the criminal justice agencies. A more realistic discussion of what criminal justice agencies—government—can and cannot achieve would surely lead us to different methods of sentencing and correction and a more selective, almost surgical use of incapacitation.

Among those who have spoken up about the impersonal nature of the criminal justice system are victims, whose needs and views have largely been ignored until recently. Unfortunately, the victims' movement has tended to focus on more severe punishment for offenders, simplistically equating this with the welfare of victims. Recent developments in the victims' movement which emphasize safety, prevention, restoration, and the avoidance of future crime are quite encouraging and seem to address more fully our individual and social needs.

There is little doubt, however, that we are exacting more punishment for more offenders than ever before, largely as a result of these developments. We rely upon prisons to achieve this, so the proportion of our populace in prison is greater than ever before in our history. Among the most chilling related developments is the manipulation of information and statistics to justify the reliance on imprisonment. The National Rifle Association has emerged as a major proponent of the death penalty and imprisonment, justifying these measures with the view that they are cost-efficient methods of crime control. These 1990s versions of the "Big Lie" fly in the face of every responsible study of the issues, yet are advanced in support of ideological views.

One irony of these developments is that we have moved responsibility for social problems to the criminal justice system. If greater use of imprisonment reduces crime, as the NRA asserts, we are absolved of addressing the underlying social and economic problems that stifle human development and lead to crime. If punishment is an effective social tool, we can abandon direct efforts to attack poverty and the problems associated with it, such as the lack of education, housing, health care, and opportunity for the poor. It is not accidental that increased emphasis on criminal justice responses allows for less attention to and compassion for the many problems associated with poverty.

Another irony is that some agencies of the criminal justice system now direct their efforts toward social intervention of a kind usually reserved for social welfare agencies. Some police departments have redefined their objectives, often under the mantle of community policing, to try to deal more directly with issues such as community development. While police have been criticized for modifying their enforcement policies in favor of social interventions, even critics acknowledge that this is done, in part, because these interventions have been abandoned by others and left to the police.

One can rationalize these developments in criminal justice policy on any number of grounds. But these developments really bespeak deep confusion about values (though this is often disguised) and the appropriate means to advance them. This confusion is very apparent when we understand the human and economic consequences and the ineffectiveness of these changes. We are in a period in which simplistic explanations for human behavior abound and in which extreme measures to deal with it dominate; in short, it is a time when policy is grossly out of balance with what we know about the limits of the criminal justice system and the complexity of human needs and behavior. Still another irony about all of this is that the problem of crime control is the one area in which we are not hearing the familiar refrain that less government and more individual and community responsibility are needed, yet it is an area in which this seems so obviously true. There is a sharp "dissonance" between real problems and the phony solutions which are offered.

Developments in Society

The confusion of criminal justice policy bespeaks a deeper confusion in society, which also appears to be in a state of transition. Now more than ever, emotion seems to dominate policy making. One writer described current sentencing trends as "expressive justice," push-button reactions of rage at all crimes that are engendered by a few highly publicized, outrageous crimes and criminals (Anderson 1995). He points out that the typical criminal looks nothing like the "monsters" portrayed in the sensationalized media reporting and that the system does not often misfire as it is so often portrayed as doing. He draws a distinction between the majority of cases and the sensationalized ones, which are atypical but which nonetheless drive criminal justice policy, affecting all cases.

Surely, radio talk show hosts and politicians have become masters of the sound bite, designed to "trigger the emotions without disturbing the mind," resulting in "the displacement of the language of ideals with the language of images" (*New York Times,* Jan. 28, 1994, p. B1).

Of course, in criminal justice, what is being triggered are the instincts for vengeance and punishment. To the extent that these instincts compete with the qualities of compassion, empathy, and forgiveness, the latter are losing the competition. It would probably be more accurate to say that these qualities can coexist in a more complex emotional and psychological life, but there is no appeal to them or to a more reflective approach. Indeed much of popular culture discourages reflection by triggering emotion. Simplistic responses dominate, complexity dies.

Facts also have a tough time today, because the whole notion of facts has been debased by ideologues, deconstructionists, and those who suggest the absurdity of the search for truth. Courteous, searching, public dialogue is now the exception, in part, because issues are presented in terms of extremes—false choices. We are either tough or soft on crime, for abortion or against it. There is no room in today's world for any more complex analysis of these difficult problems than this. The absence of leadership and of any national vision or purpose to life exacerbates the difficulty of the search for facts and principles upon which to base modern life.

There are many other currents which signify the "disconnectedness" of modern life. Among them are the enormous dislocations in our economy that have affected so many Americans. More people face uncertain economic futures than ever before, people who never anticipated this development. The women's movement has also affected the economic environment, while having a profound effect upon families and the roles of family members. Immigration has put renewed pressure on the economic and social fabric, particularly for the poor, who see new immigrants as competition for low-paying jobs. Amidst this economic uncertainty, I wonder if we are not a more materialistic society, a more competitive one, a less satisfied one. If we are, it appears to be at the expense of matters of the spirit.

Another example of our disconnectedness is in the fact that moral relativism is everywhere. Although much can be said about this, I will simply say this: It is harder than ever to know what is right. There are many reasons for this confusion. One is that, amidst all the talk about crime, many of us see a lot of unprincipled, if not criminal, behavior that goes unattended. What would we learn about the extent of crime in our society if we were to inquire further about tax, business, and investment practices with an eye toward criminal prosecution?

Whether it is falsifying the facts to get a grant, double dipping, or taking money to do one thing and then doing another (as in house building or academia), many people who feel they play by the rules see others who get ahead because they do not. Put another way, it is hard to know what the basis for living a principled life is, let alone what such a life consists of. Am I alone in wondering if I am a chump because I think I am supposed to play by the rules?

Living with uncertainty and ambiguity, both economic and moral, is very difficult. It does not bring out the best in us. It makes us afraid. In such an environment, lashing out and scapegoating are easy. Emotion easily dominates; reflection suffers. We yearn for the simple and get, at least in criminal justice policy, the simplistic. We are a "disconnected" people, looking for moorings, for reference points for ethical decisions, for community and cohesion in modern life. It is difficult, as Tocqueville observed, for a person to be confined "entirely within the solitude of his own heart."

On the other hand, there are positive developments. A major one is the new outbreak of democracy. Not only do we see it in eastern Europe, we also see it in America, in our everyday lives. In schools, in the workplace, in government, we are seeing profound attempts at involvement and participation, new ways of democratic living. In very real ways, we are in transition from authority based institutions to participatory ones. If there is a positive message from recent elections, it is that progress requires more personal and community involvement in social affairs. And, of course, the gay rights, feminist, and civil rights movements are all attempts by people to have a voice, though these voices may not agree with many of those heard in the recent elections. In business, many companies believe greater productivity comes with increased employee involvement in workplace decisions.

Now, we may not be handling the pressure for participation very well. We may need to learn better how to disagree, how to preserve standards while enlarging what we study, and how to measure performance. We may need to learn that the greatest threat to free speech is not government but the lack of courage to speak up. However, we can learn these lessons through the greater participation of people in their communities and in the institutions which so influence the shape of life. These developments are cause for optimism and are directly related to the amelioration of the harshness and to the infusion of forgiveness and related values in criminal justice.

Forgiveness and Restorative Justice

A major roadblock to the infusion of forgiveness and restorative justice into the criminal justice system is that it is essentially personal and communal in an impersonal and bureaucratic system. Forgiveness strikes me as an act of maturity, for it bespeaks a high degree of balance, self-awareness, self-possession, and connection to others. If any one word describes the dominant trend in our society and in criminal justice, it is *disconnectedness,* which involves the opposite of those qualities I associate with forgiveness, empathy, compassion, mercy, and restoration.

Despite this, if we really are in a time of transition, there is the possibility of change for the better. One reason for guarded optimism is that current dissatisfaction with criminal justice and social life is, in part, due to their imbalance, their neglect of basic human instincts and needs, their inability to "work for us." Among the missing is the instinct to be "connected" to oneself and others. From such connections forgiveness, empathy, compassion, and mercy can flow, the natural results of the restoration of balance in the human spirit. If balance is restored in the human spirit, it may be restored in institutions created by humans.

I wish I could say that there is a magic wand to bring these changes about, to take us through this period of transition to a healthier world. But implicit in the nature of the problem as I have outlined it and in the reasons for optimism is that change will come largely from individual effort, from participation, and from forging a better understanding of our interdependence, our connections.

There are already some promising developments. In criminal justice, the restorative justice movement relates directly to the needs of the system and the human spirit, already identified. Restorative justice is a model still in the process of formation. It is based on sound assumptions that are not well attended to in the criminal justice system as we know it. Let me develop them further than I already have.

Crime hurts victims, communities, and offenders. The primary goal of the system ought to be to restore all three to a state of "wholeness," measured not by how much punishment was inflicted but by how much restoration was achieved. This requires that all parties—victim, offender, and community—should be involved in the response to crime, with communities and government playing complementary roles in this response. To restore wholeness, the offender must accept responsibility for the harm and try to repair it. The community must provide an environment supportive of this reparation on the part of the offender as well as the healing process for the victim. The government should ensure community safety and protection of the rights of all people in this healing process.

Now, there is much that could be said about this movement and its many individual manifestations. It obviously strikes a balance of priorities different from those of the current system, and it accords rights and responsibilities to all involved in the process, which also sharply contrasts with the current system. The possible implications of the movement are immense.

Rather than try to outline all of them, let me instead share a few observations. While there are many interesting and innovative programs to implement this model, we have been doing it with prisoners and the victims of their crimes. (Clearly, the best "fit" would come at an earlier stage in the criminal justice process, in the community, as part of the disposition of criminal cases.) One can have little doubt about the need for victims to be restored and for offenders to comprehend better the consequences of their actions and communicate their responsibility if one has been involved in the moving encounters that occur between victims and offenders. Enormous preparation is required before the meeting of victim and offender, but the combination of preparation and an appropriate coming together appears remarkably healthy and healing. Apology plays a role in the process, but that word does not adequately convey what we have observed by way of the offenders' understanding, empathy, and acceptance of responsibility and the victims' healing. That healing is itself very complex, and it often involves the victims' new understandings of themselves and the offenders.

If one has been involved in this restoration process, there can be little doubt that our business-as-usual criminal process is relatively empty of many things that victims and offenders need. This assumes, of course, that the harm of crime is a harm to the well-being—physical, material, and spiritual—of individuals and communities. It assumes that repair requires restoration and effort, especially of offenders but also of communities and victims. It assumes that the individual and general welfare is advanced when we make rather than break connections between people. It also assumes that we have, or can develop, the means to ensure that connections are made without further harm to those already harmed.

This means that all those involved must take risks. This is always difficult, even under the best circumstances. A reader of an earlier version of this chapter referred to the situation today as one of "dangerous opportunity." This succinctly characterizes these times of transition.

References

Anderson, David C. 1995. *Crime and the politics of hysteria: How the Willie Horton story changed American criminal justice.* New York: Times Books.

Enright, R. E. 1995. The psychology of interpersonal forgiveness. Paper presented at the National Conference on Forgiveness, Madison, Wis., March.

North, J. 1987. Wrongdoing and forgiveness. *Philosophy* 62: 499–508.

10

Forgiveness in the Community: Views from an Episcopal Priest and Former Chief of Police

The Reverend David Couper

I spent thirty-four years of my adult life in the police service and twenty-five of them as a chief of police. I have a master of arts in sociology, having studied deviant behavior at the University of Minnesota in the late 1960s and early 1970s. I recently (1993) retired from the police department and entered a seminary of the Episcopal church. I am now a parish priest serving a small congregation in Portage, Wisconsin, northwest of Madison. With these kinds of life experience, I will attempt to claim some kind of authority in the area of crime, criminal behavior, vengeance, and forgiveness.

What do we mean when we talk about forgiveness? From my understanding, forgiveness can be effected only by the person affronted. And once forgiveness is accomplished, the affront or offense should no longer condition the relationship between the offender and the offended. An example of successful forgiveness is when harmony is restored between victim and offender (see *Anchor Bible Dictionary*, 2:831).

Theologically speaking, impediments to forgiveness include "stubborn unrepentance, unbelief, denial of wrongdoing, and the refusal to forgive other people" (see *Anchor Bible Dictionary*, 2:835). Probably the best theological example of forgiveness I can think of is the biblical story of the Prodigal Son (Luke 15:11–32). In it we are observers of the dynamics that can take place in a family setting when one person (the father in this case) chooses to forgive one of his children. In this story we can see how the elder, obedient, nonoffending son perceives a situation where he feels he, too, has been offended by the philandering younger brother. The father has found a lost son and calls for the celebratory killing of a fatted calf. The elder son protests to the father, "Listen! For all these years I have been working like a slave for you and I have never disobeyed your command; yet you have never given me even a young goat so that I might celebrate with my friends." The father, no doubt somewhat puzzled by the elder son's outburst, replies, "Son, you are always with me, and all that is mine is yours. But we had to celebrate and rejoice, because this brother of yours was dead and has come to life; he was lost and has been found."

Forgiveness in this setting is and is not about justice. No doubt the elder brother is offended on a couple of fronts: He is offended as a member of the family, whose youngest son ran off with his share of the family money and spent most of it on wine, women, and song. The elder brother is probably also offended because "fair is fair"; the younger brother took his share and left and now, legally, he has no claim to anything. Do we detect a certain meanspiritedness here, a need for punishment and vengeance?

Neither the elder brother nor the father knows what we, as listeners, know. We know from the storyteller that the younger brother suffered terribly, nearly starving in his plight, and that he had to work on a pig farm (doing ritually "unclean" work). The son has chosen to return to his father, not as his son, but to beg work as servant on the family farm.

When the son is coming down the road but is still far off, "his father saw him and was filled with compassion; he ran and put his arms around him and kissed him." This happens before any words are said. Afterward, the son says, "Father, I have sinned against heaven and before you. I am no longer worthy to be called your son." And what does the father do? He calls for a robe, sandals for the son's feet, and a ring for his finger. He calls for a celebration, for his son "was dead and has come to life; he was lost and has been found."

The question here is, What role does the elder son play as "victim"? Is he a victim? I ask this because much of our style of justice in this country is based on the concept of "society" as victim. In this case, is not the elder brother "society"? And what standing does he have in the relationship between his father and the younger brother? If this is all about share and assets, then the elder son really has no standing, because the property belongs to the father to distribute and redistribute, if necessary, as he sees fit. The restorative nature of this is between the father and the younger, albeit transgressing and offending, son. Forgiveness must primarily be between father and younger son. Sure, there may be some issues that need to be worked through between the two sons, and the younger brother may ask some kind of forgiveness from the elder brother, but this story is about two, not three, characters. Yet the elder son wishes to bring himself into this question and to refuse forgiveness to his brother. And that is his choice. But the full worth of this story and its effectiveness as a model for both forgiveness and restorative justice remains, despite the actions and words of the elder brother.

I believe Christians and Jews ought to be in the business of forgiveness. It is an essential fundamental of our theology. We are called to forgive others as God forgives us (Matthew 18:23–25). The Judeo-Christian heritage is overwhelmingly about forgiveness (Exodus 34:9, 34:6–7; Matthew 18:23–25). I think it is important to recall that the central purpose of forgiveness in a theological and pastoral context was originally for the benefit of the nation and of humankind in general (*Anchor Bible Dictionary,* 2:835). Christians and Jews have a moral and ethical responsibility not only for their "vertical" relationship with God but also for their "horizontal" relationships with one another, and this, in turn, leads to a great social benefit.

However, my task is not to preach but to respond to Walter Dickey. I would like us to think of forgiveness in an even broader context— beyond that between individual persons to that of the institution and the community. I suggest that not only individuals can be injured parties and wrongdoers, but so can collectives of people—institutions, communities, and even nations. There is a strong and respectable current of thought in political philosophy—at least in the Western world—which grants the status of personhood to political associations and social institutions. We can speak of the state, for example, as acting for a reason and as having rights and responsibilities, obligations and duties. Institutions, associations, and organizations are legal persons possessing the characteristics of person- hood. Such groups may also be said to commit acts of wrongdoing and to be harmed by others. An institution, for example, can be a wrongdoer by polluting the environment by not practicing proper waste disposal. On the other hand, an institution can be an injured party when it is subject to physical attack or even an attack on its business reputation by terrorists trying to extort money or other concessions from it.

I also believe that communities, societies, and governments can be wrongdoers by perpetuating racism, ageism, classism, or sexism. Nations too, as we have seen this century, can be wrongdoers through the instru- ments of warfare and other foreign policies. At the same time, a community or society can be an injured party by being the target of collective violence, widespread drug addiction, unemployment, or even by the action of gov- ernmental mandates that make it difficult for that community to achieve health or wholeness in matters such as employment and education.

As you may see, I am trying to broaden the definition of who can be injured and who can do wrong. In responding to Walter Dickey's concept of restorative justice I would like to expand the idea from merely that of an individual criminal and his or her victim, a problem between people, to the greater constituency of the community, a problem which affects us all.

Unfortunately, today we seem to be uninterested in either model— that of restoring the relationship between victim and offender or that between institutions and communities and their members. The burgeoning population of our prisons only serves to support this statement. And the process of building and maintaining criminal justice systems seems to neglect the tasks of either seeking justice or restoring harmony between individuals and between people and the institutions and associations they create.

I suggest that the soul of a society is seen not only in how it treats its children, but also in how it treats its wrongdoers—its deviants, troublemakers, and pariahs. Today, those two entities, children and wrongdoers, are coming closer together as we imprison not only more of our "wrongdoers" but also more of our children. We have even gone so far as to lower the age of the death penalty in many American states as a way of responding to children who are wrongdoers. Today, the trend seems to be to refer more and more children to adult courts and adult prisons. This greatly frightens me. My experience for many years in the police has led me to believe that, once we put a child into the criminal justice system (for any reason whatsoever), we have abandoned that child to a life of crime. The odds are greatly against saving or restoring any child that we place in or sentence to any of our formal "corrective" systems. When we transfer children under sixteen or seventeen years of age into adult courts and sentence them to adult prisons, we have stated clearly that the need to segregate that child from society is far more important than that child's life. It is interesting to speculate how the generational status of "child" and the labeling of "deviant" are becoming less and less distinguishable. Now, I am enough of a realist to know that there are children under eighteen years of age who are vicious and must be segregated from society, but there are not that many of them out there to justify changing and restructuring our entire juvenile justice system to respond to them as we are doing today. Whatever happened to intervention and prevention?

The question we need to ask ourselves today is, How does a young boy or girl find redemption in this society after he or she has made a mistake? What are his or her options? No longer can a young man or woman who drops out of high school easily find work to support himself or herself, let alone a family. They can no longer join the military service with a criminal record. What are they to do? A young man on the street without a high school education and with a petty offense record is a young man we will soon put into prison. Why? Because there are no options for him in today's society, and we are fearful to create any.

The Western world is a society of wealth and possessions. Often it appears that our economies are fueled solely by our need to acquire—to consume and to be successful consumers. There is only one problem: To be a successful consumer requires a job and some disposable income; that makes poor people expendable. And some of the poorest people in this society are our children.

Our rush to imprison people, regardless of age, is morally reprehensible as well as irresponsible. Our generation has, in fact, delayed solving the problem of criminal and social deviancy by passing the decision on to the next generation (again, to our children), who will have to figure out what they are going to do with the enormous cost of maintaining this huge population of imprisoned people. There is a second and much more costly effect of this: After a number of years of living in a prison population with some dangerous and violent cell mates, many so-called nonviolent property offenders and drug traffic offenders will themselves, as a result of this experience, be considered violent and dangerous. It is simply a matter of the consequences of a life in prison. Now, if prisons were places where a young wayward person could get an education, improve his or her reading and writing abilities, learn a trade, and have support outside the walls of the prison, I could possibly be convinced that prison life is a restorative mechanism. But that's not what I see going on today.

What I see in my present ministry to both state and federal prisoners is (primarily) young men, more often than not of African descent, doing long and hard time. It is not unusual to hear of sentences which range from seventy to eighty years with no chance of parole. When these men are finally released, the prison system has been unable to raise their reading level, they have not been able to get a general education diploma (GED), and they have learned no marketable job skills. Our prisoners are released "to the street" after being out of touch with society and their families for many years. There is truly little chance for their successful "rehabilitation." What actually has occurred is that these men have grown older, stronger, more "streetwise," and are far more physically dangerous than when they were sentenced. This is why I say that we are shifting today's problems to the next generation.

I think the death penalty is a good example of what I am trying to point out. Although no one in government will admit it, it appears that the hidden argument in implementing the death penalty is that it will reduce prison costs. But even without this hidden agenda being made apparent, there is a twisted logic among those who support the death penalty under the guise of seeking "justice." It is that we, as a society, should choose to kill persons who kill other people in order to demonstrate to others that killing is wrong because life is sacred. We can even carry this logic a step further. We put people in cages, take away their property and their rights, and do nothing to care for them or change their behavior in order to show to others that people should not be mistreated, written off, abused, or have their property confiscated.

A number of years ago we started doing something serious about victim rights and victim advocacy, and rightly so. I am sorry to say, however, that we did not think much about the important role that apology and forgiveness can play in supporting the well-being of crime victims. While I was a part of those early discussions, it never entered my mind that we need to think of the truly interpersonal nature of crime. We were too quick to deal with crime as behavior against the state and its set of laws. But crimes in a more important way are offenses against people; for the most part, crime is interpersonal. It is amazing to me today that we did not pay attention to these interpersonal needs—the victim's need to hear and receive an apology for being wronged and the offender's need to apologize for his or her behavior. I think we have begun to understand today that deciding to accept an apology from a person who has offended us and asking for forgiveness from a person whom we have offended can be an important part of each side of our healing process—both as victim and as offender. The ability to give and to ask for forgiveness is one of the unique things which make us human.

After all, crime is, for the most part, about failed relationships. We know that we are most vulnerable to physical attack from persons with whom we have a close personal relationship. When family violence or other interpersonal violence happens between persons who have been in a relationship with one another, the justice system comes into play and immediately starts talking about "cases," and not about people and the need, perhaps, to restore these failed relationships.

Reflecting on my police career, I found that I was occasionally able to use forgiveness as an instrument of healing. But I have to admit, it was more by accident than by design. It was accidental because once in a while it appeared to be so logical, so human, to use tried and tested human solutions in the workplace—a simple human solution such as, when you make a mistake, say you're sorry. I came to find that in matters of internal police discipline, when one employee is aggrieved by another, pursuing a sincere apology from the offending employee to the person offended is an effective way to maintain the social fabric of the organization and a far better way than using cumbersome rules and regulations. I came to realize that by pursuing an apology I was better able to hold together the organization's torn fabric. Pursuing an apology is a way to reinforce the principles the organization needs in order to uphold the cultivation of trust, respect, and dignity between employees in the workplace.

Unfortunately, "modern" personnel administration practices and union procedures have forced interpersonal problems in the workplace to be tackled through systems not unlike the criminal justice system with its rules, statements of charge, and mandatory hearings and aura of impersonality.

Another situation in which forgiveness can be used is when the police, either as an organization or as individual employees in the organization, make a public mistake. It could be a big mistake that is both organizational and individual, like the Rodney King incident (March 3, 1991) in Los Angeles. Or it could be something like an individual police officer making an improper remark to a citizen. Sometimes the seeking of forgiveness must be pursued by the organization as well as the individuals within it. The offended public or individual can then be in the position of deciding whether or not he or she wants to forgive the police department or the individual police officer.

A number of years ago a young female police supervisor (we'll call her Lucy) was on duty as a station commander one night. During her shift the dispatcher, whom she personally knew quite well, called to report a fire at one of the city's more troublesome apartment buildings. While concluding the informational call from the dispatcher, Lucy made a flippant remark about the place burning down and "good riddance" to it, humming the tune of "Scotland's Burning." Unfortunately, as things sometimes tragically turn out, two children died in that blaze. For further information, the police supervisor was white, and the two children, African American.

I did not hear about the matter until someone leaked to the news media that there had been an inappropriate comment that night between a police supervisor and a dispatcher. As it was, all telephone communications with the dispatch center were tape-recorded and a simple check confirmed the rumor as true.

When the supervisor's comments were printed in the newspaper, there was a call for me to fire her. I knew Lucy was a good, hardworking, and caring officer. In fact, I had hired as well as promoted her. She had definitely made a mistake. There was no doubt. I met with her and her union representative. I suggested as a course of action offering an apology and requesting forgiveness from the families of the children and the entire community.

Apology can also be used as part of the disciplinary process. The supervisor and her union representative agreed with my suggestion, and Lucy agreed to go hold a news conference with me and offer the apology. For the most part, it worked. The community was able to hear, from me, the results of my internal investigation of what actually had happened during that incident. The facts revealed that Lucy, a mother herself, did not know the extent of the fire or that anyone was in danger. But she realized immediately afterward that she had made a terrible mistake. She made the apology and, in addition, she was suspended without pay for a number of days. She kept her job, and the department learned a very valuable lesson about insensitive remarks and the worth in admitting one's mistake and apologizing. The public and families heard and accepted a sincere, tear-filled apology from Lucy's heart, and she is still employed by the police department today.

Powerful governmental organizations like the police make mistakes. They frequently offend people. I believe apologies should be made when mistakes are made; forgiveness should be pursued. But what, in fact, appears to be the practice of most governmental agencies is denial and entrenchment when they are accused of wrongdoing. Through a fear of uncontrollable consequences, they respond either by going on the defensive, or making no comment, or, in the worst case, trying to justify what they themselves know to be wrong.

Looking back, I wish I had been able to do more with the forgiveness process both inside and outside the department. I found that forgiveness reduces organizational depersonalization and invites the community into the dialogue. The pursuit of forgiveness has the potential to restore relations between people and institutions. Of course, it is the aggrieved person's choice whether or not to accept the apology. Aggrieved persons cannot be forced to forgive either other persons or institutions. By choosing whether or not to forgive, aggrieved persons can become empowered and restored by the process.

Using forgiveness theory and restorative justice is something that is not often seen in our society today. Instead, we see and hear angry and injured persons and their families screaming obscenities and hatred at court hearings and even executions. There is anger all around us in school board meetings, union halls, and executive suites. Surely, not much good and certainly no healing can come out of unresolved anger.

I would also like to comment about forgiveness in government. If there is one place besides the court room where forgiveness and restoration are profoundly lacking it is in politics. Is it possible to have ever done anything wrong and still be a candidate for national political office? If you have ever smoked and inhaled marijuana in your youth, shoplifted, or done any foolish thing, does it preclude you from political office? And if it does, must we then choose between political candidates who have little life experience or who have chosen to lie about their backgrounds? Do we want men and women as our leaders who have made mistakes, learned from those mistakes, sought forgiveness, and experienced personal growth as a result of these experiences, or do we want liars as leaders? Unfortunately, we seem to be taking the latter course.

As a Christian, I find this both puzzling and frightening. It is puzzling because our ethical values should include both forgiveness and restoration. As a people, both forgiveness and restoration are part of our theological and moral history. It is frightening because these concepts are not being taught or even practiced in our society. Instead, a number of "big lies" serve to fuel the "vengeance argument." They are as follows: (1) capital punishment prevents crime; (2) long prison sentences with harsh treatment deter crime; (3) elimination of parole is a good idea; (4) "three strikes and you're out" is a good sentencing policy; (5) prevention doesn't work; (6) lack of education, employment, and opportunity have nothing to do with crime and its causes; and (7) all criminal offenders are monsters who are different from "normal" people like you and me.

These big lies in our society persist in spite of data or experience and because the public discussion of these issues is almost entirely absent from our society. Instead, extremism reigns. It is as if we are too weary as a nation to engage in any meaningful dialogue around these issues. A short time listening to talk radio will convince most of us that we, as a nation, have lost the art of rational argument and the ability to listen to one another. What we hear instead is a constant stream of anger and cynicism spewed out over the nation's airwaves. Where is all that coming from? I cannot help but think that we have too many people out there who are in need of forgiving and being forgiven—in need of restoration.

I would like to conclude at this time, not because the issues have been thoroughly identified or argued from my point of view, but rather because the discussion has served to identify some work that needs to be done. The work is restorative justice and the method is forgiveness. If they are to succeed, then they need nurturing. One of the strengths of the restorative justice movement is that it is about improving people and their relationships. Restorative justice seeks healing between individuals and between people and their institutions. It is the seeking of the biblical "shalom": inner peace, wholeness, and completeness of both individuals and their society. The restorative movement seeks, when necessary, to maintain and make whole the connections and relationships among people that lead to their healing.

Now is the time for boldness. I think it is a time to move forward and recognize the fact that we, as a world people, are more the same than we are different, that we all seek restoration and forgiveness in our lives. Then the concept of forgiveness can be reintroduced to all peoples and societies. We need to recognize that the idea is, after all, an important theological component of all the world's major religions. Forgiveness, nevertheless, needs research, and the world needs to hear of successful forgiveness and restoration "stories" illustrating that vengeance does not work.

As a final note, if we do not incorporate a forgiveness and reconciliation mechanism into our interpersonal, institutional, and community lives, we will, I am afraid, continue to suffer the effects of broken relationships, rampant vengeance, and uncontrolled anger in our society. The ultimate result is that we will see even more murder, assault, and rape in an increasingly weapon-oriented and "vengeance happy" society. We will become even less open and less free, less nurturing, less healing; we will become a society engaging in more and more military action in the world, possessing a burgeoning prison population, and engaging in more and more behaviors to distance and polarize "them" and "us."

The result of neglecting forgiveness, reconciliation, and restorative justice in both our interpersonal and national lives will be a nation and a people distant, divided, vengeful, and unforgiving. It really is up to us— it's a matter of values, choice, and action.

Reference

Anchor Bible Dictionary. 1992. Edited by D. N. Freedman. New York: Doubleday.

11

Is There Forgiveness in Politics?
Germany, Vietnam, and America

Donald W. Shriver, Jr.

World War I was grinding to a halt when Thomas Mann remarked ruefully: "The Germans will never become democratic, for they do not love politics." In those same grim months, Max Weber (1958, 1968) advised a Munich audience that a vocation for politics requires "trained relentlessness in viewing the realities of life" (1958, pp. 126–127). But ten years later, Erich Maria Remarque (1929–30) reminded the world, on behalf of millions of war veterans on both sides, that the realities of life, in politics, encompass the reality of massive death. If Clausewitz was right that "war is nothing but a continuation of political intercourse with the admixture of different means,"[1] who could "love" politics? The hero of Remarque's great novel visits an army hospital, views the shattered bodies, declares that "a hospital alone shows what war is," and then poses these questions to the "fathers" who sent him and his generation off to the western front:

> "What would our fathers do if we suddenly stood up and came before them and proffered our account? What do they expect of us if a time ever comes when the war is over? Through the years our business has been killing—it was our first calling in life. Our knowledge of life is limited to death. What will happen afterwards? And what shall come out of us?" (pp. 228 229)

We know what came out: Versailles, Weimar, Hitler, and a second round of "great war," greater than the first. In the fourth year of that subsequent war, the Scottish poet Edwin Muir offered up his own version of Remarque's despairing questions in a poem entitled "The Wheel." "Long since rusted" knives stab us from behind, he mused. "Revengeful dust" rises up to haunt us. History plagues us like a relentless wheel. Who can "set a new mark" or "circumvent history?" (Muir 1960).

No wonder that, as that second round came to its gruesome end, millions of young people in devastated countries across the earth accepted

---

1. From *On War* [Vom Kriege], as translated in the *Encyclopaedia Britannica*, 15th ed., s.v. "Clausewitz, Karl von."

for themselves a revulsion from politics epitomized by German youth in the crisp phrase *ohne mich*.

In early February of 1995, I stood in a place where that motto had been historically, decisively reversed to democratic forms of *mit mich*. It was Berlin, where now, these fifty years later, unprecedented, hopeful answers have emerged among Germans and with their war enemies of the twentieth century. "What shall come out of us?" A democratic Germany has come, along with the dawn of new hope that, in its new global connectedness, humanity may yet learn not to live by nuclear terror alone. Edwin Muir's question has an answer, "How can I . . . set a new mark? Circumvent history?" The answer was spread out that day around Humboldt University in the former East Berlin: We set new marks in politics by repenting of old sins that will continue to haunt us if we try to forget them or deny that they *were* sins. Clausewitz's famous axiom has an empirical corollary: For skeptics politics may be war by other means; but the politics of speechmaking, as the Greeks well knew, is a vast improvement on the politics of warmaking. In human conflict carried out chiefly in speech, a democratic political philosophy has a deep investment. Politics is the negotiation of conflicting interests and conflictual humans. Even if it is a radical form of negotiation, violence is always on the edge of the degeneration of real politics into pseudopolitics.

If we are to celebrate rightly these momentous "circumventions" of previous grim history, however, our present generation of citizens would do well to ponder equally momentous, too-rarely asked questions: To the extent that some of the world's peoples have really pulled away from the dead weight, the vortex traps, of their earlier history, *how* have they done so? What are the right names of this achievement? Who was responsible for it? And of what ingredients has it consisted? The answers are complex: Among the ingredients of change in modern Germany (and German-American relations) have been the coercions of victors in war, new constructions of domestic law, the irresistible promises of economic reconstruction, the threats of power politics just short of war, surges of peaceful human resistance to outworn political orders, and cultural roots older than ideology. All these forces have contributed to the changes of the political landscape that lay around us that day in Berlin in such astonishing array.

Yet, for the proper naming of such events, there is one element which even Christians are historically prone to forget when they talk theology and ethics in relation to politics. It is only one element in political change or in social change generally, but over against the massive evils that some human collectives sometimes visit on others, it is an indispensable element. Hannah Arendt (1959), refugee from Nazism and eminent secular political philosopher, termed it one of the two essential acts for genuine social change. It is one of the oldest concepts in the history of Jews and Christians, yet it is a concept that even they have only hesitantly applied to political relationships. I speak of *forgiveness*. Does it, can it, function in the ethics of international relations? That is the question central to this paper (Shriver 1995).

What Jews and Christians Have Assumed, and Not Assumed, About Forgiveness

This is not an essay about recondite Church history, but it will clear some ground for two narratives to follow if I summarize the major assumptions which the Bible long ago rendered conventional for any careful religious use of the term *forgiveness* in the Jewish and Christian traditions.

- Forgiveness simultaneously presupposes the commission of an *evil* act by one agent against another and the effort of the victim to repair the relationship fractured by the evil. As John Dryden put it: "Forgiveness to the injured doth belong" (*The Conquest of Granada* II.1.2).
- As a transaction between agents, however, forgiveness has as its match the willingness of offenders to acknowledge their offenses and to receive the offer of forgiveness. This is the *repentance* side of the transaction. Forgiveness without repentance hangs, abstract and unconsummated, in limbo. Repentance without forgiveness cuts the nerve of the parties for moving on toward a reconciliation, which is the fulfillment of a process in which forgiveness is the beginning.
- Forgiveness itself begins *not* with a forgetting but with a remembering, a refusal to buy the repair of the relation at the cost of not mentioning the cause of the fracture. Moral forgiveness begins with the memory of immorality, with moral *judgment*.
- To forgive, or to try forgiving, is to value *the hope of relation repair* above the bare moral claim that one has inflicted evil and another has suffered it. Forgiveness is a future-oriented social transaction. It aims at a new bond for a relation now broken.
- As such, forgiveness always involves a certain *forbearance,* a step back from revenge, however morally tempting and justified revenge may be. The refusal of vengeance does not mean refusal of all punishment for evildoing, but forgiveness does refuse punishment-in-kind. It aims at breaking the cycle of evil and counterevil in endless repetition.
- It likewise involves some degree of *empathy* with the one who has committed the wrong. Forgiveness is a kind of stooping, an

acknowledgment of the humanity of another and the salvageability of victims' relation to that other.

In all of this, between humans, forgiveness takes *time*. It is a process that may take years and years to consummate, the more so if the evils are great and one of the parties has yet to confess to culpability in the matter.

These principles should be familiar and agreeable to adherents to the historic biblical tradition. Forgiveness consists of (1) a memory of evil and a moral judgment of the evil, (2) a forbearance from vengeance, (3) an empathy for the enemy, and (4) an intention of renewed positive relation with the enemy.

However, there is another set of assumptions which clash with the possibility that forgiveness has any important place in a Jewish or Christian ethic for politics. If we are to find a place for forgiveness in our political ethics, we may have to "set a new mark" in certain of these emphases that we have inherited from our forebears around the subject of forgiveness. For many of them have taught us the following:

- Forgiveness, we are often told in the Hebrew Bible, is preeminently a unique power and privilege of God. Only in some limited fashion can human beings be entitled to forgive. "There is forgiveness with thee," prays the psalmist (Psalm 130:4)—and only with thee. Critics of Jesus of Nazareth treated this belief as taken-for-granted orthodoxy. Twice in the Gospels they exclaim, "Who can forgive sins but God alone?" (Mark 2:7; Luke 5:21).
- To the contrary, according to these Gospels, Jesus insisted that forgiveness must be a primary practice in the life of his disciples. This emphasis may have been his most revolutionary innovation in his ethical interpretation of the Hebrew Scriptures. Hannah Arendt thought so. In any exegesis, forgiveness between humans has a stronger place in the core of New Testament ethics than it probably had in the Hebrew Bible.
- Partly as a result of this biblical tradition, over the next two hundred years, the word *forgiveness* acquired the connotations of a uniquely *religious* word; and by its attachment over the centuries to the Catholic sacrament of penance, it became a name for a transaction preeminently private, personal, and profoundly nonpolitical.
- In these postbiblical centuries, Christian theologians commended *justice,* after Greek and Roman precedents, as the basic norm for Christian thinking about the political order.
- Augustinian *love,* we Christians have been taught, is more central to Christian ethics than justice; and from this principle—love's transcendence of justice—the ground was laid for the concession that love has a home in the Church, not in the raw conflicts of

secular power, where justice is the highest ideal that anyone can aspire to. (*A fortiori,* for that great German-American theologian Reinhold Niebuhr, forgiveness, as the final expression of love, is only fitfully possible for "Christian realism" in politics [Niebuhr 1935, pp. 128–129].)

• Therefore it is inevitable that twentieth-century speech about forgiveness in politics, whether mouthed by Christians or secularists, should sound sentimental, idealistic, personalistic, or otherwise out of place in discourse about rough-and-tumble collective power conflicts. Collectivities do not forgive, nor are they forgiven, as Max Weber himself put it so staunchly to a 1918 Munich audience in the wake of the recently ended war: "A nation forgives if its interests have been damaged, but no nation forgives if its honor has been offended, especially by a bigoted self-righteousness" (Weber 1958, p. 118).

There in 1918, Germany was about to be offended by the bigoted self-righteousness (*pfaffische Rechthaberei*) of the Versailles treaty. Knowing, as we do, what lay ahead in 1939, had he lived till then, might not Weber have found in the Versailles treaty itself the negative lesson that, absent something like forgiveness in international politics, it degenerates again into the pseudopolitics of war? What if Weber was wrong, *and* the major streams of Christian ethical thinking about politics were wrong, to banish forgiveness from the processes of collective, mutual recovery from gross, unjust, collective suffering? What if Dietrich Bonhoeffer (1955, pp. 53–54) was beginning to break down the wall of separation between forgiveness and politics when early in his *Ethik* he allowed that, "even within the history of the internal and external political struggle of the nations, there is something in the nature of forgiveness" (*etwas wie Vergebung*)? And what if fifty years of American-German relations offer us evidence that forgiveness in human collective affairs consists of a dynamic interaction, over time, between moral and political developments that Bonhoeffer himself (Bonhoeffer 1955, pp. 53–54) named when he went on to say that "this forgiveness within history can come only when the wound of guilt is healed, when violence has become justice, lawlessness has become order, and war has become peace"?

The Long Road to Reconciliation: What Forgiveness Means for Fifty Years of German-American Relations

Perhaps for God, forgiveness is one mighty act, but between human beings—even if only two of them—the classic components of forgiveness take time to bring together, as do most changes in human affairs. The more complex the description of an act of forgiveness, the more likely the forgiveness has taken some time to achieve. I have posited that the act is fourfold, involving (1) the open naming of wrong, (2) the drawing back from revenge-in-kind, (3) the development of empathy for the wrongdoer, and (4) the extending of a tentative hand toward renewed community still in the future. These are the minimal four steps on the road to reconciliation, which is paved simultaneously with corresponding steps of repentance, all of which intertwine like eight matching strands of cable. A party offered forgiveness matches the offer with repentance, with gratitude that revenge is not in the offing, with counterempathy for victims' suffering, and with hope that reconciliation is now possible. Perhaps it is best to distinguish ethically between "reconciliation," as finally achieved, and these steps that take sinful humans down the road toward reconciliation. The reconciliation promised in the New Testament retains profound dimensions of futurity. It remains eschatologically connected to the "Kingdom of God" language in the Lord's Prayer, where the Greek verbs strain (through aorist tenses) toward an eschatological Kingdom-Not-Yet-Come. *Not* so connected to futurity, however, is the forgiveness petition of this famous prayer. There, in present and perfect tenses (in St. Luke's version of the prayer in Greek), forgiveness is the one requested kingdom gift wrapped inexorably in the present time of the life of disciples (Matthew 6:12; Luke 11:4). And there, in an apparent great theological difficulty, divine and human forgiveness are made reciprocal and interdependent.

What might that mean in a Christian ethic for secular politics? Over the past fifty years, the history of German-American relations encompasses a series of events, each of which offers some answer. In my recent book, *An Ethic for Enemies: Forgiveness in Politics* (1995), I have a chapter that chronicles these events in some detail. People familiar with this history will know how to rehearse it in a series of official meetings, laws, and symbols: Nüremberg, Stuttgart, Darmstadt, the Marshall Plan, *Grundgesetz, Laste-nausgleichsgesetz, Wiedergutmachung, Ruckerstattung, Ost Memorandum, Ostpolitik,* the Warsaw Treaty. All these events are relevant to an answer to the question, What is forgiveness in German politics? and the companion question, What is repentance? Rather than attempting further abstract summaries or cursory historical surveys of this string of events, let me single out one omitted from the above list: Bitburg.

Preliminarily let me state a methodological maxim that governs my own pursuit of my vocation as a student of Christian ethics: You shall know their ethics by their slant on history. To "do" social ethics as Christians or secular persons, citizens of our century should deal not just with concepts but with history—with the relativities, the uncertainties, the imprecisions, the pains, the sufferings, and, above all, the concretions of human events. Only those who immerse themselves in the ambiguities of human history have a right to claim *some* ethical clarity about that history.

Bitburg: "A Most Necessary Grief"

The word *forgiveness* is so foreign to ordinary public rhetoric that, when it appears repeatedly in journalistic accounts of any event over a period of six or eight weeks, one's curiosity, at least, is aroused. Such was the case on the American side of the Bitburg cemetery event (*New York Times,* Feb.–May 1985).

The debate, in fact, was almost a year in the making. Excluded from the June 6, 1984, ceremony marking the fortieth anniversary of the Normandy invasion, Chancellor Helmut Kohl visited President Ronald Reagan the following November and invited him to Germany for the fortieth anniversary of the May 8 end of the European war. It would be a sign of reconciliation between our two countries, the chancellor urged.

Over the next four months, the Reagan White House vacillated about the proposal. Should the president include a visit to a concentration camp site? Should he lay a wreath on the graves of German soldiers in the Kolmeshöhe Cemetery in the Rhineland town of Bitburg? On March 21, 1985, Mr. Reagan announced that, no, he would not visit Dachau or any other concentration camp, because that would just "reawaken the memories" of a long-past war. Instead, on April 11, he announced that he would visit Bitburg.

One must be prepared to acknowledge the importance of symbol, ceremony, and gesture in international relations if one is to understand the furor that ensued. And one must also acknowledge the wisdom (rare in the minds of many Americans) in the words of our novelist William Faulkner: "The past is never dead. It's not even past." (*Requiem for a Nun*).

The next four weeks were an extended lesson in that wisdom for the president of the United States. In these weeks the White House was flooded with telegrams, phone calls, and press commentary: Why *not* a presidential visit to a concentration camp? Did the president want to remember the graves of soldiers to the neglect of the ashes of the Holocaust? By April 16, the president had changed his mind again: He would visit Bergen-Belsen.

But that left Bitburg. On that April day, in answer to a reporter's question, Mr. Reagan uttered words that immediately threw him into a sea of political trouble: " . . . there's nothing wrong with visiting that cemetery where those young men are victims of Nazism also. . . . They were victims, just as surely as the victims of the concentration camp." Oh?

Do the "victims" also include the forty-nine bodies of the SS men in that cemetery? To millions of American ears, it was a facile moral mistake; to no ear was it more shocking than that of the man who, three days later, was to face the president of the United States in the White House itself in what was already a high ceremonial occasion: Nobel Peace Prize winner Elie Wiesel, youthful survivor of Auschwitz, now to receive the Congressional Gold Medal, highest civilian honor which the Congress awards.

Early in Reagan's administration, some American journalists had awarded him the title "Great Communicator." But it was his misfortune on April 19, 1985, to face a greater communicator, a Jewish leader determined to mobilize all the literary skill and moral passion at his command to say publicly to the president: "That place, Mr. President, is not your place. Your place is with the victims of the SS" (*New York Times,* Apr. 20, 1985). That was the theme of Wiesel's impassioned plea. It must have been an embarrassing speech for this White House audience to listen to. Here are some excerpts:

> Mr. President, I have seen children, I have seen them thrown into the flames alive. Words, they die on my lips. So I have learned, I have learned the fragility of the human condition. . . .
>
> What can I do? I belong to a traumatized generation. As to us, as to you, symbols are important. And furthermore, following our ancient [Jewish] tradition . . . our tradition commands us to "speak truth to power. . . ."
>
> I am convinced . . . that you were not aware of the presence of SS graves in the Bitburg cemetery. . . . But now we all are aware. . . .
>
> Oh, we know there are political and strategic reasons, but this issue, as all issues related to this awesome event, transcends politics and diplomacy.
>
> The issue here is not politics, but good and evil. . . .
>
> Mr. President, I know and I understand, we all do, that you seek reconciliation. . . . I too wish to attain true reconciliation with the German people. I do not believe in collective guilt, nor in collective responsibility. Only the killers were guilty. Their sons and daughters are not.
>
> And I believe, Mr. President, that we can and we must work together with them and with all people. And we must work to bring peace and understanding to a tormented world that, as you know, is still waiting redemption.

Reagan was said to be deeply moved by these words, but not moved to cancel his visit to Bitburg. And so the controversy continued to mount. Fifty-three (out of a hundred) U.S. senators signed a petition urging him not to go. Rallies of American Jews and their friends multiplied across the land. In one of those rallies in Philadelphia, Elie Wiesel spoke even more harshly than he had spoken in Washington: "This is the beginning [of] . . . the rehabilitation of the SS. To go to that place" means "that in a few years it would be acceptable to honor the SS. . . . We believe in reconciliation with all people but the killers" (*New York Times*, Apr. 22, 1985). On the same occasion, Menachem Z. Rosensaft, born in Bergen-Belsen, called the Bitburg visit "a calculated, deliberate insult to the victims of the Holocaust. . . . there must be at least one cemetery in all of Germany which does not contain SS men" (*New York Times*, Apr. 22, 1985).

Try as his staff did to claim that the Bitburg visit paid presidential respect to Germany's war dead generally, American critics insisted that the merest breath of respect for the forty-nine bodies of SS men buried in Bitburg, even a floral wreath, was a moral outrage, a crossing of the line between relative evil and absolute evil. Perhaps there was some earthly moral limbo to which the troops of the German armies could be assigned, but the SS was in the lowest reaches of the Nazi hell, and they should be left there.

Meantime in Germany, the old questions of the Nazi past rose up again for public debate. Reporters interviewed members of the Bundestag. The member from Bitburg (a town that had voted against the Nazi party in 1933), Alois Mertes, said that he hoped the resolution of the fifty-three American senators "does not represent the feelings of the American people"—a hope that sounded odd to the ears of many Americans, who expect their senators often, if not always, to represent their feelings. In America, the polls began to show an even division in the electorate over the Bitburg visit; and ominously enough in both the United States and Germany, polls and interviews surfaced some stubborn strains of anti-semitism. With marked lack of empathy, 60 percent of Americans who favored the visit agreed with the statement: "Jewish leaders in the United States protested" it "too much" (*New York Times*, May 8, 1985). Then there was a sample of Bitburgers who convinced an American reporter that both Germans and Americans have citizens in their ranks who view Jews as "an indigestible lump, a foreign body in both countries" (*New York Times*, May 14, 1985). One Bitburger found himself quite out of democratic tune with the Hebrew tradition of "speaking truth to power." "Imagine the nerve of a Jew," he said acidly, "lecturing President Reagan. I saw him on television, making trouble the way they all do." It is not clear whether he knew that his interviewer, the reporter, was Jewish as well as American.

Amidst these rising tides of bitterness on both sides, the leaders of the two nations were apparently learning something about the uses of more measured, historically realistic, and even more repentant-sounding public rhetoric. Citizens must sometimes speak truth to power, but power must sometimes speak truth to citizens. Before they had made their painful way through this event, four major leaders—two Germans and two Americans —presented to the world something of what it means to speak truth about the past, to put that truth to the service of public repentance in the present, and to infuse civil discourse with "something in the nature" of a forgiveness matched to that public repentance. In America the chief teacher was Elie Wiesel, and the most prominent learner, Ronald Reagan. In Germany, Chancellor Helmut Kohl was one of the learners, and he seemed to learn more rapidly than his counterpart in Washington. Two weeks before Bitburg, the chancellor stood in Bergen-Belsen and spoke more concretely about guilt, responsibility, and reconciliation than many had ever heard him speak before: "Reconciliation with . . . the [Holocaust] victims is only possible if we accept our history as it really was, if we Germans acknowledge our shame and our historical responsibility, and if we perceive the need to act against any efforts at undermining human freedom and dignity" (*New York Times,* Apr. 22, 1985). And, remembering what the victors of the war had done to reverse the precedent of Versailles, he praised those former enemies and even the former concentration camp inmates and relatives who "reached out their hands to us in reconciliation."

A few days later Ronald Reagan went to Bitburg and repeated much the same words: "Many of you are worried that reconciliation means for-getting. I promise you, we will never forget." But we remember, too, that "too often . . . each war only planted the seeds of the next. We celebrate today the reconciliation between our two nations that has liberated us from that cycle of destruction" (*New York Times,* May 6, 1985).

Because such words were so long in coming, Mr. Reagan left behind him in America an internal problem of fractured, damaged reconciliation. Again, Elie Wiesel identified the problem most eloquently: "In the long run, I'm sure the wounds will heal. After all, he is the President and we must deal with his policies, with his staff, with his Administration. But the wounds are there and the wounds are deep. I felt excluded, rejected, almost unnecessary, when I watched the Bitburg visit" (*New York Times,* May 6, 1985).

It was an indirect way of speaking about the difference between war and democratic politics: "We must deal with" this president, his policies, his inept knowledge of history, and with his misguided advisors. For in dealing with our governments we citizens are dealing with each other; and a commitment to deal with one another, even in our antagonism, is the essential discipline of democratic citizenship. It is also near-relative of forgiveness in politics. To stop speaking to each other is to close off one of the last political bridges away from war.

What did leaders and citizens, in Germany and the United States, learn about forgiveness in politics in their public conflict over Bitburg? Some, at least, learned certain primary lessons about our existence as social beings:

- Victims of very great evil remember that evil for a very long time.
- For neighbors to forget the evil is an assault on the humanity of the victims.
- The first step, therefore, and the repeated step of forgiveness in politics is accurate, painstaking, pain-sharing remembering. We begin to forgive by not forgetting.
- Citizens who have no personal share in guilt for the commission of dreadful political deeds have a responsibility for the past in the sense that they are responsible both for remembering it and for holding in check those current forces that threaten a repetition of it, or worse. Collective guilt across generations may be a morally dangerous idea, but collective responsibility across generations may be a morally necessary idea.
- If a collective memory is ever to be unburdened from the weight of an evil past, the institutions of public life—government, education, the media, the religious communities—must keep the memory accessible to upcoming generations. On occasion they must be willing to rehearse the past in the context of the maxims: We remember the past in order not to repeat it. We remember evil in order to build a new community with the descendants of the evildoers.

An American journalist, William Safire, on May 6, 1985 (*New York Times*), gave an account of how a central character in this drama learned what he had not learned while a Hollywood actor. Safire, himself Jewish and a speechwriter for Richard Nixon during the Watergate crisis, wrote as follows:

> Ronald Reagan, a month ago, had no real grasp of the moral priorities of the Holocaust or the fear of forgetfulness that prevents forgiveness. His journey of understanding—his own "painful walk into the past"—opened the minds of millions to the costs of reconciliation in a way no other process could have accomplished. In driving home the lessons of history, his incredible series of blunders turned out to be a blessing. . . .
>
> In seeking at first to sidestep the smouldering resentments, the President brought on a firestorm 40 years after the Holocaust, which in turn forced a forgetful world through a most necessary grief.

There was one other national leader in this tense incident who found public words that rivaled the eloquence, the realism, the recall, and the moral passion of Elie Wiesel. He was Bundespräsident Richard Freiherr von Weizsäcker. On May 8, 1985, he delivered a speech to a hushed Bundestag audience in Bonn that the *New York Times* dubbed "the week's only memorable presidential speech" (May 12, 1985). A year later, columnist

Anthony Lewis of that newspaper called it "one of the great speeches of our time" (May 1, 1986).

It was the first time in forty years when a major politician of the conservative party had spoken in detail about the atrocities of the Nazi era. Here are some excerpts from that speech:[2]

> . . . six million Jews . . . the unthinkable number of citizens of the Soviet Union and Poland . . . our own countrymen who lost their lives . . . the murdered Sinti and Roma [Gypsies] . . . the homosexuals . . . the mentally ill . . . the hostages . . . the Resistance of all countries . . . the German resistance . . . [and all those] who accepted death rather than humble their consciences. . . .
>
> [It all added up to an] unimaginably vast army of the dead . . . a mountain of human suffering;
>> suffering from the dead,
>> suffering through wounding and crippling,
>> suffering through inhuman enforced sterilization,
>> suffering in nights of bombing,
>> suffering through flight and expulsion,
>>> through oppression and plunder,
>>> through forced labor, through injustice and torture,
>>> through hunger and need,
>> suffering through fear of imprisonment and death,
>> suffering through the loss of all that one had mistakenly believed in
> and for which one had worked.
> [And were Germans in general unaware of these crimes? Hardly. Take the case of the Jews:]
> . . . every German could witness what Jewish fellow citizens had to suffer, from cold indifference through veiled intolerance to open hatred.
>
> Who could remain innocent after the burning of the synagogues, the looting, the stigmatizing with the Jewish star, the withdrawal of rights, the unceasing violations of human worth?
>
> Whoever opened his eyes and ears, whoever wanted to inform himself, could not escape knowing that deportation trains were rolling. The imagination of men is insufficient to encompass the means and the scale of the annihilation. But in reality the crime itself was compounded by the attempts of all too many people—in my generation as well, we who were young and who had no part in the planning and execution of the events—not to take note of what was happening. . . .
>
> [And why go into all these historical details? Precisely because] . . . whoever closes his eyes to the past becomes blind to the present. Whoever does not wish to remember inhumanity becomes susceptible to the dangers of new infection.

---

2. English text for these and other quotations from this speech was supplied to me by the Embassy of the Federal Republic of Germany in Washington, D.C., May 1985.

On and on went the speech to what one journalist described as a "hushed parliament." The likes of it would have hushed any parliament in the world—and stirred deep anger as well. The political truth is clear: There are moments in the history of nations when what leaders *say* to their publics constitutes "political action" in a very constructive form. Abraham Lincoln was an American master of this truth. In his Gettysburg Address, he coined words that virtually redefined the United States as united in a "new birth" of equality as well as freedom. Later in his brief Second Inaugural Address at the end of our Civil War, Lincoln again practiced the high art of moving a people through their inexpressible suffering toward its moral meaning and the repair of a collective relation fractured by 600,000 deaths (McPherson, New York: Ballantine Books, 1988, p. 854) and other vast destruction in a fratricidal war, "with malice towards none, with charity towards all."

Like Lincoln, von Weizsäcker in his May 8 speech sought to tame the legacies of "malice" and hatred left over from war while acknowledging many reasons for that malice and hatred. Not once in his Bundestag speech did he use the word *Vergebung* or *Verzeihung*, and it would have violated the spirit of the whole utterance had he added the gratuitous note, "On grounds of this confession, I hope that the nations of the world will forgive Germany." Yet the speech touches on almost all the requirements to be met by offending parties if genuine forgiveness is to be extended to them by the offended: (1) acceptance of moral judgment, (2) grateful acknowledgment that forbearance from revenge is being tendered from an enemy, (3) reciprocal empathy for the hurt that has been so unjustly inflicted, and (4) a political turn in principle, policy, and behavior toward reconciliation between offended and offenders. If the von Weizsäcker speech was not a demonstration of the relevance of forgiveness to politics, it is nonetheless a powerful example of the relevance of public *repentance* to politics, a public verbal embodiment of the process by which nations plant their feet firmly on the road to reconciliation. The peoples of the world, not least Americans, are fortunate when their leaders re-present a shameful past and hail a different future with such historical, moral, and political integrity.

Forgiving America: A "Necessary Grief" Yet to Be Politically Experienced in This Country

I would not want to end this chapter, nor would I be a suitable representative of the seminary in which Reinhold Niebuhr taught for so long, without acknowledging the reality to which his political theology so regularly called attention: how, in the tortured relations of human collectivities, great wrongs are usually committed on all sides. Among America's theologians, none more regularly tried to puncture that American innocence, which so annoys many of America's friends and enemies in the world. In the conduct of World War II, for example, Americans perpetrated some destructions of life that left the theory of "just" war in tatters. For Germans, the memory of Dresden will probably lead the list of candidates for American war crimes during that war. For the Japanese, the list will begin with Hiroshima and Nagasaki. Unless we Americans, too, reckon with our own excesses of violence in our history, we shall not be good partners of others in our mutual exploration of political guilt and reconciliation. Even if Americans of my generation remain in considerable disagreement about the justification of a military strategy that kills cities, it will be hard for both Americans and Japanese to review the history of the Pacific war without stumbling over the vast evidence that it was a *racist* war on both sides. If one's memory of the war does not fuel that thought, one should read John W. Dower's (1986) important book, *War without mercy.*

The general truth here has many a painful, specific illustration: In politics, as between persons, nothing is more false or damaging to human relations than self-righteousness. Max Weber did well to warn victors against *pfaffische Rechthaberei.* As Reinhold Niebuhr was fond of saying, the universality of sin is the one Christian doctrine that is empirically verifiable.

However, I must end by remaining true to my methodological principle: Only those who wrestle with specific histories have a right to moral clarity about that history, especially in matters of guilt, forgiveness, and reconciliation. Early in 1995 a colleague in Germany gently delivered to me the message: "Germans are impressed with the generosity of America in victory; we are not so sure that America is generous in defeat. And we wonder about America's dealing with its great modern defeat: the Vietnam War."

Americans, too, should wonder. When in 1991 President George Bush called for a "just" war against aggressive Iraq, many Americans rose in support of this military effort as an occasion to "put Vietnam behind us." The analogy to Germany in 1939 would have been all too apt: putting World War I behind us. *Not* analogous, surely, is what Germans did, after 1945, to put Nazism behind them. Once the concentration camp gates were opened, once the gaunt faces of surviving inmates stared out, Germans in increasing numbers began the long journey toward acknowledging that the defeat of 1945 was morally necessary to them as well as to the world. In no mature similar way, however, have Americans put Vietnam behind them. Though the public turned against the war finally in the late 1960s, as late as 1992, in campaigning for the presidency, Bill Clinton seemed compelled to shy away from making a *virtue* of his own youthful opposition to that war. Moral assessment of that war does not yet win votes in democratic America.

Perhaps Americans' nearest approach to symbolic *grief* for the Vietnam War is that remarkable war monument which erupts from a patch of earth in Washington, D.C. Designed by Asian American Maya Lin and rightly described by James Fallows as "a work of genius," it is unique among all American war monuments in that it names in one place every American citizen known to have died in the war. Across that long granite wall, stretch names of fifty-eight thousand Americans. Berliners needed to tear down a wall; we Americans needed to build one. Veterans and their families come to that wall every day of the year now, many putting their hands and their tears on the names of their lost friends, sons, and daughters.

Nonetheless, my country has ahead a long struggle with dimensions of our defeat in Vietnam that have much to do with the repair of our relation to Vietnam but even more to do with guilt and reconciliation *internal* to the United States. Guilt and reconciliation with Vietnam are part of our agenda, but they may be the easier part. The Vietnamese civil war generated some two million deaths, and Americans should not take the blame for all of them. But something else died in the Vietnam War that Americans have not yet had the leaders or the collective courage to identify and grieve: our classic American image of ourselves as a moral nation among immoral nations.

A former Presbyterian missionary to Zaire, Walter T. Davis, now a professor at San Francisco Theological Seminary, has recently published a book, *Shattered Dreams,* in which he probes this American malady through the eyes of our still-living citizens who suffered most in this war: our Vietnam veterans. Out of interviews with hundreds of them, Davis uncovers the real depths of the American defeat in Vietnam. He writes:

> When the curtain fell on Vietnam, John Wayne was dead (figuratively speaking) and with him the ideal of masculine heroism as well as the hubris of America's civilizing mission in the world. (Davis 1994, p. 72)
>
> . . . in Vietnam the American story backfired. Science and technology proved insufficient; nation-building was ineffectual; and American "cowboys" met "Indians" they could not defeat.
>
> Loren Bariz uses the term "American exceptionalism" to describe the controlling myths of U.S. national identity and purpose. . . . America [was supposed to] be different—an exception—from the corrupt and oppressive societies of the Old World. . . .
>
> Two components of the myth have been linked historically in a particularly nefarious manner: the division of the world into two camps—one good, the other evil—and the necessity of violence to produce the good. . . .
>
> [For example, President Woodrow Wilson carried Americans into World War I with the words,] "I will not cry 'peace' as long as there is sin and

wrong in the world. . . ." When his turn at the helm of state came, President Kennedy would describe the defense of freedom and human rights around the world as "God's work." And in 1991 President Bush would use the same Manichaean categories to mobilize American support for Desert Storm. (pp. 113–115)

We learned in the Vietnam War [that] no president is willing to admit defeat or error. Thus, in the absence of rituals of confession or a common religious perspective that would call the nation to repentance, [our] national story rarely comes under judgment. (p. 117)

In Vietnam, "Americanism" failed. Power, innocence, purity, organiza-tion, technology, can-do optimism, the defense of civilization—the whole myth turned in upon itself. . . . The national story [became] no longer cred-ible. The web of myths that holds that story together has come unraveled. (pp. 118–119)

In an astute summary of his entire study, Davis (1994) quotes our neighbor, Canadian theologian Douglas John Hall: "Americans are not educated for darkness. [They] are 'the officially optimistic society,' with little sense of limits or of the tragic. Therefore, the[ir] temptation is avoidance, denial, flight" (p. 165).

Who are the Americans who might stem our national propensity for avoidance, denial, and flight from "the dark side" of American history? To our greatest internal national crime—African slavery—African Americans will always bear witness; to our almost-as-great crime, Native Americans bear witness. But in regards to Vietnam, Walter Davis is sure who the proper witnesses are: living American veterans of the war. Americans generally have only begun to listen to their testimony, and that has only deepened the traumatic impact of the war upon the veterans still in our midst. At least 2.5 million Americans served in the military in Vietnam. One-fourth of them, 800,000, have suffered from what the psychiatrists have called posttraumatic stress disorder. Since the late 1960s, at least sixty thousand combat veterans have committed suicide, and one in three homeless people on the streets of American cities is a Vietnam veteran (Davis 1994, pp. 130ff.). If and when they are encouraged to talk about their war experience, they speak in ways that few war veterans have ever spoken in American history:

"[Upon my return to the States] it didn't take long to realize that I was a casualty of war. My country did not want me, was embarrassed by me. No one cared what happened to me; no one wanted to listen to the horrors of war. My country sent me to do evil and then hid from me because I reminded them of it. I was a victim of America's arrogance, and I was being blamed for it."

. . . The major task for vets, says marine veteran Rev. Michael Stewart, is not their need to reconcile with the Vietnamese . . . but "the need to reconcile with the American people in their midst. . . . For many Vietnam veterans feel that they have no good reason to trust anyone here again and cannot find within themselves the ability to forgive." (Davis 1994, pp. 108–109)

[Ten years after returning from Vietnam, said one veteran, a medical doctor,] "I explored my anger. I'm Jewish, and as an adolescent I had been obsessed with the Nazis and angry that the Jews didn't fight back. . . . But anger wasn't all I had been repressing. In 1988 during a session of . . . therapy the therapist touched me . . . and I was flooded with guilt and shame, and the terrible recognition that I am like the Nazis. I had done my job, obeyed the orders, never questioned my superiors. . . . I am no better than my own worst enemy! That is what I have to live with." (pp. 85–86)

Might there have been a *public, politically relevant therapy* for these damaged Americans? The Vietnam wall was a beginning, but it is not enough. Few American politicians seem up to the painful task. They could have offered returning veterans a more genuine "welcome," says Davis, if they had greeted the returnees with a "bipartisan governmental admission of error . . . and a request that the vets forgive the nation for sending them to fight" a war that destroyed villages it was supposed to save and destroyed the inner morale of many an American who fought it. "What was 'wasted' in Vietnam was the continuity of the American story. To face the demise of the American national identity was too painful then, and for most it is still too painful now" (Davis 1994, pp. 108–109).

Possibly the people of a recently reunited Germany know this agenda only too well in their task of national reconciliation, still in the future, between the two former Germanys. Might a Germany, sobered by the human capacity for evil, teach an optimistic America to abandon its vulnerability to national self-righteousness? Yes, it might. I reluctantly remember that in many an American Protestant church, within reaching distance of the pulpit, there stands an American flag. I think about that flag in connection with Bonhoeffer's essay about his impression of the American churches in the 1930s: "Protestantism without Reformation." Were I replicating such an essay in the 1990s, I would focus it on "Patriotism without Reformation." Huey Long said once that, if totalitarianism ever comes to the United States of America, it will come wrapped in an American flag. We Protestants should take that flag out of our church sanctuaries.

Our helpers in the revision of our characteristic cultural optimism and our unreformed patriotism should include contemporary South Africans. Not long before the collapse of apartheid, I heard one of them, Desmond Tutu, speak a wise, implicitly theological word: "In South Africa, it is not possible to be optimistic. Therefore it is necessary to hope." One of Walter Davis' last words is equally wise:

Optimism, not despair, is the enemy of hope. Optimism blinds us to the shadow side of life. Optimism wears a forced smile, represses intuitive danger signals, and projects its own evil onto others. Optimism is a lie that denies the truth and therefore prevents necessary change. Hope, then, arises not amid optimism but amid the ruins of crumbled dreams. (Davis 1994, p. 165)

Writing in the first years of the cold war, Reinhold Niebuhr called Americans to "a sense of contrition about the common human frailties and foibles which lie at the foundation of both the enemy's demonry and our vanities." He warned us all against great political power afflicted by a blindness "induced not by some accident of nature or history but by hatred and vainglory" (Niebuhr 1952, p. 174).

The truth about our history is the first step in forgiveness for some aspects of our history. If there remain in Germany or in America those who have yet to internalize that political wisdom, let them read again Lincoln's Second Inaugural, and let them imagine what the American equivalent might be to that speech which Richard von Weizsäcker delivered on May 8, 1985.

We older people do not owe youth the fulfillment of dreams, but rather integrity. . . . We learn from our own history what [humans are] capable of. Therefore we must not imagine that we have become, as human beings, different and better. There can be no finally achieved moral perfection— neither for any individual nor for any country! As human beings we have learned, as human beings we remain endangered. Yet we always have the strength to overcome dangers afresh. . . . Our request to young people is this: do not allow yourselves to be driven into enmity and hatred. . . . See that we too, as democratic politicians, take this advice to heart, and provide us with an example. . . . Let us . . . look truth in the eye as well as we are able.

And, empowered by truth, let us become neighbors again in spite of our sins. That is the hope which forgiveness serves in human affairs.

References

Arendt, H. 1959. *The human condition: A study of the central conditions facing modern man.* New York: Doubleday.

Arendt, H. 1969. *On violence.* New York: Harcourt, Brace and World, Inc.

Bonhoeffer, D., 1955. *Ethics.* Trans. by E. Bethge. London: SCM Press, Ltd. (Originally published as *Ethik* [München: Chr. Kaiser Verlag, 1949]).

Davis, W. T. 1994. *Shattered dreams: America's search for its soul.* Valley Forge, Pa.: Trinity Press International.

Dower, J. W. 1986. *War without mercy: Race and power in the Pacific war.* New York: Pantheon Books.

Hartman, G., ed. 1986. *Bitburg in moral and political perspective.* Bloomington, Ind.: Indiana University Press.

Keegan, J. 1993. *A history of warfare.* New York: Knopf.

Muir, E. 1960. The wheel. *Collected poems.* London: Oxford University Press.

McPherson, James. *Battle cry of freedom.*

Niebuhr, Reinhold. 1935. *An interpretation of Christian ethics.* New York: Harper and Row.

Niebuhr, Reinhold. 1952. *The irony of American history.* New York: Charles Scribner's Sons.

Remarque, E. M. 1929–30. *All quiet on the western front.* (Eng. trans.). New York: Fawcett Crest.

Shriver, D. W., Jr. 1995. *An ethic for enemies: Forgiveness in politics.* New York: Oxford University Press.

Weber, M. 1958. Politics as a vocation. *Essays in sociology.* Trans. by H. H. Gerth and W. Mills. New York: Oxford University Press.

Weber, M. 1968. *Politik als Beruf* Berlin: Dunker and Humbolt.

12

Expanding Our Options: The Challenge of Forgiveness

Joseph W. Elder

Archbishop Desmond Tutu introduces this volume, *Exploring Forgiveness,* with the proposition: " . . . forgiveness is an absolute necessity for continued human existence" (p. xiii).

Each chapter in this book, directly or indirectly, raises questions about this proposition, the evidence on which it is based, and its implications. In this chapter I subsume, under three overarching queries, the many questions raised in this book: (1) What are the defining characteristics of forgiveness? (2) What are the consequences of forgiveness for individuals/clients? and (3) What are the consequences of forgiveness for collectivities (such as communities or nations)? After examining the rich variety of answers this book provides to these three queries, I raise some additional questions.

What Are the Defining Characteristics of Forgiveness?

Marietta Jaeger provides a dramatic illustration of forgiveness in her account of how she forgave the man who kidnapped and killed Susie, her seven-year-old daughter. In forgiving him, Jaeger drew on her belief, based in the Hebrew and Christian Scriptures, that God is a God of mercy and compassion, who works unceasingly to help and heal. She concluded that Susie's kidnapper and murderer "was a son of God, and, as such . . . he had dignity and worth . . ." (p. 12). When this man phoned her in the middle of the night to taunt her and Jaeger asked him what she could do to help him, he wept. In the end, after he was apprehended and convicted, he confessed to Susie's death. Drawing on the agony and relief of her own experience, Jaeger concludes: "I believe the only way we can be whole, healthy, happy persons is to learn to forgive" (p. 14). In propositional terms, Jaeger suggests that learning to forgive is a necessary condition for being a whole, healthy, happy person. Without learning to forgive, one cannot be a whole, healthy, happy person. This is a proposition for which data could be gathered.

Bob Enright, Suzanne Freedman, and Julio Rique, in their chapter, provide a detailed description of what interpersonal forgiveness is and what it is not. Interpersonal forgiveness is *not* accepting or tolerating injustice or ceasing to be angry about injustice; nor is it forgetting, condoning, or excusing wrongdoing; nor is it making oneself feel good, or granting a legal pardon, or achieving a reconciliation. Forgiveness must be separated from "pseudo-," or false, forgiveness, which is a ploy to exercise superiority over the one who has ostensibly been forgiven.

These authors define interpersonal forgiveness as "a willingness to abandon one's right to resentment, negative judgment, and indifferent behavior toward one who unjustly injures us, while fostering the unde-served qualities of compassion, generosity, and even love toward him or her" (pp. 46–47). This definition incorporates a number of assumptions. It assumes that people have a "right" to resentment, negative judgment, and indifferent behavior. Is this a psychological right, a moral right, or a legal right? This definition assumes there are "unjust" injuries (distinguish-able from "just" injuries). It assumes there are "undeserved" qualities of compassion, generosity, and even love (distinguishable from "deserved" qualities of compassion, generosity, and even love). These assumptions could be explored profitably through further philosophical and psycho-logical research.

Enright, Freedman, and Rique go on to identify a four-phase pathway that many victims follow when they forgive. In the first (uncovering) phase, the victim becomes aware of the emotional pain associated with the injury, with the sense of injustice, and (implicitly) with the desire for revenge. In the second (decision) phase, the victim gives up the idea of revenge and considers forgiving the offender. In the third (forgiving) phase, the victim works on the process of forgiving the offender. This requires the victim to "reframe" *cognitively* the offender's narrative, to identify *emotionally* with the offender, and to commit *morally* not to pass on the pain of her or his injury to the offender who caused that injury. Interestingly enough, these cognitive, emotional, and moral processes appear to be independent of the assumptions of rights and unjustness incorporated in this chapter's definition of interpersonal forgiveness. These authors assume that, if one rationally believes one's rights were violated, then proceeding with the four-phase process is appropriate. I will have more to say about one's perceptions and forgiveness later in the chapter.

According to Enright, Freedman, and Rique, in the fourth (outcome) phase, the victim finds meaning in the forgiveness process and experiences improved psychological health. The authors note the paradox that, "when we give to others the gift of mercy and compassion, we ourselves are healed" (p. 54). They also note that "a merciful reaching out to the offender is consistent with ancient Hebrew, Christian, Islamic, and Confucian texts" (p. 47). Later in this chapter I shall suggest that, for a variety of reasons, Hindu and Buddhist texts say less about "merciful reaching out to the offender" than Hebrew, Christian, Islamic, and Confucian texts do.

Enright and his colleagues define reconciliation as different from forgiveness: Forgiveness is an individual act, whereas reconciliation is an interactive process involving at least two people. They suggest that forgiveness (in some situations, offered separately by *both* individuals involved) may be a necessary condition for reconciliation between two people. Here we have another proposition for which data could be gathered.

Joanna North, in her chapter, provides a philosophical analysis of forgiveness and its related ideas. The discussion takes place within the sphere of interpersonal relations between an "injured party" (IP) and a "wrongdoer" (WD). She positions them in a shared moral community in which *both* the injured party *and* the wrongdoer agree that the wrongdoer has done something wrong. Then, through a series of cognitive, emotional, and volitional steps (implying a process that is both gradual and sequential), the injured party may reach a point where he or she is capable of expressing forgiveness to the wrongdoer. Most important in reaching this point is the process of "reframing," whereby the injured party, through trying to understand the wrongdoer's perspective and narrative, separates the wrongdoer from the "wrong" he or she has committed. Through a similar series of cognitive, emotional, and volitional steps, the wrongdoer may reach a point where he or she feels regret for his or her past "wrong" actions and wishes to be forgiven by the injured party. In the end, reconciliation between the injured party and the wrongdoer is possible (albeit not guaranteed). Once again, reconciliation is seen as an interactive process, not as an individual act.

Beverly Flanigan's chapter deals with forgiveness in terms of degrees, and she cautions us that there may be several levels of forgiving experienced with differing degrees of intensity. She draws on Michelle Nelson's three types of forgiveness: *detached forgiveness* (a reduction in negative affect toward the offender but no restoration of the relationship), *limited forgiveness* (a reduction in negative affect toward the offender along with partial restoration of and decreased emotional investment in the relationship), and *full forgiveness* (a total cessation of negative affect toward the offender along with full resotration and growth of the relationship). Flanigan reports that injured individuals in her sample of just over seventy made a distinction between "full forgiveness" and "complete forgiveness." They considered forgiveness *complete* when they (1) no longer harbored resentment against their offenders, (2) felt neutral toward their offenders, (3) once again experienced some degree of trust in their offenders, or (4) reconciled with their offenders, or when they experienced some combination of these four end-states. Only end-state 4 can be considered identical with full forgiveness. Flanigan proposes a possible relationship between the degree of damage an offender inflicts on an injured person's basic world assumptions and the degree to which the injured person is capable of forgiving the offender. Close examination of Flanigan's distinctions suggests that full forgiveness, as she defines it, coincides with reconciliation as defined, for example, by Enright, Freedman, and Rique. Limited forgiveness and most of the complete forgiveness possibilities are individual acts, whereas the final complete forgiveness possibility (involving reconciliation with the offender) and full forgiveness (full restoration and growth of the relationship with the offender) involve two people interacting with each other.

Flanigan urges intrafamily therapists to accept varying degrees of forgiveness as acceptable goals for their clients, and not to insist that their clients achieve full forgiveness. Inasmuch as full forgiveness, as she defines it, involves client-offender interaction, and inasmuch as the offender is usually not part of the therapy session, Flanigan's recommendation to intrafamily therapists may prove to be of great practical help to therapists.

In addition, Flanigan raises such interesting questions as: Do men and women forgive differently? Does socio-economic status influence forgiveness? Does forgiveness vary from culture to culture? She concludes with the comment, "If forgiving is truly a tool of peacemaking, . . . then it seems imperative that we understand its various forms, degrees, and subtleties" (p. 104). Here again, there are opportunities for future research and scholarship.

Keith Yandell identifies forgiveness as being fully successful when a victim's negative feeling (e.g., desire for revenge) toward her or his offender is completely gone, even if the consequences of the offender's actions continue to harm the victim. Yandell extends the definition of forgiveness by distinguishing it from retribution, rehabilitation, and "the desire for justice." Yandell notes that in the reframing process being carried out by the victim, increasing the *victim's* narrative, the victim's and the offender's *relational* narrative, and the *cosmic* narrative may be as important as increasing the *offender's* narrative in enabling the victim to forgive the offender (pp. 43–44). Here we are reminded that the highly complex nature of interpersonal relations requires us to develop and foster conceptions of forgiveness that are capable of doing these relations justice.

What Are the Consequences of Forgiveness for Individuals/Clients?

The psychiatrist Richard Fitzgibbons draws on over twenty years of clinical experience to write his chapter. He explains that the majority of mental health professionals have urged their patients to deal with any denied resentments or thoughts of revenge by expressing their anger. Fitzgibbons has tried another approach. He has urged his patients to deal with any denied resentments or thoughts of revenge by forgiving. Fitzgibbons has observed that many of his patients, by forgiving, have gained control over their anger and have resolved it in an appropriate manner. He describes how the process of forgiveness proceeds on three levels: cognitive (understanding the life struggles of the offender), emotional (developing empathy for the offender), and spiritual (relinquishing to God any remaining anger against the offender). Fitzgibbons' three levels of forgiveness and Enright and colleagues' three processes of forgiveness (cognitive, emotional, and moral) bear remarkable similarity to each other.

According to Fitzgibbons, "Forgiveness has remarkable healing power in the lives of those who utilize it. . . . [It] may be as important to the treatment of emotional and mental disorders as the discovery of sulfa drugs and penicillin have been to the treatment of infectious diseases" (p. 71). Supporting evidence can be found for Fitzgibbons' proposition regarding the remarkable healing power of forgiveness clinically in the lives of those who utilize it and empirically in the studies done by Enright and his colleagues.

The family systems therapist Paul Coleman defines forgiveness as the decision to offer love to someone who has betrayed that love. Forgiveness is not approval of that betrayal, nor does it ignore injustice or indignity. It does involve giving the betrayer a second chance (pp. 78–79). Phase 1 of forgiving requires that the injured person identify the hurt that has been done to her or him by the betrayer. In phase 2 the injured person confronts the betrayer. Phase 3 is a dialogue between the injured person and the betrayer in which reframing and understanding play useful parts. In phase 4 the injured person forgives the betrayer, taking a "giant leap of faith" that the betrayer will not betray again. And in phase 5 the injured person lets go of any remaining pain or resentment. This may sometimes be helped by the injured person attempting to make the suffering meaningful. According to Coleman, the attempt may generate pain, but the pain may be necessary as part of a process of experiencing a quality of one's life that one might otherwise not have known. "Forgiveness is more than a moral imperative, more than a theological dictum. It is the only means, given our humanness and imperfections, to overcome hate and condemnation and proceed with the business of growing and loving" (p. 94). Again we have a proposition for which further data could be gathered.

What Are the Consequences of Forgiveness for Collectivities (Such as Communities or Nations)?

Walter Dickey discusses the possibility of forgiveness in criminal justice. Accepting Robert Enright's definition of forgiveness, Dickey asserts that forgiveness plays a role in restorative justice (i.e., "the restoration to wholeness of those whose lives and relationships have been broken or deeply strained by a criminal offense" [p. 107]). Dickey maintains that restorative justice has much in common with forgiveness. "[Restorative justice] is not forgetting; it is not condoning or pardoning; it is not indifference or a diminishing of anger; it is not inconsistent with punishment; it does not wipe out the wrong or deny it" (p. 108). Indeed, restorative justice requires that an offender recognize the wrong he or she has committed and take responsibility for it.

One form of restorative justice involves victim-offender reconciliation meetings. In such meetings (held after careful staff planning and preparation), the victim and the offender exchange information relating to the facts of the offense and the consequences of the offense for the victim. The results of such meetings might include greater understanding on the part of both victim and offender for why the crime occurred, apology and/or restitution efforts by the offender, forgiveness by the victim, and even eventual rehabilitation of the offender. According to Dickey,

> Crime hurts victims, communities, and offenders. The primary goal of the [criminal justice] system ought to be to restore all three to a state of "wholeness," measured not by how much punishment was inflicted but by how much restoration was achieved. . . . To restore wholeness, the offender must accept responsibility for the harm and try to repair it. The community must provide an environment supportive of this reparation on the part of the offender as well as the healing process for the victim. (pp. 118–19)

Dickey's injunction raises an interesting question: How can a community provide the support environment needed for the victim to be healed?

Rev. David Couper, a former Madison police chief, in his response to Walter Dickey's chapter, broadens the concept of forgiveness beyond individuals to institutions, communities, and even nations: " . . . communities, societies, and governments can be wrongdoers by perpetuating racism, ageism, classism, or sexism. Nations . . . can be wrongdoers through the instruments of warfare and other foreign policies" (p. 123). Reflecting on his days as police chief, Couper says,

> We were too quick to deal with crime as behavior against the state and its set of laws. But crimes in a more important way are offenses against people. . . . It is amazing to me today that we did not pay attention to . . . the victim's need to hear and receive an apology for being wronged and the offender's need to apologize for his or her behavior. . . . The ability to give and ask for forgiveness is one of the unique things which make us human. (p. 126)

Couper holds that powerful governmental organizations, like police, make mistakes. When they make mistakes, they should apologize and seek forgiveness. According to Couper, the Judeo-Christian heritage is overwhelmingly about forgiveness. And, historically, a central purpose of forgiveness has been to benefit the nation in particular and humankind in general. Couper concludes: "The result of neglecting forgiveness, reconciliation, and restorative justice *in both our interpersonal and national lives* will be a nation and a people distant, divided, vengeful, and unforgiving" (p. 130; emphasis added). Couper suggests that individual and organizational acts of apology, forgiveness, and reconciliation may benefit the quality of life of an entire community. Here, too, is a proposition for which data could be gathered.

Donald Shriver, professor of Christian ethics in Union Theological Seminary, asks: Can forgiveness function in the ethics of international relations? Can formerly hostile nations ever achieve reconciliation?

The Hebrew Bible reserves forgiveness for God. The psalmist sang, "There is forgiveness with thee." When Jesus forgave people, his critics exclaimed, "Who can forgive sins but God alone?" During the next two millennia the word *forgiveness* became attached to the Christian sacrament of penance and acquired the connotations of an essentially private, personal, and nonpolitical transaction.

According to Shriver, the biblical tradition sees both forgiveness (by the victim) and repentance (by the offender) to be necessary for reconciliation. Forgiveness and repentance go through four stages to make reconciliation possible (p. 136). *Forgiveness* by the victim includes: (1) openly naming the wrong, (2) drawing back from revenge-in-kind, (3) developing empathy for the offender, and (4) extending to the offender a tentative hand toward renewed community still in the future. *Repentance* by the offender includes: (1) offering repentance for the wrong, (2) feeling gratitude that revenge-in-kind is not in the offing, (3) developing empathy for the victim's suffering, and (4) hoping for reconciliation with the victim. Shriver points out that, in the Lord's Prayer, "divine and human forgiveness are made reciprocal and interdependent" (p. 136). As we forgive, may we be forgiven.

Shriver moves the discussion of forgiveness and repentance from the individual level to the national level, drawing on an event that occurred in

1985. That year, U.S. president Ronald Reagan planned to visit Chancellor Helmut Kohl in Germany to mark the fortieth anniversary of the end of the war on the European front and to serve as a sign of post-World War II reconciliation between the United States and Germany. Shriver describes the storm of protest that followed President Reagan's announced plan, while on his visit to Germany, to lay a wreath on the graves of German soldiers in the town of Bitburg. Among the graves were those of forty-nine men who had been members of the notorious Nazi SS, which had played a major part in the Jewish Holocaust.

Nobel Peace Prize winner Elie Wiesel, a survivor of the Jewish Holocaust, denounced President Reagan. He was appalled that Reagan would show respect for members of the SS by placing a wreath in a cemetery containing their graves. This would be a moral outrage, a crossing of a line between relative evil and absolute evil, an abandonment of the victims of the SS.

In his visit to Germany, President Reagan did lay a wreath in the Bitburg cemetery and repeated his desire for reconciliation between the United States and Germany. But he stressed the fact that reconciliation and the establishment of mutual trust between the United States and Germany would never erase remembering—for one thing, the horrors of the Holocaust. Forgiving was not forgetting.

In any war, great wrongs are committed by all nations. Reconciliation between warring nations may have to begin by each nation acknowledging the evils for which it, as a nation, is responsible. According to Shriver,

> Citizens who have no personal share in guilt for the commission of dreadful political deeds have a responsibility for the past in the sense that they are responsible both for remembering it and for holding in check those current forces that threaten a repetition of it, or worse. Collective guilt across generations may be a morally dangerous idea, but collective responsibility across generations may be a morally necessary idea. (p. 141)

Following that observation, Shriver calls upon U.S. citizens to acknowledge the responsibility of their nation for evils of the slave trade, the annihilation of Native Americans, the bombing of Dresden, Hiroshima, and Nagasaki, and the abandoning of Vietnam veterans.

Some Further Questions

What if the injured party and/or the wrongdoer accepts a cosmology with no formal place for forgiveness? Most of the chapters in this book accept a world view based upon a philosophical tradition infused with a broadly Judeo-Christian-Muslim cosmology. This is a cosmology in which God punishes those who sin and forgives those who repent. In the Old Testament the children of Israel and their prophets repeatedly called upon Yahweh for forgiveness. Jesus asked his Heavenly Father to forgive his tormenters. Muslims pray for forgiveness to Allah, the all-forgiving. Within the Judeo-Christian-Muslim cosmology, divine punishment and forgiveness provide a context within which human repentance and human forgiveness acquire meaning.

Virtually every chapter in this book assumes a "victim" and a "wrong-doer" as two essential ingredients for forgiveness. The victim has been wronged, betrayed, unjustly injured, and so on. In most cases it is assumed that the victim desires revenge for the wrong that has been committed. Indeed, in several of the chapters one of the first steps toward forgiveness is the victim's abandonment of the desire for revenge. After that, it is easier to repent and to forgive.

To what extent are abandoning the desire for revenge, forgiving, and repenting universal patterns of human behavior, and to what extent are they patterns of behavior unique to Judeo-Christian-Muslim cosmology? The basic Buddhist and Hindu cosmology, shared by about one-fifth of the world's population, differs from the Judeo-Christian-Muslim cosmology in that it has no formal place for human repentance and divine forgiveness.

Central to the Buddhist-Hindu cosmology is the law of karma. According to the law of karma, every virtuous act is rewarded and every sinful act is punished in an inexorable manner similar to the laws of physics. The punishments and rewards might happen in this life or in subsequent lives, but they *will* happen. There is no process of repentance or forgiveness that can affect the inevitability of the punishments and rewards. It would be both wrong and unnecessary to seek revenge. Punishment will happen on its own. Justice will be done through the dynamics of the law of karma.

In the center of the Tibetan Buddhist "Wheel of Life" are pictured a pig, a rooster, and a snake. These are identified, respectively, as the "three poisons": ignorance, attachment, and hatred. Within the Buddhist cosmol-ogy, ignorance, attachment, and hatred are the central causes of suffering. They infect all sentient creatures everywhere and generate countless lives of misery. To overcome them, one must acquire wisdom and compassion.

Revenge, or a desire for revenge, would incorporate all three of the poisons: ignorance, attachment, and hatred. According to these Buddhist teachings, one should not feel attachment to self (the injured sentient being) any more than one should feel attachment to all sentient beings (all of whom experience injury). One should not feel hatred toward the "wrongdoer" any more than one should feel hatred toward all wrongdoers (including oneself). And one should not be ignorant of the knowledge that, through the dynamics of the law of karma, the wrongdoer will inevitably be fully and fairly punished. There is no place for revenge, or a desire for revenge, within this cosmology.

Conversely, neither is there a place for forgiveness. The thought that one person can "forgive" another reflects ignorance. In instances of wrongdoing, one should recognize that the wrongdoing is a result of the wrongdoer's three poisons. One should strive to remove the three poisons of the wrongdoer, and of all wrongdoers (including oneself), through acquiring wisdom. And at all times one should feel compassion for the wrongdoer, as one should feel compassion for all sentient beings.

Although Buddhist and Hindu cosmologies may have no formal place for forgiveness, a Buddhist or a Hindu attempting to end ignorance, attachment, and hatred may engage in conceptual processes that differ in only minor ways from the reframing conceptual processes described in this book, for example, by Enright, Freedman, and Rique. The Dalai Lama, one of the world's most distinguished Buddhists, has supported the study of forgiveness, perhaps in part because of the close parallels he recognizes between the reframing dynamics endorsed by Judaism, Christianity, and Islam and the dynamics of acquiring wisdom and overcoming ignorance, attachment, and hatred endorsed by Buddhism.

What if the injured party and the wrongdoer do not share the same moral community? The examples of wrongdoing discussed in this book seem "wrong" by any definition: kidnapping, murder, physical abuse, marital infidelity, and so on. The injured party and the wrongdoer agree that a wrong was done and that the wrongdoer did it. To that extent they share a "moral community." Virtually every chapter in this book assumes such a moral community. But what if the injured party and the wrongdoer do *not* share the same moral community? What if the wrongdoer insists that within her or his moral community what she or he did *was not wrong?* How does the process of forgiveness proceed?

Consider one example involving a nuclear-missile protester and a law-enforcement officer. The protester trespasses on government property and attempts to damage a missile silo, the law enforcement officer arrests the protester and presses charges against him or her that result in imprisonment and a heavy financial fine.

In this instance, what dynamics occur if the protester "forgives" the officer? Any forgiving carries with it an explicit or implicit accusation of wrongdoing, since forgiveness is granted by victims to their wrongdoers. In this instance, the protester, in forgiving the law enforcement officer, would simultaneously be stigmatizing the officer as a "wrongdoer." The officer might well feel that being forgiven by the protester is gratuitous, undeserved, and unacceptable, inasmuch as the law enforcement officer did nothing wrong and was *not* a wrongdoer. When the victim and the wrongdoer do not share the same moral community, forgiveness may be an empty, and indeed offensive, gesture.

Consider another example: the North and the South in the U.S. Civil War. What if, during the U.S. Civil War, Northerners felt they needed to invade the South in order to preserve the Union, and Southerners felt they needed to drive the Northerners out of the South in order to preserve states' rights? How could either side forgive the other or seek forgiveness from the other if neither side felt it engaged in wrongdoing? Once again, in the absence of a shared moral community, forgiveness may be an empty gesture.

When violent conflicts continue between two parties over any length of time, who the injured party is and who the wrongdoer is typically become thoroughly intertwined. Revenge counters revenge. Atrocities are met by counter atrocities. Before long each side can, with accuracy, recite a litany of wrongs the other side has perpetrated against it. And each side can demand apologies and indemnities from the other side before talking of any peace settlement. At a certain point, if there is to be any move toward a peace settlement, each side must put the past behind it. If forgiveness (because of its stigmatization of the "wrongdoer") will not put the past behind, then some process of recognizing the pain, suffering, and loss both sides have experienced may be called for, as well as each side's acknowledgment of its contribution to the other side's pain, suffering, and loss. This process of recognition may have been one of the contributing factors to the historical handshake between Israel's prime minister Yitzhak Rabin and the PLO chairman Yasir Arafat on September 13, 1993, after decades of hatred and violence between Israelis and Palestinians.

Current efforts to define universal human rights, identify and punish "war crimes," and so on, may reflect a move toward an international moral community in which one can speak of wrongdoers, repentance, and forgiveness. But at present the existence of an international moral community is still in the future.

What if the dynamics of collective decision making are so complex that it is virtually impossible to identify who in a collective is responsible for (and hence should be forgiven for) some wrong inflicted on a victim? In Shriver's account of the passions aroused by Ronald Reagan's cemetery announcement, virtually everyone agreed that the Holocaust was an enormous evil. But who were the wrongdoers responsible for the evil? all Germans? the German "high command"? all Germans in uniform? only Germans in SS uniforms?

Similarly, generations of settlers in the United States as well as their government in Washington, D.C., pursued policies of harassment, relocation, and genocide of Native Americans. There is widespread agreement that what was done to the Native Americans was wrong. But who were the wrongdoers? the president? the Congress? the Bureau of Indian Affairs? the settlers? the military? all of them? a few specific persons among them?

In a national collectivity that has done wrong, how can the wrong-doer be identified? Without identifying the wrongdoer, how (and whom) can one forgive? In the war crime trials after World War II, a Japanese general was executed for atrocities his troops had committed without his knowledge. German military personnel were condemned to long terms of imprisonment for obeying orders from superiors they had pledged to obey. Where collectivities are involved in wrongdoing, the issue of respon-sibility can become quite tangled. "Facts" can be interpreted differently by different people. And mistakes in assigning moral responsibility can be made (and often are). This should not lead us to abandon efforts to create an international moral community. But we should remain aware of how difficult creating such a moral community will be and just how crucial sympathetic dialogue is to its development.

Where collectivities are involved, the issue of forgiveness becomes much more complicated than in the one-to-one model of an injured person and a wrongdoer sharing a moral community. The increased complexity of the situation need not lead us to abandon efforts to encourage "forgive-ness" or the attitudes that accompany forgiveness. If, ultimately, one is in-terested in processes of reconciliation, the study of forgiveness as a potential contributor to reconciliation becomes of prime importance. There is ample evidence in this book and elsewhere that, in certain contexts, forgiveness is a crucial component of reconciliation. In the final analysis it may be that attitudes defined in this book as accompanying forgiveness—attitudes expressed also in religions such as Buddhism and Hinduism: abandoning the desire for revenge, reframing participants' narratives, and refusing to pass on one's pain to others—may be as important as forgiveness itself in achieving peace and/or reconciliation.

The increased moral complexity of collective behavior *does* call for an awareness of the limits of our own perceptions. It calls for an acknowledg-ment that our perceptions might be inaccurate. It calls for recognition of our own frequent involvement in wrongdoing since we are part of collectives that engage in wrongdoing. It calls for wisdom and compassion.

None of the problems I have identified here seriously challenges Desmund Tutu's introductory proposition: "Forgiveness is an absolute necessity for continued human existence." If anything, the difficulties serve to supplement his proposition and extend its applicability worldwide. What this book achieves as a whole is that it provides us with a first, stimulating attempt to appreciate fully the complexity and richness of the notion of forgiveness.

Bibliography
Index

COMPREHENSIVE BIBLIOGRAPHY
ON INTERPERSONAL FORGIVENESS

Robert D. Enright

This bibliography represents my imperfect attempt to amass the writings on interpersonal forgiveness that have been published or that have appeared as doctoral dissertations. I focused primarily on those works that make forgiveness the central theme, although when a work gives some thought to the topic, I tried to include it as well. Those works emphasizing person-to-person forgiveness are the primary focus. I inadvertently may have eliminated some works that center on divine-to-human forgiveness and then discuss person-to-person forgiveness as a secondary issue. I most certainly missed some large works in which interpersonal forgiveness is given a small place.

Not appearing here are early works (prior to 1980) that discuss such tangential (to our purposes) themes as trust and guilt. Most works in languages other than English are not here, but I hope that those with a facility in other languages will furnish bibliographies in the future. Papers presented at conferences also do not appear here.

My apologies in advance to those scholars whose works I omitted because of my own need to delve further into the topic. I am open to correction and feedback so that the next bibliography will be more complete.

Adams, J. E. 1989. *From forgiven to forgiving*. Wheaton, Ill.: Victor Books.
Aden, L. 1988. Forgiveness and fulfillment in pastoral counseling. In *The church and pastoral care,* ed. L. Aden and J. J. Ellens, Grand Rapids, Mich.: Baker Books.
Alexander, J. F. 1980. A feeling of passionate mercy: You don't have to keep the rules but you do have to take care of the kids. *The Other Side* 107: 8–11.
Allender, D. B., and T. Longman. 1992. *Bold love*. Colorado Springs, Colo.: Navpress.
Al-Mabuk, R. H. 1990. The commitment to forgive in parentally love-deprived college students. Doctoral dissertation, University of Wisconsin–Madison. *Dissertation Abstracts International—A,* 51(10), 1991, p. 3361.
Al-Mabuk, R. H., and W. R. Downs, 1996. Forgiveness therapy with parents of adolescent suicide victims. *Journal of Family Psychotherapy* 7(2): 21–39.

Amanecida Collective. 1987. *Revolutionary forgiveness: Feminist reflections on Nicaragua.* Maryknoll, N.Y.: Orbis Books.

Arendt, H. 1958. *The human condition.* Chicago: University of Chicago Press.

Arnodei, M. 1996. *Decide to forgive.* Notre Dame, Ind.: Ave Maria Press.

Atkinson, D. 1982a. Forgiveness and personality development. *Third Way* 5(11): 18–21.

Atkinson, D. 1982b. The importance of forgiveness. *Third Way* 5(10): 4–7.

Augsburger, D. 1970. *The freedom to forgive.* Chicago: Moody Press.

Augsburger, D. 1981a. *Caring enough to forgive: True forgiveness.* Chicago: Moody Press.

Augsburger, D. 1981b. *Caring enough to not forgive.* Ventura, Calif.: Regal Books.

Aune, M. B. 1984. A Lutheran understanding and experience of repentance and forgiveness. *New Catholic World* 227: 33–36.

Baker, D. 1984a. *Beyond forgiveness: The healing touch of church discipline.* Portland, Oreg.: Multnomah Press.

Baker, D. 1984b. Beyond forgiveness: The healing touch of church discipline. *Leadership* 5(3): 96–97.

Bandler, E., and J. Grinder. 1979. *Frogs into princes: Neurolinguistic programming.* Moab, Utah: Real People Press.

Bangley, B. 1986. *Forgivng yourself.* Wheaton, Ill.: Harold Shaw.

Bass, E., and L. Davis. 1988. *The courage to heal: A guide for women survivors of child sexual abuse,* pp. 150–154. New York: Harper and Row.

Bauer, L., J. Duffy, E. Fountain, S. Halling, M. Holzer, E. Jones, M. Leifer, and J. O. Rowe. 1992. Exploring self-forgiveness. *Journal of Religion and Health* 31(2): 149–160.

Baures, M. M. 1996. Letting go of bitterness and hate. *Journal of Humanistic Psychology* 36(1): 75–91.

Beahm, W. M. 1955. *The cross and God's forgiveness.* Elgin, Ill.: Church of the Brethren.

Beals, I. A. 1987. *What it means to forgive.* Kansas City, Mo.: Beacon Hill Press.

Beatty, J. 1970. Forgiveness. *American Philosophical Quarterly* 7: 246–252.

Beck, J. R. 1995. When to forgive. *Journal of Psychology and Christianity* 14: 269–273.

Beck, T. V. 1988. Forgiving. In *Daughters of the elderly: Building partnerships in caregiving,* ed. J. Norris. Bloomington, Ind.: Indiana University Press.

Benson, C. K. 1992. Forgiveness and the psychotherapeutic process. *Journal of Psychology and Christianity* 11(1): 76–81.

Bent, R. F. 1990. *Forgiving your parents.* New York: Warner Books.

Bergan, J. J., and S. M. Schwan. 1985. *Forgiveness: A guide for prayer.* Winona, Minn.: Saint Mary's Press.

Bergin, A. E. 1980. Psychotherapy and religious values. *Journal of Consulting and Clinical Psychology* 48(1): 95–105.

Bergin, A. E. 1988. Three contributions of a spiritual perspective to counseling, psychotherapy, and behavior change. *Counseling & Values* 33: 21–31.

Bernardin, J. 1995. A story of reconciliation. *Origins: CNS documentary service* 24(31): 513–515.

Bishop, J., and M. Grunte. 1993. *How to forgive when you don't know how.* Barrytown, N.Y.: Station Hill Press.

Bloomfield, H. H., and L. Felder. 1983. *Making peace with your parents*. New York: Ballantine Books.

Boersma, F. J. 1989. Gifts from the unconscious: Spiritual healing and forgiveness within a family. *Medical Hypnoanalysis Journal* 4(1): 6–10.

Bonar, C. 1989. Personality theories and asking forgiveness. *Journal of Psychology and Christianity* 8(1): 45–51.

Boobyer, G. H. 1954. Mark II, 10a and the interpretation of the healing of the paralytic. *Harvard Theological Review* 47: 115–120.

Borysenko, J. 1977. *Guilt is the teacher, love is the lesson: A book to heal you, heart and soul*. New York: Warner Books.

Bosk, C. L. 1979. *Forgive and remember: Managing medical failure*. Chicago: University of Chicago Press.

Boyer, M. G. 1994. Do Catholics forgive as they have been forgiven? *U.S. Catholic* (Sept.): 6–15.

Bradshaw, J. 1992. Forgiveness. *Homecoming: Reclaiming and championing your inner child*, pp. 170–172. New York: Bantam Books.

Brakenhielm, C. R. 1993. *Forgiveness*. Trans. T. Hall. Minneapolis: Augsburg Fortress.

Brandsma, J. M. 1982. Forgiveness: A dynamic, theological and theoretical analysis. *Pastoral Psychology* 3(1): 40–50.

Brandsma, J. M. 1985. Forgiveness. In *Baker's Encyclopedia of Psychology*, ed. G. D. Benner. Grand Rapids, Mich.: Baker Books.

Branscomb, H. 1934. Mark 2:5, "Son thy sins are forgiven." *Journal of Biblical Literature* 53: 53–60.

Brasch, R. 1996. *A book of forgiveness*. New York: Harper Collins World.

Brien, A. 1989. Can God forgive us our trespasses? *Sophia* 28: 35–42.

Brink, R. L. 1985. The role of religion in later life: A case of consolation and forgiveness. *Journal of Psychology and Christianity* 4(2): 22–25.

Bristol, G., and C. McGinnis. 1982. *When it's hard to forgive*. Wheaton, Ill.: Victor Books.

Bryant, D. 1987. Forgiveness: Learning forgiveness as a way of life. *World Christian* 6. 40–42.

Bucello, G. L. 1991. Family of origin and personality characteristics as predictive of a high capacity for forgiveness in ongoing relationships. Doctoral dissertation, United States International University, San Diego. 1991. *Dissertation Abstracts International—B*, 52(09), p. 4968.

Bürkle, H. 1989. Guilt and its resolution outside of the Christian tradition. *Communio* 6: 172–196.

Burquest, D. A. 1982. A celebration feast of forgiveness: Confession is the first step in establishing a new beginning in our fellowship with God. *Christian Today* 26: 24–25.

Buscaglia, L. 1984. *Loving each other: The challenge of human relationships*. New York: Holt, Rinehart and Winston.

Calian, C. S. 1981. Christian faith as forgiveness. *Theology Today* 37: 439–443.

Callahan, J. 1993. Forgiving the unforgivable. *New Age Journal* (Sept.-Oct.): 76–81,141.

Campbell, J. M. 1996. *The nature of atonement*. Grand Rapids, Mich.: William B. Eerdmans.

Canale, J. R. 1990. Altruism and forgiveness as therapeutic agents in psychotherapy. *Journal of Religion and Health* 29: 297–301.

Caplan, B. 1992. Forgiving the loss of a parent in childhood: Three case studies. Doctoral dissertation, Harvard University, Cambridge, Mass. *Dissertation Abstracts International—B*, 53(09), 1993, p. 4993.

Caro, C. 1972. On mercy. *Philosophical Review* 81: 182–207.

Carter, K. S. 1977. Forgiveness revisited: God's and ours. *Brethren Life and Thought* 22: 199–209.

Casarjian, R. 1992. *Forgiveness: A bold choice for a peaceful heart.* New York: Bantam Books.

Caserta, T. G. 1993. *Beyond the darkness into the light: Thinking about sin and forgiveness today.* Boston: St. Paul Books and Media.

Cavanaugh, C. 1986. *Love and forgiveness in Yeats' poetry.* Ann Arbor, Mich.: UMI Research Press.

Cechinato, L. 1983. *Reconcilia: -vos: Reflexões sobre o sacramento do perdaõ.* Petrópolis, Brazil: Editora Vozes.

Childs, B. H. 1981. Forgiveness in community in light of Pauline literature and the experience among pre-school children. Doctoral dissertation, Princeton Theological Seminary. *Dissertation Abstracts International—A,* 42(04), p. 1683.

Chödrön, P. 1994. *Start where you are: A guide to compassionate living.* Boston: Shambhala.

Clarke, J. F. 1867. *The Christian doctrine of forgiveness of sin.* Boston: American Unitarian Association.

Cloke, K. 1993. Revenge, forgiveness, and the magic of mediation. Special issue: Beyond technique: The soul of family mediation. *Mediation Quarterly* 11(1): 67–78.

Close, H. T. 1970. Forgiveness and responsibility: A case study. *Pastoral Psychology* 21: 19–25.

Cobb, W. F. 1913. Forgiveness. In *Encyclopedia of religion and ethics,* Vol. 6, ed. Geoffrey W. Bromiley. Edinburgh: T. & T. Clark.

Cochran, L. 1996. *Forgiven and set free: A post-abortion Bible study for women.* Grand Rapids, Mich.: Baker Books.

Coleman, P. W. 1989. *The forgiving marriage: Resolving anger and resentment and rediscovering each other.* Chicago: Contemporary Books.

Compaan, A. 1985. Anger, denial and the healing of memories. *Journal of Psychology and Christianity* 4(2): 83–85.

Cook, J., and S. C. Baldwin. 1979. *Love, acceptance and forgiveness.* Ventura, Calif.: Regal Books.

Copeland, K. 1987. A time to remember . . . a time to forget. *Believer's Voice of Victory* 15(2): 2–5. (Kenneth Copeland Ministries).

Cornwall, J. 1978. *Let us enjoy forgiveness.* Old Tappan, N.J.: Revell.

Cotroneo, M. 1982. The role of forgiveness in family therapy. In *Questions and answers in the practice of family therapy,* ed. A. Gurman, pp. 241–244. 2d ed. New York: Brunner/Mazel.

Coyle, C. 1995. The moral development of forgiveness among post-abortion men. Unpublished doctoral dissertation, University of Wisconsin–Madison.

Cummins, M. 1831. *A sermon on confession and forgiveness of sins: Preached in the Roman Catholic Church of Utica.* Utica, N.Y.: E. A. Maynard Printing.

Cunningham, B. B. 1985. The will to forgive: A pastoral theological view of forgiving. *Journal of Pastoral Care* 39(2): 141–149.

Curtis, N. C. 1989. The structure and dynamics of forgiving another. Doctoral dissertation, United States International University, San Diego. *Dissertation Abstracts International—B,* 50(03), p. 1152.

Darby, B. W., and B. R. Schlenker. 1982. Children's reactions to apologies. *Journal of Personality and Social Psychology* 43(4): 742–753.

Daube, D. 1960. *Sin, ignorance, and forgiveness.* Claude Montefiore Lecture. London: Liberal Jewish Synagogue.

Davidson, D. L. 1993. Forgiveness and narcissism: Consistency in experience across real and hypothetical hurt situations. Doctoral dissertation, Georgia State University, Atlanta. *Dissertation Abstracts International—B,* 54(05), p. 2746.

Davies, W. W. 1920. The law of forgiveness. *Methodist Review* 103: 807–813.

Davis, R. L. 1984. *A forgiving God in an unforgiving world.* Eugene, Oreg.: Harvest House.

Dayton, T. 1992. *Daily affirmation for forgiving and moving on.* Deerfield Beach, Fla.: Health Communications.

Dealing with religious issues in counseling and psychotherapy: A symposium. 1979. *Journal of Religion and Health* 18(3): 176–201.

de Cantanzaro, C. J. 1962. Forgiveness in the Old Testament. *American Church Quarterly* 2: 26–39.

De Jong, P. 1951. Divine and human forgiveness: An investigation into the biblical data about God's and man's forgiveness and the relation between them, followed by a comparison of the biblical data and some of the systematic and ethical approaches to the problem. Doctoral dissertation, Union Theological Seminary, New York. *Dissertation Abstracts International—A,* 49(01), 1988, p. 103.

Denison, N. 1992. To live and forgive. *On Wisconsin* (Nov.–Dec.): 22–23, 44.

DiBlasio, F. A. 1992. Forgiveness in psychotherapy: Comparison of older and younger therapists. *Journal of Psychology and Christianity* 11(2): 181–187.

DiBlasio, F. A. 1993. The role of social workers' religious beliefs in helping family members forgive. *Journal of Contemporary Human Services* 74: 163–170.

DiBlasio, F. A., and B. B. Benda. 1991. Practitioners, religion and the clinical use of forgiveness. *Journal of Psychology and Christianity* 10: 168–172.

DiBlasio, F. A., and J. H. Proctor. 1993. Therapists and the clinical use of forgiveness. *American Journal of Family Therapy* 21: 175–184.

Dickinson, H. 1986. Bound or free? *Theology* 89(728): 102–108.

Dobel, J. P. 1980. The Vietnam War: Is it time to forgive and forget? Three views. *Worldview* 23: 13–16.

Dodge, J. W. 1870. *The true foundation.* Boston: William White.

Domeris, W. R. 1986. Biblical perspectives on forgiveness. *Journal of Theology for Southern Africa* 54: 48–50.

Donnelly, D. 1979. *Learning to forgive.* New York: Macmillan.

Donnelly, D. 1980. Learning to forgive. *Theology Today* 37: 388–390.

Donnelly, D. 1982. *Putting forgiveness into practice.* Allen, Tex.: Argus Communications.

Donnelly, D. 1983. Fall and rise of confession. *Christianity and Crisis* 43: 312–314.

Donnelly, D. 1984a. Forgiveness and recidivism. *Pastoral Psychology* 33(1): 15–24.

Donnelly, D. 1984b. The human side of forgiveness and what it tells us about how God forgives. *New Catholic World* 227:28–30.

Donnelly, D. 1991. The benefits of forgiving. (Interview by Art Winter). *Praying* 41: 22–28.

Dooley, K. 1984. Reconciliation in the early Church: Lessons from history. *New Catholic World* 227: 16–21.

Downie, R. S. 1965. Forgiveness. *Philosophical Quarterly* 15: 128–134.

Downie, R. S. 1971. *Roles and values: An introduction to social ethics*. London: Methuen.

Dreelin, E. D. 1994. Religious functioning and forgiveness. Doctoral dissertation, Fuller Theological Seminary, Pasadena, Calif. *Dissertation Abstracts International—A*, 55(06), p. 2397.

Droll, D. M. 1984. Forgiveness: Theory and research. Doctoral dissertation, University of Nevada-Reno. *Dissertation Abstracts International—B*, 45(08), 1985, p. 2732.

Eastin, D. L. 1988. The treatment of female incest survivors by psychological forgiveness processes. Unpublished doctoral dissertation, University of Wisconsin–Madison.

Editors, *U. S. Catholic*. 1990. How to forgive when it seems impossible: An interview with Lewis B. Smedes. *U.S. Catholic* 55(11): 7–13.

Educational Psychology Study Group. 1990. Must a Christian require repentance before forgiving? *Journal of Psychology and Christianity* 9: 16–19.

Ellis, G. E. No date [1800s]. *Repentance: The condition of forgiveness*. Boston: Crosby, Nichols. Printed for the American Unitarian Association.

Elwin, V. 1962. *A philosophy of love*. Faridabad, India: (Delhi) Publications Division, Ministry of Information and Broadcasting.

Emerson, J. G. 1964. *The dynamics of forgiveness*. Philadelphia: Westminster.

Engel, B. 1989. *The right to innocence—healing the trauma of childhood sexual abuse*. Los Angeles: Jeremy P. Tarcher, Inc.

Enright, R. D. 1996. I forgive you. *McCall's*, Dec., pp. 82, 85, 87.

Enright, R. D., and the Human Development Study Group. 1991. The moral development of forgiveness. In *Handbook of moral behavior and development*, vol. 1, ed. W. Kurtines and J. Gerwirtz, pp. 123–152. Hillsdale, N.J.: Erlbaum.

Enright, R. D., and the Human Development Study Group. 1994. Piaget on the moral development of forgiveness: Reciprocity or identity? *Human Development* 37: 63–80.

Enright, R. D., and the Human Development Study Group. 1996. Counseling within the forgiveness triad: On forgiving, receiving forgiveness, and self-forgiveness. *Counseling and Values* 40: 107–126.

Enright, R. D., and G. L. Reed. 1995. *Forgiveness as a first step in the reduction of racism and violence*. Proceedings of the UNESCO Conference on Racism and Violence, Austria, June.

Enright, R. D., and R. Zell. 1989. Problems encountered when we forgive one another. *Journal of Psychology and Christianity* 8(1): 52–60.

Enright, R. D., E. A. Gassin, and C. Wu. 1992. Forgiveness: A developmental view. *Journal of Moral Education* 21(2): 99–114.

Enright, R. D., M. J. O. Santos, and R. H. Al-Mabuk. 1989. The adolescent as forgiver. *Journal of Adolescence* 12:95–110.

Enright, R. D., E. A. Gassin, T. Longinovic, and D. Loudon. 1995. Forgiveness as a solution to social crisis. In *Morality and social crisis,* ed. S. Krnjajic. Belgrade, Serbia: Belgrade Institute for Pedagogic Research.

Enright, R. D., I. Sarinopoulos, R. H. Al-Mabuk, and S. Freedman. 1992. The moral development approach: Justice and forgiveness. In *Psychological interventions,* ed. R. C. D'Amato and B. A. Rothlisberg. New York: Longman.

Enright, R. D., D. L. Eastin, S. Golden, I. Sarinopoulos, and S. Freedman. 1992. Interpersonal forgiveness within the helping professions: An attempt to resolve differences of opinion. *Counseling and Values* 36: 84–103.

Estés, C. P. 1992. Marking territory: The boundaries of rage and forgiveness. *Women who run with the wolves: Myths and stories of the wild woman archetype,* pp. 347–501. New York: Ballantine Books.

Evans, C. T. 1985. *Start loving, keep loving: The miracle of forgiveness.* Garden City, N.Y.: Doubleday.

Everett, W. H. 1995. Free to forgive. *Alive Now* 25(4): 48–51.

Farrell, W. 1949. No place for rain. *Thomist* 12: 397–424.

Feather, N. T. 1986. Value systems across cultures: Australia and China. *International Journal of Psychology* 21: 697–715.

Ferch, S. R. 1995. The experience of touch in love relationships: An interpretation of its significance in forgiveness. Unpublished doctoral dissertation, University of Alberta, Edmonton.

Ferrini, P. 1991. *The twelve steps of forgiveness: Essential reading for students of a course in miracles.* Brattleboro, Vt.: Heartways Press.

Fittipaldi, S. E. 1982. Zen-mind, Christian-mind, empty-mind. *Journal of Ecumenical Studies* 19(1): 69–84.

Fitzgibbons, R. P. 1986. The cognitive and emotional uses of forgiveness in the treatment of anger. *Psychotherapy* 23(4): 629–633.

Flanigan, B. 1987. Shame and forgiving in alcoholism. *Alcoholism Treatment Quarterly* 4(2): 181–195.

Flanigan, B. 1992a. *Forgiving the unforgivable.* New York: Macmillan.

Flanigan, B. 1992b. War crimes of the heart. *Psychology Today* 25(5): 36–39, 78–79, 90–92.

Flanigan, B. 1996. *Forgiving yourself.* New York: Macmillan.

Fleming, T. 1988. The healing power of forgiveness. *Reader's Digest,* June, pp. 100–102.

Floristan, C., and C. Duquoc, eds. 1986. Forgiveness. *Concilium* (Special Issue, Apr.) (Edinburgh: T. & T. Clark).

Forest, J. 1979. Mercy, mercy: Why I struggle to let the mercy of God make me a merciful person. *The Other Side* 150: 28–29.

Forgiveness. 1987. *Parabola* (Special issue). 12(3).

Forgiveness. 1992. *Weavings, a Journal of the Christian Spiritual Life* (Special issue). 7(2).

Forgiveness and its power to heal. 1993. *Christian Science Sentinel* (Special issue). 95(18).

Fow, N. R. 1988. An empirical-phenomenological investigation of the experience of forgiving another. Doctoral dissertation, University of Pittsburgh. *Dissertation Abstracts International—B,* 50(03), 1989, p. 1097.

Fow, N. R. 1996. The phenomenology of forgiveness and reconciliation. *Journal of Phenomenological Psychology* 27(2): 219–233.

Foward, S. 1989. *Toxic parents.* New York: Bantam Books.

Freedman, S. R. 1995. Forgiveness as an educational intervention goal with incest survivors. Doctoral dissertation, University of Wisconsin–Madison. *Dissertation Abstracts International—B,* 55(07), 1995, p. 3034.

Freedman, S. R., and R. D. Enright. 1996. Forgiveness as an intervention goal with incest survivors. *Journal of Consulting and Clinical Psychology* 64: 983–992.

Freiburg, C. 1958. The forgiving king. *The Expository Times* 69: 120–121.

Fuchs, L. 1990. *Forgiveness: God's gift of love.* New York: Alba House.

Galloway, P. 1992. Forgive, not forget. *Chicago Tribune,* Sept. 30, pp. 1–2.

Gardner, E. P. 1873. The sinfulness of the heart before God. *The Cleveland Pulpit* 1(15): 169–177.

Gartner, J. 1988. The capacity to forgive: An object relations perspective. *Journal of Religion and Health* 27(4): 313–320.

Gassin, E. A. 1995. Social cognition and forgiveness in the context of adolescent romance: An intervention study. Doctoral dissertation, University of Wisconsin–Madison. *Dissertation Abstracts International—A,* 56(04), 1995, p. 1290.

Gassin, E. A., and R. D. Enright. 1995. The will to meaning in the process of forgiveness. *Journal of Psychology and Christianity* 14(1): 38–49.

Gayton, R. R. 1995. *The forgiving place.* Waco, Tex.: WRS Publishing.

Gentilone, F., and J. R. Regidor. 1986. The political dimension of reconciliation: A recent Italian experience. In Forgiveness, ed. C. Floristan and C. Duquoc, pp. 22–31. *Concilium* (Special issue, Apr.) (Edinburgh: T. & T. Clark).

Gerber, L. A. 1987. Experiences of forgiveness in physicians whose medical treatment was not successful. *Psychological Reports* 61: 236.

Gerber, L. A. 1988. A piece of my mind. *Journal of the American Medical Association* 259 (Apr. 22–29): 2461.

Gerber, L. A. 1990. Transformations in self understanding in surgeons whose treatment efforts were not successful. *American Journal of Psychotherapy* 44: 75–84.

Getting over. 1993. *The New Yorker,* Apr. 5, pp. 4, 6.

Gingell, J. 1974. Forgiveness and power. *Analysis* 34: 180–183.

Gladson, J. A. 1992. Higher than the heavens: Forgiveness in the Old Testament. *Journal of Psychology and Christianity* 11: 125–135.

Glende, N. H. 1993. *Forgiving is the only real solution to violence.* Cleveland, Ohio: Noelani Publishing.

Glenn, J. 1974. Kierkegaard's ethical philosophy. *Southwestern Journal of Philosophy* 5: 121–127.

Godfrey, H. C. 1992. The evolution of forgiveness. *Nature* 355(6357, Jan.): 206–207.

Goins, S. L. 1987. The concept of forgiveness as reflected in the writings of Albert Ellis and Jay Adams. Master's thesis, University of West Florida, Pensacola. *Masters Abstracts International* 26(03), 1988, p. 291.

Golding, M. P. 1984. Forgiveness and regret. *The Philosophical Forum* 16(1): 121–137.

Good, D. 1983. Abraham Lincoln: Paradigm of forgiveness. *Fides et Historia* 15(2): 28–43.

Gorsuch, R. L., and J. Y. Hao. 1993. Forgiveness: An exploratory factor analysis and its relationships to religious variables. *Review of Religious Research* 34: 333–347.

Govier, G. 1995. Choosing forgiveness opens "deep well of power." *The Capital Times* (Madison, Wis.), Apr. 22–23, p. 12A.

Grace and forgiveness. 1992. *Journal of Psychology and Christianity* (Special issue). 11(2).

Graham, K. H. 1994. Forgiveness: A personal and pastoral imperative. Doctoral dissertation, Fuller Theological Seminary, Pasadena, Calif. *Dissertation Abstracts International—A,* 55(04), 1994, p. 991.

Graham, W. A. 1982. Transcendence in Islam. In *Ways of transcendence,* ed. E. Dowdy. Bedford Park, South Australia: Australian Association for the Study of Religion.

Greenberg, S. 1978. Some reflections on God's forbearance, forgiveness, and related concepts. In *Perspectives on Jews and Judaism: Essays in honor of Wolfe Kelman,* ed. A. A. Chief. New York: Rabbinical Assembly.

Grudem, W. 1980. Forgiveness: Forever and today. *HIS,* Feb. 15–16.

Guest, J. L. 1988. *Forgiving your parents.* Downers Grove, Ill: InterVarsity Press.

Gunnell, R. A. 1977. *Adventures in successful thinking,* pp. 118–129. Lakemont, Ga.: CSA Printing and Binding.

Guzie, T. W. 1979. *The forgiveness of sin.* Chicago: Thomas More.

Haber, J. 1991. *Forgiveness.* Savage, Md.: Rowman and Littlefield.

Halifax, S. 1846. *The works of the Right Reverend Father in God, Joseph Butler, D.C.L., late Lord Bishop of Durham.* New York: Robert Carter.

Halling, S. 1979. Eugene O'Neill's understanding of forgiveness. In *Duquesne studies in phenomonological psychology,* Vol. 3, ed. A. Giorgi, R. Knowles, and D. L. Smith, pp. 193–208. Pittsburgh: Duquesne University Press.

Halling, S. 1994. Shame and forgiveness. *Humanistic Psychologist* 22(1): 74–87.

Halling, S. 1995. Embracing human fallibility: On forgiving oneself and forgiving others. *Journal of Religion and Health* 33(2): 107–113.

Hamilton, D. 1980. *Forgiveness.* Downers Grove, Ill.: InterVarsity Press.

Hamilton, D. S. 1984. The ethics of forgiveness: A response to Butler. Doctoral dissertation, Johns Hopkins University, Baltimore. *Dissertation Abstracts International—A,* 45(11), 1985, p. 3377.

Hamrogue, J. M. 1987. *Forgive and be forgiven.* Ligouri, Mo.: Ligouri Publications.

Hancock, M., and K. B. Mains. 1987. *Child sexual abuse: A hope for healing.* Wheaton, Ill.: Harold Shaw Publishers.

Haney, J. 1996. *How to forgive when it's hard to forget.* Green Leaf, Ariz.: New Leaf Press.

Hansen, E. K. 1978. Earth mother/mother of God: The theme of forgiveness in the works of Eugene O'Neill. Doctoral dissertation, School of Theology at Claremont, Calif. *Dissertation Abstracts International—A,* 39 (03), 1978, p. 1567.

Hargrave, T. D. 1994. *Families and forgiveness.* New York: Brunner/Mazel.

Harkas, S. S. 1983. Let mercy abound: Social concern in the Greek Orthodox church. *Greek Orthodox Theological Journal* 28: 291–293.

Harris, J. W. 1986. Lawyers and forgiveness: Until seventy times seven? *Modern Christianity* 28(2): 32–41.

Harvey, J. 1993. Forgiving as an obligation of the moral life. *International Journal of Moral and Social Studies* 8(3): 211–222.

Harvey, R. W., and D. G. Benner. 1996. *Choosing the gift of forgiveness: How to overcome hurts and brokenness.* Grand Rapids, Mich.: Baker Books.

Hauerwas, S. 1983. Constancy and forgiveness: The novel as a school for virtue. *Notre Dame English Journal* 15: 23–54.

Hebl, J. H. 1990. Forgiveness as a psychotherapeutic goal with elderly females. Doctoral dissertation, University of Wisconsin–Madison. *Dissertation Abstracts International—A,* 51(04), 1990, p. 1119.

Hebl, J. H., and R. D. Enright. 1993. Forgiveness as a psychotherapeutic goal with elderly females. *Psychotherapy* 30: 658–667.

Henderlite, R. 1961. *Forgiveness and hope: Toward a theology for protestant Christian education.* Richmond, Va.: John Knox Press.

Hepp-Dax, S. 1996. Forgiveness as an intervention goal with fifth grade inner city children. Unpublished doctoral dissertation, Fordham University, New York.

Herford, R. T. 1964. Repentance and forgiveness in the Talmud: With some reference to the teaching of the gospels. *Hibbert Journal* 40: 55–64.

Herhold, R. M. 1979. The joy of forgiveness. *The promise beyond the pain.* Nashville: Abingdon.

Hession, R. 1977. You must forgive. *Moody Monthly* (May): 54–56.

Hestevold, H. S. 1985. Justice to mercy. *Philosophy and Phenomenological Research* 46: 281–291.

Heuslin, E. R. 1991. *Forgiven and free.* Nashville: Thomas Nelson.

Holeman, V. T. 1994. The relationship between forgiveness of a perpetrator and current marital adjustment for female survivors of childhood sexual abuse. Doctoral dissertation, Kent State University, Kent, Ohio. *Dissertation Abstracts International—B,* 55(10), 1994, p. 4592.

Hollenbach, B. 1983. Lest they should turn and be forgiven: Irony. *Bible Translator* 34(3): 312–321.

Holmgren, M. R. 1993. Forgiveness and the intrinsic value of persons. *American Philosophical Quarterly* 30(4, Oct.): 341–352.

Hong, E. H. 1984. *Forgiveness is a work as well as a grace.* Minneapolis: Augsburg.

Hootman, M., and P. Perkins. 1982. *How to forgive your ex-husband (and get on with your life).* New York: Warner Books.

Hope, D. 1987. The healing paradox of forgiveness. *Psychotherapy* 24(2): 240–244.

Hopkins, J. H. 1857. *The American citizen: His rights and duties, according to the spirit of the constitution of the United States.* New York: Pudney and Russell.

Hora, T. 1983. *Forgiveness.* Orange, Calif.: Pagl Press.

Horsbrugh, H. J. 1974. Forgiveness. *Canadian Journal of Philosophy* 4: 269–289.

Howard, B. 1986. *Journal of forgiveness.* Independence, Mo.: Herald Publishing House.

Huang, S. T. 1990. Cross-cultural and real-life validations of the theory of forgiveness in Taiwan, the Republic of China. Doctoral dissertation, University of Wisconsin–Madison. *Dissertation Abstracts International—B,* 51(05), 1990, p. 2644.

Hughes, M. 1975. Forgiveness. *Analysis* 35: 113–117.

Hughes, P. M. 1993. What is involved in forgiving? *Journal of Value Inquiry* 27: 331–340.

Human Development Study Group. 1991. Five points on the construct of forgiveness within psychotherapy. *Psychotherapy* 28: 493–496.

Hunt, M. 1988. Forgiveness: The best revenge. *Woman's Day*, Dec. 20, pp. 78, 82–84.

Hunter, R. C. A. 1978. Forgiveness, retaliation, and paranoid reactions. *Canadian Psychiatric Association Journal* 23(3): 167–173.

Hyde, C. 1984. *To declare God's forgiveness*. Wilton, Conn.: Morehouse Barlow Company.

Ingersoll, R. E. 1995. Construction and initial validation of the spiritual wellness inventory. Doctoral dissertation, Kent State University, Kent, Ohio. *Dissertation Abstracts International—B*, 56(10), 1995, p. 5827.

Ingram, K. J. 1993. *Blessing your enemies, fogiving your friends*. Ligouri, Mo.: Ligouri Publications.

Jacobson, S. T. 1959. The interpersonalism of guilt and forgiveness as seen in the writings of Harry Stack Sullivan and Emil Brunner. Doctoral dissertation, Princeton Theological Seminary. *Dissertation Abstracts International.* ADD X1959.

Jacoby, S. 1983. *Wild justice: The evaluation of revenge*. New York: Harper and Row.

Jampolsky, G. G. 1980. The future is now. *Journal of Clinical Child Psychology* 9(2): 182–184.

Jampolsky, G. G. 1985. *Good-bye to guilt*. New York: Bantam.

Jankelevitch, V. 1967. *Le pardon*. Paris: Editorus Montaigne.

Jenco, L. M. 1995. *Bound to forgive: The pilgrimage to reconciliation of a Beirut hostage*. Notre Dame, Ind.: Ave Maria Press.

Jennings, T. W., Jr. 1988. *The liturgy of liberation: The confession and forgiveness of sins*. Nashville: Abingdon.

Johnson, B. 1996. *Good guilt, bad guilt: And what to do with each*. Downer's Grove, Ill.: InterVarsity Press.

Johnson, P. 1985. Why I must believe in God. *Reader's Digest*, June, pp. 124–127.

Johnson, K. A. 1986. A model of forgiveness: Theory formulations and research implications. Unpublished doctoral dissertation, Rosemead School of Psychology, La Mirada, Calif.

Johnston, G. 1960. Soul care in the ministry of Jesus (II). *Canadian Journal of Theology* 6(1): 25–30.

Jones, L. G. 1995. *Embodying forgiveness: A theological analysis*. Grand Rapids, Mich.: William B. Eerdmans.

Joy, S. S. 1985. Abortion: An issue to grieve? *Journal of Counseling and Development* 63(6): 375–376.

Kahrhoff, R. E. 1988. *Forgiveness: Formula for peace of mind*. St. Charles, Mo.: Capital Planning Corp.

Kaplan, B. H. 1992. Social health and the forgiving heart. *Journal of Behavioral Medicine* 15(1): 3–14.

Kaplan, B. H. 1993. Two topics not covered by Aldridge: Spirituality in children and forgiveness and health. *Advances* 9(4): 30–33.

Kasper, W. 1989. The Church as a place of forgiveness. *Communio: International Catholic Review* 16: 160–171.

Kaufman, G. 1980. *Shame: The power of caring*. Cambridge, Mass.: Schenkman Publishing Co.

Kaufman, M. E. 1984. The courage to forgive. *Israeli Journal of Psychiatry and Related Sciences* 21(3): 177–187.

Kellems, J. 1926. *Study in the forgiveness of sins.* New York: Doran.

Kennedy, C. A. 1960. An exegetical study of "aphiemi" and its cognates with special reference to the Jewish idea of forgiveness in Jesus' day. Doctoral dissertation, Southwestern Baptist Theological Seminary, Grand Rapids, Mich. *Dissertation Abstracts International,* ADD X1960.

Kennington, P. A. 1994. Encouraging friendship relationships between women who volunteer and women who live in shelters: An educational action research study focusing on social justice, interpersonal forgiveness, and womanist identity. Doctoral dissertation, North Carolina State University, Raleigh. *Dissertation Abstracts International—A,* 55(04), 1994, p. 868.

Keysor, C. W. 1982. *Forgiveness is a two-way street.* Wheaton, Ill.: Victor Books.

Kidder, J. 1975. Requital and criminal justice. *International Philosophical Quarterly* 15: 255–278.

Kiel, D. V. 1986. I'm learning how to forgive. *Decisions* (Feb.): 12–13.

Kierkegaard, S. 1938. *Purity of heart.* New York: Hayes and Brothers.

King, J. N. 1982. *The God of forgiveness and healing in the theology of Karl Rahner.* Washington, D.C.: University Press of America.

King, M. L., Jr. 1963. *Strength to love.* Philadelphia: Fortress Press.

Kirkpatrick, C. K. 1995. The interpersonal construct of human forgiveness: Comparing perceptions of clinical psychologists and pastoral counselors. Doctoral dissertation, United States International University, San Diego. *Dissertation Abstracts International—A,* 56(02), 1995, p. 463.

Kirkup, P. A. 1993. Some religious perspectives on forgiveness and settling differences: Beyond techniques: The soul of family mediation. *Mediation Quarterly* 11(1): 79–94.

Klassen, W. 1966. *The forgiving community.* Philadelphia: Westminster Press.

Klein, C. 1995. *How to forgive when you can't forget.* Bellmore, N.Y.: Liebling Press.

Kleining, J. 1969. Mercy and justice. *Philosophy* 44: 341–342.

Koerbel, P. 1986. *Abortion's second victim.* Wheaton, Ill.: Victor Books.

Kohn, N. C. 1983. Guilt as a dynamic of depression, and the priestly ministry of the pastor in mediating forgiveness toward healing. Thesis abstract in *Calvin Theological Journal* 18: 295.

Kolenda, K. 1986. The wisdom of youth. *The Humanist* 46(2): 40.

Kolnai, A. 1973–74. Forgiveness. *Proceedings of the Aristotelian Society* 74: 91–106.

Kraft, K. 1986. The aftermath. *Guideposts* (May): 34–37.

Krass, A. 1983. Seeking the peace of the city. *The Other Side,* 52–53.

Krentz, G. 1993. Kassens' killer is offered a Bible: Girl's mother tells him, "I forgive you." *Milwaukee Sentinel,* Mar. 1.

Krondorfer, B. 1995. *Remembrance and reconciliation: Encounters between young Jews and Germans.* New Haven, Conn.: Yale University Press.

Kus, R. 1992. Spirituality in everyday life: Experiences of gay men of Alcoholics Anonymous. *Journal of Chemical Dependency Treatment* 5: 49–66.

Kushner, H. S. 1996. *How good do we have to be? A new understanding of guilt and forgiveness.* Boston: Little, Brown and Company.

Lambert, J. C. 1985. *The human action of forgiving.* New York: University Press of America.

Landman, I., et al., ed. 1941. Forgiveness. *The universal Jewish encyclopedia,* Vol. 4. New York: Universal Jewish Encyclopedia, Inc.

Lang, B. 1994. Forgiveness. *American Philosophical Quarterly* 31(2): 105–117.

Laporte, J. 1986. Forgiveness of sins in Origen. *Worship* 60(6): 520–527.

Lapsley, J. N. 1966. Reconciliation, forgiveness, lost contracts. *Theology Today* 22: 45–49.

Larsen, E. 1992. *From anger to forgiveness.* New York: Hazelden.

Larsen, S., and D. Larsen. 1984. *Forgiveness: No guilt no grudges.* Wheaton, Ill.: Shaw.

Lauritzen, P. 1987. Forgiveness: Moral prerogative or religious duty? *Journal of Religious Ethics* 15: 141–150.

Lawry, J. D. 1987. Forgiveness: Key to happiness. *Today's Catholic Together* (Mar.): 73.

LeGuin, U. K. 1996. *Four ways to forgiveness.* New York: Harper Collins.

Lehmann, P. 1940. *Forgiveness: Decisive issue in Protestant thought.* New York: Harper and Brothers Publishers.

Lena, M. 1984. Education in the sense of forgiveness. Trans. J. Lyon. *International Catholic Review* 11: 308–321.

Lester, J. 1996. *And all our wounds forgiven.* New York: Harcourt Brace and Company.

Lewis, M. 1980. On forgiveness. *Philosophical Quarterly* 30:236–245.

Libby, B. 1992. *The forgiveness book.* Cambridge, Mass.: Cowley Publications.

Lilly, G. 1977. *God is calling his people to forgive.* Kingwood, Tex.: Hunter Books.

Linn, D., and M. Linn, 1974. *Healing our memories.* New York: Paulist Press.

Linn, D., and M. Linn. 1978. *Healing life's hurts: Healing memories through the five stages of forgiveness.* New York: Paulist Press.

Little, H. M. 1996. Forgiving Mom and Dad for their sins. *Chicago Tribune,* No. 26, p. 9.

Lockerbie, J. 1981. *Forgive—forget and be free.* Chappaqua, N.Y.: Christian Herald Books.

Loewen, J. A. 1970. Four kinds of forgiveness. *Practical Anthropology* 11(4, Pt. 2): 153–168.

Loewen, J. A. 1976. The social context of guilt and forgiveness. *Practical Anthropology* 17(2): 80–96.

Lofthouse, W. F. 1915. Forgiveness. In *Dictionary of the Apostolic Church,* ed. J. Hastings. Edinburgh: T. & T. Clark.

Lomax, E. 1996. *The railway man: A true story of war, brutality and forgiveness.* New York: Norton.

Londey, D. 1986. Can God forgive us our trespasses? *Sophia* 25: 4–10.

Luzzatto, M. H. 1932. Cleanness. In *Understanding Jewish theology: Classical issues and modern perspectives,* ed. J. Neusner. New York: Ktan Publishing House, Inc.

Lynch, L. W. 1983. Fear, freedom, and forgiveness: A goal toward wholeness and healing for single parents with custody. Doctoral dissertation, Claremont School of Theology, Claremont, Calif. *Dissertation Abstracts International—A,* 44(03), 1983, p. 789.

McAll, K. 1982. *Healing the family tree.* London: Sheldon Press.

McAllister, E. W. C. 1983. Christian counseling and human needs. *Journal of Psychology and Christianity* 2(3): 50–60.

McCullough, M. E. 1995. Forgiveness as altruism: A social-psychological theory of interpersonal forgiveness and tests of its validity. Doctoral dissertation, Virginia Commonwealth University, Richmond. *Dissertation Abstracts International—B*, 56(09), 1995, p. 5224.

McCullough, M. E., and Worthington, E. L., Jr. 1994. Encouraging clients to forgive people who have hurt them: Review, critique, and research prospectus. *Journal of Psychology and Theology* 22(1): 3–20.

McCullough, M. E., and Worthington, E. L., Jr. 1995. Promoting forgiveness: Psychoeducational group interventions with a wait-list control. *Counseling and Values* 40: 55–68.

McDonald, H. D. 1984. *Forgiveness and atonement*. Grand Rapids, Mich.: Baker Books.

McDowell, J. H. 1990. *Sex, guilt & forgiveness*. Wheaton, Ill.: Tyndale House Publishers.

McGary, H. 1989. Forgiveness. *American Philosophical Quarterly* 26(4): 343–351.

McGee, R. S., and D. W. Sapaugh. 1996. *The search for peace: Release from the torments of toxic unforgiveness*. Ann Arbor, Mich.: Servant Publications.

Mackintosh, H. R. 1927. *The Christian experience of forgiveness*. New York and London: Harper and Brothers Publishers.

McNally, R. E. 1977. The Counter-Reformation's views of sin and penance. *Thought* 52: 151–166.

McNeill, D. P. 1971. The dynamics of forgiveness in community: A study of the theological meaning and pastoral implications of processes of forgiveness in experiences other than the celebration of the sacrament of penance. Doctoral dissertation, Princeton Theological Seminary. *Dissertation Abstracts International—A*, 32(05), 1971, p. 563.

Mains, K. B. 1984. *The key to an open heart*. Elgin, Ill.: David C. Cook.

Mains, K. B. 1985. *The key to a loving heart*. Carmel, N.Y. Guideposts.

Marino, G. D. 1995. The epidemic of forgiveness. *Commonweal* 122(Mar.): 9–11.

Marks, M. 1988. Remorse, revenge, and forgiveness. *The Psychotherapy Patient* 5(1–2): 317–330.

Maroda, K. J. 1991. Saint or sadist: Who is the self-righteous patient? *The Psychotherapy Patient* 7(3–4): 125–135.

Martin, A. 1994. Forgiving the unforgivable. *Detroit Free Press Magazine,* Aug. 21, pp. 7, 10, 12–15.

Martin, J. A. 1953. A realistic theory of forgiveness. In *The return to reason,* ed. J. Wild. Chicago: Regnery.

Martin, R. P. 1974. Reconciliation and forgiveness in the letter to the Colossians. In *Reconciliation and hope,* ed. R. Banks. Exeter, England: Paternoster Press.

Martindale, L. S. 1985. *Only once forgiven*. Winona, Minn.: Apollo Books.

Mauger, P. A., T. Freeman, A. G. McBride, J. E. Perry, D. C. Grove, and K. E. McKinney. 1992. The measurement of forgiveness: Preliminary research. *Journal of Psychology and Christianity* 11(2): 170–180.

Mauldin, F. L. 1983. Singularity and a pattern of sin, punishment and forgiveness. *Perspectives in Religious Studies* 10: 41–50.

Meek, K. R., J. S. Albright, and M. R. McMinn. 1995. Religious orientation, guilt, confession, and forgiveness. *Journal of Psychology and Theology* 23(3): 190–197.

Meniger, W. A. 1996. *The process of forgiveness*. New York: Continuum Publishing.

Merritt, M. J. G. 1983. The interpretive context for struggle: A response to R. Duane Thompson. *Wesleyan Theological Journal* 18: 93–99.

Messenger, J. C. 1959. The Christian concept of forgiveness and Anang morality. *Practical Anthropology* 6: 97–103.

Miller, W. E. 1994. *Forgiveness: The power and the puzzle*. Warsaw, Ind.: ClearBrook Publishers.

Minas, A. 1975. God and forgiveness. *Philosophical Quarterly* 25: 138–150.

Mitchell, C. E. 1995. A model for forgiveness in family relationships. *Family Therapy* 22(1): 25–30.

Molander, P. 1985. The optimal level of generosity in a selfish, uncertain environment. *Journal of Conflict Resolution* 29(4): 611–618.

Moore, D. B. 1993. Shame, forgiveness, and juvenile jusice. *Criminal Justice Ethics* 12(2): 3–25.

Morison, P. H. 1987. *Forgive! As the Lord forgave you*. Phillipsburg, N.J.: Presbyterian and Reformed Publishing Co.

Morris, H. 1988. Murphy on forgiveness. *Criminal Justice Ethics* 7: 15–19.

Morrissey, K. 1982. *A women's workshop on forgiveness*. Grand Rapids, Mich.: Zondervan Publishing.

Morrow, L. 1984. Why forgive? *Time*, Jan. 9, pp. 26–33.

Morrow, L. 1985. Forgiveness to the injured doth belong. *Time*, May 20, p. 90.

Moskal, J. 1994. *Blake, ethics, and forgiveness*. Tuscaloosa, Ala.: University of Alabama Press.

Moss, D. B. 1986. Revenge and forgiveness. *American Imago* 43(3): 191–210.

Moule, C. F. D. 1971. The theology of forgiveness. In *From fear to faith: Studies of suffering and wholeness*, ed. N. Autton. London: S.P.C.K.

Moule, C. F. 1978. As we forgive: A note on the distinction between desserts and capacity in the understanding of forgiveness. In *Donum gentilicium, New Testament studies in honour of David Daube*, ed. E. Bammel, C. K. Barrett, and W. Davis. Oxford: Clarendon Press.

Mow, J. B. 1975. Rawls on mercy: Pardon and amnesty *Journal of the West Virginia Philosophical Society* (Spring): 2–5.

Mueller, J. 1996. *Why can't I forgive you?* Chicago: Thomas More.

Murphy, J. G. 1982. Forgiveness and resentment. *Midwest Studies in Philosophy* 7: 503–516.

Murphy, J. G. 1988a. Forgiveness, mercy, and the retributive emotions. *Criminal Justice Ethics* 7: 3–15.

Murphy, J. G. 1988b. A rejoinder to Morris. *Criminal Justice Ethics* 7: 20–22.

Murphy, J. G., and J. Hampton. 1988. *Forgiveness and mercy*. Cambridge: Cambridge University Press.

Murray, M. 1975. Spirituality and forgiveness. Master's thesis, Dusquesne University, Pittsburgh. *Masters Abstracts International*, 13(04), 1995, p. 455.

Narramore, B., and W. Counts. 1974. *Freedom from guilt*. Irvine, Calif.: Harvest House.

Neblett, W. R. 1974. Forgiveness and ideals. *Mind* 83: 269–275.

Nelson, M. K. 1992. A new theory of forgiveness. Doctoral dissertation, Purdue University, West Lafayette, Ind. *Dissertation Abstracts International—B,* 53(08), 1992, p. 4381.

Newberry, P. A. 1995. Forgiveness and emotion. Doctoral dissertation, Claremont Graduate School, Claremont, Calif. *Dissertation Abstracts International —A,* 56(06), 1995, p. 2269.

Newman, L. E. 1987. The quality of mercy: On the duty to forgive in the Judaic tradition. *Journal of Religious Ethics* 15: 141–150.

Niebuhr, R. 1975. Criticism: A sense of limits. In *Justice and mercy,* ed. U. M. Niebuhr. New York: Harper and Row.

Nietzsche, F. W. 1887. *The genealogy of morals.* Trans. P. Watson. London: S.P.C.K.

Norris, D. A. 1983. Forgiving from the heart: A biblical and psychotherapeutic exploration. Doctoral dissertation, Union Theological Seminary, New York. *Dissertation Abstracts International—A,* 44(10), 1984, p. 3091.

North, J. 1987. Wrongdoing and forgiveness. *Philosophy* 62: 499–508.

Noveck, S., ed. 1963. Atonement. *Contemporary Jewish Thought: A Reader.* B'nai B'rith Department of Adult Jewish Education, Clinton, Mass.: Colonial Press, Inc.

Nygren, A. 1953. *Agape and eros.* Trans. P. Watson. London: S.P.C.K.

Oberholzer, F. 1984. The transformation of evil into sin and into sorrow and forgiveness: Lessons from analytic psychology and theology. Doctoral dissertation, Graduate Theological Union, Berkeley, Calif. *Dissertation Abstracts International—A,* 45(05), p. 1444.

O'Driscoll, L. H. 1983. The quality of mercy. *Southern Journal of Philosophy* 21: 229–258.

O'Shaughnessy, R. J. 1967. Forgiveness. *Philosophy* 42: 336–352.

Owen, L. 1976. The representation of forgiveness in Shakespeare and medieval drama. Doctoral dissertation, University of Virginia, Charlottesville. *Dissertation Abstracts International—A,* 36(07), 1976, p. 4516.

Parish, T., R. Rosenblatt, and B. Knappes. 1979–80. The relationship between human values and moral judgment. *Psychology: A Quarterly of Human Behavior* 16(4): 1–5.

Park, S. R. 1994. Measuring interpersonal forgiveness in Korea. Unpublished master's thesis, Department of Educational Psychology, University of Wisconsin–Madison.

Park, Y. O. 1987. The psychological structure and process of interpersonal forgiveness: A social cognitive developmental approach. Preliminary examination paper, Department of Educational Psychology, University of Wisconsin–Madison.

Park, Y. O. 1989. The development of forgiveness in the context of friendship conflict. Doctoral dissertation, University of Wisconsin–Madison. *Dissertation Abstracts International—A,* 51(03), 1989, p. 799.

Park, Y. O., and R. D. Enright. In press. The development of forgiveness in the context of adolescent friendship conflict in Korea. *Journal of Adolescence.*

Parsons, R. D. 1988. Forgiving-not-forgetting. *Psychotherapy Patient* 5(1–2): 259–273.

Pastor, M. 1986. The nature of forgiveness in the Christian tradition, modern Western psychology and a course in miracles. Doctoral dissertation, California

Institute of Integral Studies, San Francisco. *Dissertation Abstracts International —A,* 47(03), 1986, p. 940.

Paton, M. 1982. Can God forget? *Scottish Journal of Theology* 35(5): 385–402.

Paton, M. 1988. Can God forgive? *Modern Theology* 4(3): 225–233.

Pattison, E. M. 1965. On the failure to forgive or to be forgiven. *American Journal of Psychotherapy* 19: 106–115.

Patton, J. 1985. *Is human forgiveness possible?* Nashville: Abingdon.

Peck, D. L. 1989. Teenage suicide expressions: Echoes from the past. *International Quarterly of Community Health Education* 10(1): 53–64.

Peck, S. M. 1993. *Further along the road less traveled,* pp. 20–47. New York: Touchstone.

Pelke, B. 1994. Forgiving Paula. *Miracles Magazine* 8 (Fall): 23–25, 50–51.

Perkins, P. 1984. Reconciliation in the New Testament. *New Catholic World* 227: 25–27.

Phillips, A. 1986. Forgiveness reconsidered. *Christian Jewish Relations* 19: 14–21.

Phillips, C. E. 1994. Forgiveness in the healing process. Doctoral dissertation, Northern Arizona University, Flagstaff. *Dissertation Abstracts International— A,* 55(04), 1994, p. 871.

Phillips, L. J., and J. W. Osborne. 1989. Cancer patients' experiences of forgiveness therapy. *Canadian Journal of Counseling* 23(3): 236–251.

Pingleton, J. P. 1989. The role and function of forgiveness in the psychotherapeutic process. *Journal of Psychology and Theology* 17(1): 27–35.

Pollard, M. W. 1995. The construction of a family forgiveness scale. Doctoral dissertation, Texas Woman's University, Denton. *Dissertation Abstracts International —A,* 56(03), 1995, p. 829.

Power, C. 1994. Commentary. *Human Development* 37: 81–83.

Quanbeck, W. A. 1962. Forgiveness. *The interpreter's dictionary of the Bible,* ed. G. A. Buttrick, Vol. E-J, p. 318. New York: Abingdon Press.

Rackley, J. V. 1993. The relationship of marital satisfaction, forgiveness, and religiosity. Doctoral dissertation, Virginia Polytechnic Institute and State University, Blacksburg. *Dissertation Abstracts International—A,* 54(04), 1993, p. 1556.

Rainbolt, G. W. 1990. Mercy: An independent, imperfect virtue. *American Philosophical Quarterly* 27(2): 169–173.

Ramsey, I. 1971. The theology of wholeness. In *From fear to faith: Studies of suffering and wholeness,* ed. N. Autton. London: S.P.C.K.

Ranck, L. 1990. A capacity for forgiveness and reconciliation. *Christian Social Action* (May 28–29).

Raybon, P. 1996. *My first white friend: Confessions on race, love, and forgiveness.* New York: Viking Penguin.

Redding, D. A. 1988. The healing power of forgiveness. *Plus* 39(7, Pt. 2): 13–23.

Redmond, S. A. 1993. The father God and traditional Christian interpretations of suffering, guilt, anger and forgiveness as impediments to recovery from father-daughter incest. Doctoral dissertation, University of Ottawa, Canada. *Dissertation Abstracts International—A,* 54(09), 1993, p. 475.

Reed, J. R. 1995. *Dickens & Thackeray: Punishment and forgiveness.* Athens, Ohio: Ohio University Press.

Rhode, M. G. 1990. Forgiveness, power, and empathy. Doctoral dissertation, Fuller Theological Seminary, School of Psychology, Pasadena, Calif. *Dissertation Abstracts International—B,* 51(05), 1990, p. 2606.

Richards, L. 1996. *Forgiveness: The gift that heals and sets free.* Nashville: Thomas Nelson.

Richards, N. 1988. Forgiveness. *Ethics* 99: 77–97.

Richardson, A. 1950. *A theological word book of the Bible.* London: SCM Press.

Ritzman, T. A. 1987. Forgiveness: Its role in therapy. *Journal of the American Academy of Medical Hypnoanalysts* 2: 4–13.

Roberts, H. R. 1971. Mercy. *Philosophy* 46: 352–353.

Roberts, R. C. 1995. Forgivingness. *American Philosophical Quarterly,* 32(4, Oct.): 289–306.

Robinson, L. J. 1988. The role of forgiving in emotional healing: A theological and psychological analysis. Doctoral dissertation, Fuller Theological Seminary, Pasadena, Calif. *Dissertation Abstracts International—B,* 49(07), 1989, p. 2872.

Rogness, A. N. 1970. *Forgiveness and confession: Keys to renewal.* Minneapolis: Augsburg.

Rooney, A. J. 1989. Finding forgiveness through psychotherapy: An empirical phenomenological investigation. Doctoral dissertation, Georgia State University, College of Arts and Sciences, Atlanta. *Dissertation Abstracts International—B,* 51(02), 1989, p. 1001.

Rosberg, G. 1992. *Do-it-yourself relationship mender.* Colorado Springs, Colo.: Focus on the Family Publishing.

Roscoe, B., L. E. Cavanaugh, and D. R. Kennedy. 1988. Dating infidelity: Behaviors, reasons and consequences. *Adolescence* 23(89): 35–43.

Rosenak, C. M., and G. M. Harnden. 1992. Forgiveness in the psychotherapeutic process: Clinical applications. *Journal of Psychology and Christianity* 11(2): 188–197.

Rosenzweig-Smith, J. 1988. Factors associated with successful reunions of adult adoptees and biological parents. *Child Welfare* 67(5): 411–422.

Rowe, J. O., S. Halling, E. Davies, M. Leifer, D. Powers, and J. van Bronkhorst. 1989. The psychology of forgiving another: A dialogical research approach. In *Existential phenomenological perspectives in psychology,* ed. R. S. Valle and S. Halling, pp. 233–244. New York: Plenum.

Ruman, M., and C. Johnson. 1994. The unforgiven. *New Woman,* Apr., pp. 80–83.

Sandage, S. J., K. Wibberly, and E. L. Worthington. 1995. Christian counselors' resources for multi-cultural understanding and counseling. *Journal of Psychology and Theology* 23(1): 30–36.

Santos, M. 1986. A cognitive developmental view of forgiveness. Unpublished master's thesis, University of Wisconsin–Madison.

Sawyerr, H. 1964. Sin and forgiveness in Africa. *Frontier* (Spring): 60–63.

Schell, D. W. 1990. *Getting bitter or getting better: Choosing forgiveness for your own good.* St. Meinrad, Ind.: Abbey Press.

Sch-he-rie, M. 1984. *The scale of wisdom,* chap. 6 (In Arabic). Qum, Iran: Propagation Center.

Schmidt, M. I. 1986. Forgiveness as the focus theme in group counseling. Doctoral dissertation, North Texas State University, Denton. *Dissertation Abstracts International—A,* 47(11), 1986, p. 3985.

Scott, J. A. 1976. Self-forgiveness. *Journal of the American Institute of Hypnosis* 17(3): 131–132.

Scott, J. W. 1911. Idealism and the conception of forgiveness. *International Journal of Ethics* 21:189–198.

Senkbeil, H. L. 1994. *Dying to live: The power of forgiveness.* St. Louis, Mo.: Concordia Publishing House.

Server, R. C. 1986. The freedom of forgiveness. *Discipleship Journal* 6: 44–46.

Sharma, A., and H. E. Cheatham. 1986. A women's center support group for sexual assault victims. *Journal of Counseling and Development* 64: 525–527.

Sherrer, Q., and R. Garlock. 1989. *How to forgive your children.* Lynwood, Wash.: Aglow Publications.

Shontz, F. C., and C. Rosenak. 1988. Psychological theories and the need for forgiveness: Assessment and critique. *Journal of Psychology and Christianity* 7(1): 23–31.

Shriver, D. W. 1980. The pain and promise of pluralism. *Christian Century* 97: 345–350.

Shriver, D. W. 1995. *An ethic for enemies: Forgiveness in politics.* Oxford: Oxford University Press.

Siebert, D. 1994. Forgiveness: Healing life's deepest hurts. Unpublished master's thesis, Notre Dame College, Manchester, N.H.

Sigwela, E. 1990. Forgive infinitely. *The Plough* 24:6–8.

Simmons, D. 1982. Is there compassion in principled moral judgement? *Psychological Reports* 50(2): 553–554.

Simon, S. B., and S. Simon. 1990. *Forgiveness: How to make peace with your past and get on with your life.* New York: Warner Books.

Sinton, V. 1990. *How can I forgive?* Oxford, England: Lion Pocketbook.

Smart, A. 1968. Mercy. *Philosophy* 43: 345–359.

Smedes, L. B. 1983a. Forgiving people who do not care. *Reformed Journal* 33: 13–18.

Smedes, L. B. 1983b. Forgiveness: The power to change the past. *Christianity Today* 27: 22–26.

Smedes, L. B. 1984. *Forgive and forget: Healing the hurts we don't deserve.* New York: Harper and Row.

Smedes, L. B. 1996. *The art of forgiving.* Nashville: Morrings.

Smedslund, J. 1991. The psychologic of forgiving. *Scandinavian Journal of Psychology* 32(2): 164–176.

Smith, I. 1942. The militant Christian virtues. *Thomist* 4: 193–220.

Smith, M. 1981. The psychology of forgiveness. *The Month* 14: 301–307.

Smith, M. C. 1989. Penitential bread: The Eucharist as locus of forgiveness. *Saint Luke's Journal of Theology* 32(2): 99–106.

Snow, N. E. 1993. Self-forgiveness. *Journal of Value Inquiry* 27: 75–80.

Solomon, N. 1986. The forgiveness debate. *Christian Jewish Relations* 19(1): 3–24.

Spidell, S., and D. Liberman. 1981. Moral development and the forgiveness of sin. *Journal of Psychology and Theology* 9: 159–163.

Stanley, C. 1987. *Forgiveness*. Nashville: Thomas Nelson.

Stanley, C. F. 1995. *Freedom through forgiveness*. Wheaton, Ill.: Victor Books.

Starkey, A. D. 1987. Embracing forgiveness. *InterVarsity* (Summer): 6–7, 10–11.

Stauffer, E. R. 1987. *Unconditional love and forgiveness*. Burbank, Calif.: Triangle Publishers.

Stipe, A. M. 1996. Forgiveness and psychotherapy. Doctoral dissertation, University of Maryland at Baltimore. *Dissertation Abstracts International—A,* 56(08), 1996, p. 3312.

Stoop, D., and J. Masteller. 1991. *Forgiving our parents forgiving ourselves*. Ann Arbor, Mich.: Vine Books.

Strasser, J. A. 1984. The relation of general forgiveness and forgiveness type to reported health in the elderly. Doctoral dissertation, Catholic University of America, Washington, D.C. *Dissertation Abstracts International—B,* 45(06), 1984, p. 1733.

Strazzabosco, J. 1996. *Learning about forgiveness from the life of Nelson Mandela*. New York: Rosen Publishing Group.

Strong, S. R. 1977. Christian counseling. *Counseling and Values* 20: 151–160.

Subkoviak, M. J., R. D. Enright, C. Wu, E. A. Gassin, S. Freedman, L. M. Olson, and I. C. Sarinopoulos. 1995. Measuring interpersonal forgiveness in late adolescence and middle adulthood. *Journal of Adolescence* 18: 641–655.

Suerdlik, S. 1985. Justice and mercy. *Journal of Social Philosophy* 16 (Fall): 6–47.

Swindoll, C. R. 1989. *Forgiving and forgetting*. Fullerton, Calif.: Insight for Living.

Tavuchis, N. 1991. *Mea culpa: A sociology of apology and reconciliation*. Stanford, Calif.: Stanford University Press.

Taylor, M. J., ed. 1971. *The mystery of sin and forgiveness*. Staten Island, N.Y.: Alba House.

Taylor, V. 1941. *Forgiveness and reconciliation: A study in New Testament theology*. London: Macmillan.

Taylor, V. 1946. *Forgiveness and reconciliation*. 2d ed. London: Macmillan.

Ten Boom, C. 1971. *The hiding place*. Old Tappan, N.J.: Revell.

Thompson, M. S. 1981. *Grace and forgiveness in ministry*. Nashville: Abingdon.

Thompson, R. D. 1983. The Wesleyan and the struggle to forgive. *Wesleyan Theological Journal* 18: 81–92.

Thompson, S. H., et al. 1873–74. *Discussion of the doctrine of human depravity*. Madison, Ind.: Courier Steam Printing.

Tobin, E. 1983. *How to forgive yourself and others*. Ligouri, Mo.: Ligouri Publications.

Tobin, E. 1993. *How to forgive yourself and others: Steps to reconciliation*. Ligouri, Mo.: Ligouri Publications.

Todd, E. 1985. The value of confession and forgiveness according to Jung. *Journal of Religion and Health* 24(1): 39–48.

Torrance, A. 1986. Forgiveness: The essential socio-political structure of personal being. *Journal of Theology for Southern Africa* 56: 47–59.

Towner, J. 1982. *Forgiveness is for giving*. Nashville: Impact Books.

Trainer, M. F. 1981. Forgiveness: Intrinsic, role-expected, expedient, in the context of divorce. Doctoral dissertation, Boston University. *Dissertation Abstracts International—B,* 45(04), 1984, p. 1325.

Trzyna, T. N. 1987. Forgiveness and truth: Literary reflections of Christian ethics. *Seattle Pacific University Review* 5: 7–36.

Trzyna, T. N. 1992. Forgiveness and time. *Christian Scholar's Review* 22(1): 7–21.

Trzyna, T. N. In press. The social construction of forgiveness. *Christian Scholars Review.*

Twambley, P. 1976. Mercy and forgiveness. *Analysis* 36: 84–90.

Veenstra, G. 1992. Psychological concepts of forgiveness. *Journal of Psychology and Christianity* 11(2): 160–169.

Veenstra, G. 1993. Forgiveness: A critique of adult child approaches. *Journal of Psychology and Christianity* 12(1): 58–68.

Wade, S. H. 1989. The development of a scale to measure forgiveness. Doctoral dissertation, Fuller Theological Seminary, School of Psychology, Pasadena, Calif. *Dissertation Abstracts International—B,* 50(11), 1990, p. 5338.

Wahking, H. 1992. Spiritual growth through grace and forgiveness. *Journal of Psychology and Christianity* 11(2): 198–206.

Walker, N. 1995. The quiddity of mercy. *Philosophy* 70: 27–37.

Walker, P. J. 1993. The relationship between forgiveness and marital adjustment. Master's thesis, University of Alberta, Canada. *Masters Abstracts International,* 33(01), 1993, p. 26.

Wallington, D. 1992. *Forgive forget forever.* Nashville: Winston-Derek.

Wallis, J. 1980. We could just ask them to forgive us. *Sojourner* 9 (Jan.): 3–4.

Walters, R. P. 1983. *Forgive and be free: Healing the wounds of past and present.* Grand Rapids, Mich.: Zondervan Publishing.

Walters, R. P. 1984. Forgiving: An essential element in effective living. *Studies in Formative Spirituality* 5(3): 365–374.

Wapnick, K. 1983. *Forgiveness and Jesus: The meeting place of "A course in miracles" and Christianity.* Farmingdale, N.Y.: Colemann.

Wapnick, K. 1985. Forgiveness: A spiritual psychotherapy. *Psychotherapy Patient* 1(3): 47–53.

Watson, P. J., R. W. Hood, Jr., and R. J. Morris. 1985. Religiosity, sin and self-esteem. *Journal of Psychology and Theology* 13(2): 116–128.

Watts, R. E. 1992. Biblical agape as a model of social interest. *Individual Psychology* 48(1): 35–40.

Weatherspoon, J. B. 1944. The spirit of forgiveness. *Review and Expositor* 41: 361–371.

Wedderspoon, R. J. 1945. The debt of the forgiver. *The Expository Times* 60: 19–21.

Weil, B. E. 1993. *Adultery: The forgivable sin.* Mamaroneck, N.Y.: Hastings House.

Weiner, B. A. 1994. The sins of the parents. Doctoral dissertation, University of California, Berkeley. *Dissertation Abstracts International—A,* 55(09), 1995, p. 2978.

Weiner, B., S. Graham, O. Peter, and M. Zmuidinas. 1991. Public confession and forgiveness. *Journal of Personality* 59(2): 281–312.

White, D. 1913. *Forgiveness and suffering: A Study of Christian belief.* Cambridge: Cambridge University Press.

White, G. 1996. Forgiven. *Atlanta Journal/Constitution,* Mar. 3, p. M3.

White, J. 1988. *When the heart has healed again: A memoir of tragedy and forgiveness.* Bryan, Tex.: Centerpoint Press.

Wiener, J. 1989. The responsibilities of friendship: Jacques Derrida on Paul De Man's collaboration. *Critical Inquiry* 15 (Summer): 797–803.

Wiesenthal, S. 1969. *The sunflower.* New York: Schocken Books.

Willetts, A. 1964. *What the New Testament says about forgiveness.* New York: Association Press.

Williams, D. D. 1968. Paul Tillich's doctrine of forgiveness. *Pastoral Psychology* 19: 17–23.

Williams, J. G. 1985–86. The Sermon on the Mount as a Christian basis of altruism. *Humboldt Journal of Social Relations* 13(1–2): 89–112.

Willmer, H. 1979. The politics of forgiveness: A new dynamic. *The Furrow* (Apr.): 207–218.

Wilson, F. T. 1982. Sin and forgiveness: The ultimate liberation. *Journal of the I.T.C.* 9: 115–119.

Wilson, H. P. 1994. Forgiveness and survivors of sexual abuse: Relationships among forgiveness of the perpetrator, spiritual well-being, depression and anxiety. Doctoral dissertation, Boston University. *Dissertation Abstracts International—A,* 55(03), 1994, p. 616.

Wischmann, L. 1990. With mercy and sorrow. *The Other Side* (May-June): 34–37.

Wolter, D. L. 1989. *Forgiving our parents: For adult children from dysfunctional families.* Minneapolis: CompCare Publishers.

Woodenboek, B. 1963. Forgiveness. *Encyclopedic dictionary of the Bible.* New York: McGraw-Hill.

Woodman, T. A. 1992. The role of forgiveness in marriage and marital therapy. Doctoral dissertation, Fuller Theological Seminary, Pasadena, Calif. *Dissertation Abstracts International—B,* 53(04), 1992, p. 2079.

Worthington, E. L., and F. A. DiBlasio. 1990. Promoting mutual forgiveness within the fractured relationship. *Psychotherapy* 27(2): 219–233.

Yancey, P. 1985. Are we forgiving too much? *Christianity Today* (Nov. 22): 30–31.

Young, H. S. 1984. Practicing RET with Bible-Belt Christians. *British Journal of Cognitive Psychotherapy* 2(2): 60–77.

Ziglar, Z. 1985. *Raising positive kids in a negative world.* Nashville: Thomas Nelson.

Zunkel, C. W. 1976. Can a divorce be forgiven? *Brethren Life and Thought* 21: 155–160.

INDEX

Acting: from a rule, 37; in accordance with a rule, 37

Affair: infidelity and the forgiveness process, 83, 90

African Americans: the national crime of slavery, 146

Al-Mabuk, R., 52, 59

Anderson, D. C., 116

Anger: during forgiveness, 20, 84, 91; and God, 40, 42, 93; and therapy, 52, 53, 70, 72, 79, 84; danger of expression, 64; defined, 64; denial of, 64; expression, 64; passive-aggressive, 64; varieties of expression, 64; measured, 68; misconceptions, 68; intensity related to forgiveness, 70, 79, 91; depression, 72; eating disorders, 72; related to clinical diagnoses, 72; attacks, 73; in clinical disorders of attention deficity/hyperacitvity disorder, 73; conscious anger, 77; at one's parents, 85–87; appropriate and inappropriate, 86; displacement onto spouse, 87, at God, 88, 93; as a precursor to guilt, 93. *See also* Guilt

Anxiety, 58, 71

Apology: police department example, 125–27; as a disciplinary tool, 127

Arafat, Yasir, 160

Arendt, H., 132

Assumptive sets: degrees of damage, 102; relationship to forgiveness, 102

Attention deficit/hyperactivity disorder, 73

Axelrod, R., 82

Barefoot, J. C., 71

Beavers, W. R., 91

Bergin, A., 53

Billings, A. G., 96

Bitburg Cemetery: visit of Ronald Reagan, 1985, 137–43

Bloomfield, H., 89

Bonhoeffer, D., 135, 147

Bound to Forgive, 7

Buddhism, 7

Buddhist cosmology: central causes of suffering are ignorance, attachment, hatred, 158; wisdom and compassion overcome suffering, 158

Buddhist-Hindu cosmology: no process of divine forgiveness, Law of Karma punishes and rewards individuals' actions, 158

Bundestag: President von Weizsacker's speech to, 1985, 141–43

Bush, George, 144

Cardis, P., 59

Casarjian, R., 51

Childhood: hurts that impede forgiveness, 86–87

Children: poor, 124

Civil War: United States, 160

Clausewitz, Karl von, 131, 132

Clinical considerations, 104–5

Clinton, Bill, 144

Close, H. T., 53

Coleman, P., 6, 47, 82, 95, 98; forgiveness offers love to betrayer, five phases of forgiveness, 154

Confrontation: as a step toward forgiving, 89–90

Couper, D., 6; institutions and nations should ask forgiveness for their mistakes, 156

Crime: matching punishment to, 41; as failed relationships, 126

Crime control: "big lies," 128–29